THE

THE
Sewtionary

AN A TO Z GUIDE TO 101 SEWING TECHNIQUES + DEFINITIONS

TASIA ST. GERMAINE

KP CRAFT
CINCINNATI, OHIO

Contents

Introduction

Sewing, like any new interest, comes with a whole new language of terms. Basting? Stitch in the ditch? Underlining? What *are* they talking about, and which definitions do I need to learn right away? People who sew use many of these terms, so often it becomes second nature. Because they're so familiar with sewing vocabulary, they may assume that you know what they mean! You may also recognize some of these terms from clothing, like shoulder pads and hemming, but aren't sure how to use them in your sewing projects.

This book defines and explains 101 common sewing terms, complete with step-by-step photo tutorials so you can practice and master each one.

I wanted this book to be an easy reference guide with great visuals. Many sewing books are a great read from start to finish, but they aren't the easiest to use as a reference later on. When you're wondering where you read that great tutorial on bound buttonholes, or you can't remember which side of a blouse overlaps on top on a woman's blouse (answer: the right!), this is the book for you.

I also want to give you options and real-life examples of what each technique is used for. Why should you bother to learn how to make a French tack? What's the point of horsehair braid? When I'm learning a new skill, I want to know why a technique is important and how to apply it to my projects—tell me *why* I should want to learn this skill. It's even more useful to see real-life examples and ways to apply the different skills, so I've included these as well as useful tips and suggestions to help you master these techniques.

HOW TO USE THIS BOOK

Have you come across a sewing term you don't understand or a technique that's new to you? Simply look it up alphabetically! This book is organized alphabetically, which makes it quick and easy to find the answer to your sewing question.

For each term, I've explained what it is, when you might use it and how to apply it to your sewing projects. Each tutorial is clearly photographed so it's easy to follow. I've used contrast thread in many of the demonstrations, so it stands out and you can see what's happening, even though you may want to use matching thread on your projects. Whenever possible, I've included ideas, variations and suggestions to take your sewing to the next level.

This book's wire-bound design allows it to open flat and stay open, so you can keep it at your sewing machine or on your workstation. It's easy to look up terms as you sew, or you can keep the book open beside you as you work through some of the more challenging techniques.

Whenever a tutorial or definition mentions another sewing term, the page number is provided for easy cross-referencing. There's also an index at the back, so you'll have many ways to find the info you need. From *A* to *Z*, I have you covered!

If you're brand new to sewing, flip through the book and stop when you see a term that's familiar but you aren't sure how it applies to sewing. Do you have sewing patterns ready for your first couple of projects? Read through the pattern instructions and highlight any new terms to look up in *Sewtionary*. Or simply read through the book from start to finish. No matter what stage you're at on your sewing journey, I'm certain these pages will teach you many new things.

Happy sewing!

Abutted Seam

WHAT IS IT?

An abutted seam is a flat seam used to join two layers of fabric without overlapping them. Instead the two layers are butted close to each other, without either layer going on top of the other. There is no seam allowance in an abutted seam; the two pieces touch along the seam line without overlapping and are sewn together with a zigzag stitch or other type of wide stitch. Seam binding or stay tape can be used to bridge the gap and strengthen the seam at the same time.

Abutted seam from the front

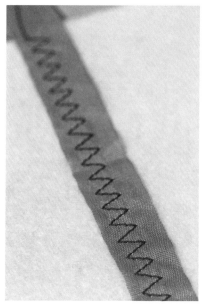

Abutted seam from the back

Abutted seam

▶ WHEN DO YOU USE IT?

An abutted seam is good for sewing flat, nonbulky seams in heavy or stiff fabrics. It's most often used as part of the interior construction, where the seams are hidden and not visible on the outside of the garment. You wouldn't want to use this seam for actual garment seams unless it's an intentional design detail. This type of seam construction isn't used frequently, but it does come in handy! If you are adding a layer of padding to a garment—for example, cotton batting in the bodice of a dress—then abutted seams are a good choice. A regular seam sewn and pressed open in cotton batting would be thick and lumpy. If you need to sew seams or darts in hair canvas interfacing (page 92), abutted seams work nicely because they don't add bulk.

Tips + Notes

You may find it easier to sew the abutted seams with the seam binding side up. I sew them with the seam binding on the underside so the batting doesn't get caught in the machine.

To sew abutted seams on curved seam lines, pin the first side of the curved seam normally. When you pin the other side, drape it over your other hand to form the curve.

For extrastrong seams, stitch up and down the seam a few times.

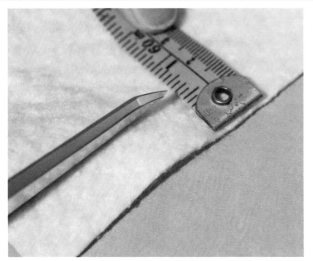

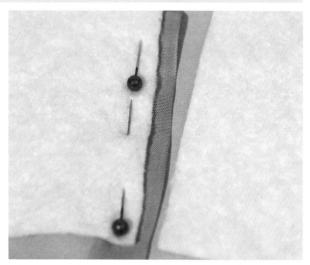

1 To prepare the pieces for sewing an abutted seam, trim off the seam allowances. To do this, measure the seam allowance amount from the raw edge, and draw in the seam line. Then trim along this line evenly.

2 Measure the seam, and cut a piece of seam binding, stay tape or any type of stable, nonstretch, thin tape. Cut your seam binding a little bit longer than your seam line, about ½" (1.3cm) longer on each end, so you can see where it is at the top and bottom of the seam. Pin the tape underneath one side of the seam, letting the fabric cover about half of the tape.

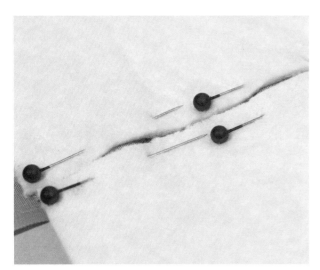

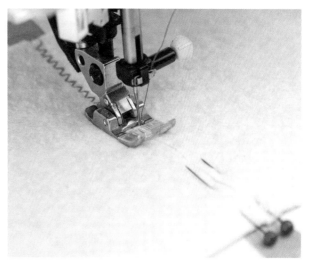

3 Pin the other side of the fabric to the seam binding or stay tape so that the edges meet. Using the stay tape makes it easier to sew the zigzag stitch and adds a protective layer to strengthen the seam. Pin with the points facing upward, so the pin heads are easy to remove as you sew.

4 Set your machine to a zigzag stitch. You could use a fancier wide stitch, but a zigzag is simple and effective. Center your work under the machine needle, and zigzag over the seam line. If the edges of the fabric pull apart as you sew, stop and readjust the layers so the zigzag catches both sides.
Trim off the extra seam binding after the seam is sewn.

Appliqué

WHAT IS IT?

Appliqué is a technique featuring pieces of fabric stitched on top of the main fabric as decoration. Appliqué can be sewn to a garment by hand or machine. Instead of cut pieces of fabric, you can buy premade appliqués to attach to your garment.

Purchased appliqué on Saltspring Dress

Appliqué detail

▶ WHEN DO YOU USE IT?

Use appliqués as decoration on just about anything—blouses, dresses or skirts; pocket openings, bodices, necklines, monograms, skirt hems or anywhere you like. Appliqués can be sewn all over the garment, placed evenly along hemlines or edges, or used to highlight specific areas like the waistline.

Depending on the project, you can either apply the appliqué before the garment is constructed or once the garment is fully sewn. Applying it before the garment is sewn is the easiest to do, since the fabric pieces are flat. This is the best way to add appliqués to small areas and the easiest to machine-appliqué. This is also the best method if you are confident on where to place the appliqué.

Sewing the appliqué in place after the garment is finished lets you pick the perfect placement. Try the garment on a dress form or yourself, pin the appliqué in place and adjust until it's in the perfect place, then sew it on securely. To sew an appliqué to a completed garment, handsewing is best unless the area is easy to access by machine, such as the hemline.

Tips + Notes

If your purchased appliqué is cotton or a natural fiber, you may want to prewash the appliqué first, before applying it to your project, especially if the finished project will be washed and not dry-cleaned. Wet the appliqué thoroughly and let it dry before sewing it on.

Consider where you're placing delicate or intricate appliqués, like beaded ones. Are they going to be abrasive? Are they located in a spot that's going to be rubbed and worn?

Beaded appliqués are best applied by hand. The machine's presser foot could damage the beads and the bumpiness makes it difficult to feed through the machine.

For interesting appliqués, cut out motifs from a printed fabric. Shapes with well-defined edges work best, like flowers with distinct outlines.

1 Cut out the appliqué shape, adding a ¼" (6mm) seam allowance all around the edges. If you are cutting multiple pieces of the same shape, make a template from cardboard.

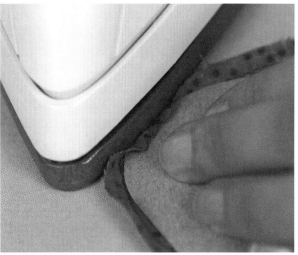

2 Staystitch (page 202) around the edges and fold the seam allowance to the wrong side. Clip edges (page 221) where necessary so the curves form nicely.

To press the edges, use the cardboard template and wrap the edges around the cardboard edge to the wrong side. Press with the iron.

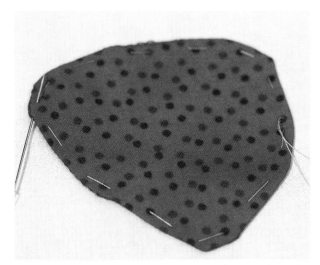

3 Hand baste (page 18) the appliqué in place, catching the folded seam allowance so it doesn't flip out to the right side.

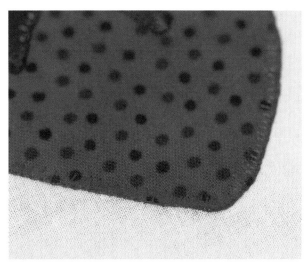

4 Handsew the appliqué around the edges. You can use a blanket stitch (page 31), slipstitch (page 194) or any stitch you prefer. Blanket stitches will be visible, while a slipstitch will hide your stitches.

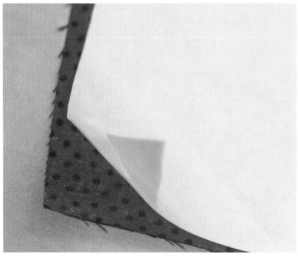

1 Apply a fusible adhesive to the wrong side of the appliqué fabric. This adhesive comes with a paper backing that peels off like a sticker. Use it to stick the appliqué to the garment fabric. Apply to the wrong side of your fabric, with the paper side up.

2 Trace around your template , or draw your appliqué design directly onto the paper backing. Cut out the appliqué shape through both the fabric and the backing, without adding any seam allowance.

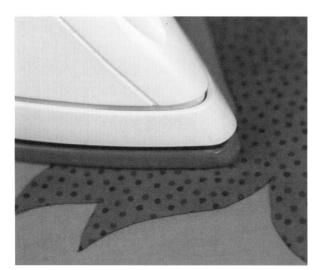

3 Peel off the backing and place the appliqué sticky side down on the right side of your garment. Fuse the appliqué in place with an iron.

4 Set your machine to sew a satin stitch by switching it to the zigzag function and shortening the stitch length to nearly zero. Doing so creates a very dense zigzag stitch that looks like a thick solid line. Sew around the edges of the appliqué, pivoting around curves and at corners. I find it easier to pivot when the needle is in position at the outer edge of the appliqué. When you reach the starting point, pull the threads to the back, tie in a knot and clip threads.

HOW TO APPLIQUÉ PIECES OF FABRIC WITH EDGES FINISHED

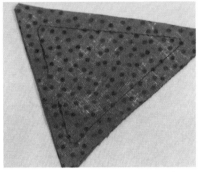

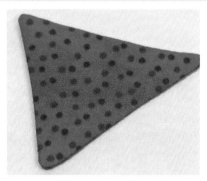

1 Cut out the appliqué shape, adding a ¼" (6mm) seam allowance. If you are cutting multiple pieces of the same shape, make a template from cardboard. For each appliqué, cut **two** pieces of fabric. Sew each appliqué pair together with a ¼" (6mm) seam, right sides together, and leave a small opening for turning. Clip curves, notch outer edges and trim corners (page 221).

2 Turn right side out and press the shape flat, then turn in the edges of the opening in line with the sewn edges.

3 Position the appliqué and hand baste (page 18) the appliqué in place. Catch the folded seam allowance so it doesn't flip out to the right side. Edgestitch (page 69) around the appliqué with a straight machine stitch, sewing your row of stitching an even distance from the turned edge.

HOW TO APPLY A PURCHASED APPLIQUÉ BY HAND

Place the appliqué where you want it and hand baste. Some purchased appliqués will come with an adhesive backing. If yours does, read the directions on the packaging to adhere the appliqué to your project. Thread a sewing needle with thread to match the appliqué. I'm using a contrast thread so it's easy to see. Handsew around the appliqué with a blanket stitch (page 31). Place the stitches close together to create a satin-stitch effect. Continue around the edges of the appliqué until you reach the starting point.

HOW TO APPLY A PURCHASED APPLIQUÉ BY MACHINE

Decide where to place the appliqué. Hand baste it in place before sewing permanently, or use a fabric glue or the adhesive backing to secure the appliqué without pins. Pins will make it bumpy and harder to sew the appliqué on evenly. Sew around the edges of the appliqué. Use a zigzag stitch or satin stitch set to the same width as the appliqué's edging. Sew around the edges of the appliqué until you reach the starting point.

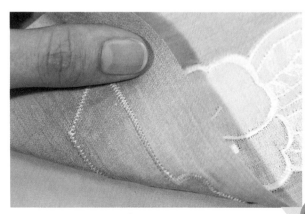

Backstitch

WHAT IS IT?

Backstitching refers to two different types of stitching, depending on whether it is done by hand or by machine. Backstitching by machine is when you stitch backward over the previous stitching to secure the ends. Without backstitching, seams can unravel at the start and end points. *Backstitch* also refers to a type of hand stitching that is worked backward. Hand backstitching is strong and flexible. Most times, when you see the term "backstitch" in modern sewing instructions, it refers to the machine stitching definition.

Backstitching done by machine

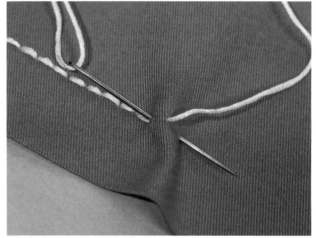

Backstitching done by hand

▶ WHEN DO YOU USE IT?

Backstitch every time you sew a seam by machine. The only time you don't backstitch is when you're planning to remove the line of stitching later, for example, when basting (page 18) or gathering (page 86). Permanent stitching is always backstitched; temporary stitching is not.

Backstitching by hand is used when sewing seams by hand. It's the strongest hand stitch! Before sewing machines, this was the most frequently used stitch for sewing seams in clothing. Hand backstitching is still used in couture sewing, even though it has rarely been used in home sewing since the introduction of home sewing machines.

Tips + Notes

When machine backstitching, if you don't want visible backstitches at the ends of your stitching, you can "zero stitch" instead. Change the stitch length to zero, and make several (five to eight) machine stitches in place to secure the row of stitching. This is effective when you are topstitching (page 218) in a visible area, especially when sewing with a contrast thread color. Substitute zero stitching for backstitching anywhere that backstitching would be unsightly.

Another way to secure the threads by machine is to stop stitching without backstitching, clip the threads but leave long thread tails and remove the piece from the sewing machine. Use a pin to pull the top thread tail to the underside of the fabric, then tie both thread tails in a knot to secure.

HOW TO BACKSTITCH BY MACHINE

Find the backstitch function on your sewing machine. Most modern machines have a backstitch button that has to be pressed down to keep the machine sewing backward; when you release the button, it will sew forward again. Older machines might have a backstitch switch or lever that allows you to switch between sewing forward and sewing in reverse. Check your sewing machine's manual if you aren't sure.

1 Starting at the top of your seam, sew about five stitches forward, then press the backstitch button and sew four or five stitches backward. Release the button and sew the rest of the seam normally.

2 When you reach the end of your seam, sew right to the edge of the fabric, press the backstitch button and sew five stitches in reverse, then continue sewing to the edge of your fabric. Trim the thread tails on each end of your seam.

HOW TO BACKSTITCH BY HAND

Thread a handsewing needle with thread. Tie both ends of the thread in a knot so you're working with a doubled thread. In the demonstration, I'm using embroidery thread and a big needle, so it's easy to see. Stitches will be smaller and less noticeable with regular sewing thread.

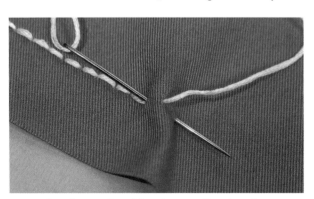

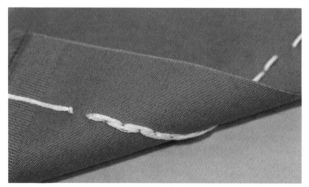

1 Working from right to left, take a small stitch in the seam and bring the needle through to the right side of the fabric. Insert the needle back into the starting point, slide it under the first stitch and bring the needle through the right side, one stitch ahead of the previous stitch. Repeat until you reach the end. There should be no space between the stitches.

2 Here's what it will look like on the opposite side. You're essentially sewing loops of thread around the two layers to hold them together. The reverse side shows the loops of thread.

Bar Tack

WHAT IS IT?

A bar tack is a set of close, dense zigzag stitches used to reinforce stress points of a garment. It will look like a thick, straight bar of stitches. Bar tacks prevent clothing from ripping or tearing as it's worn.

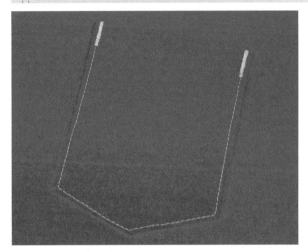

Bar tack on patch pocket

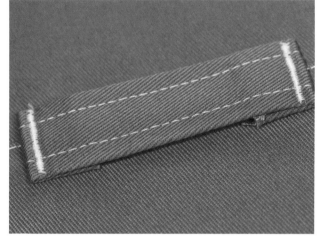

Bar tack on belt loop

WHEN DO YOU USE IT?

Use a bar tack to strengthen areas of a garment that may be under stress and need reinforcement. Bar tacks are often sewn to secure the edges of patch pockets (page 145), hold down the top and bottom of belt loops (page 20), and strengthen stress points on trouser fly closures (page 79) and at the top of slits. Sew bar tacks in contrast thread as a design feature or make them in matching thread so they blend in.

Tips + Notes

After sewing the straight stitch to mark where the bar tack goes, if the placement looks wrong or if the line is crooked, now is a good time to rip it out and start again!

If your bar tack doesn't look dense enough, shorten the stitch length (switch to a smaller number) so the zigzags are closer together.

Loosen the top tension on your machine for smoother bar tacks. This means that more of the top thread is pulled to the bottom layer and results in a smoother bar tack on the top as the top thread is pulled tightly over the fabric surface.

When sewing bar tacks at the top corners of pockets, work from the pocket toward the edge. This way you only have to mark the start point, as the end is the end of the pocket. Mark the start point ½" (1.3cm) from the edge, and sew toward the edge. Stop once you reach the end of the pocket.

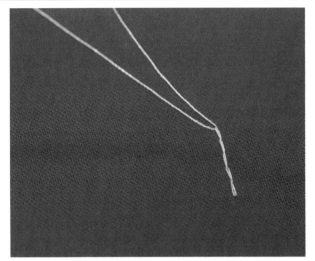

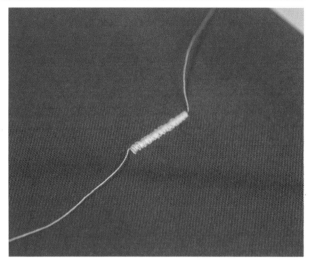

1 Decide on the length and placement of the bar tack; ½" (1.3cm) is a standard length, so use this as a starting point. Starting at one end of the tack placement, sew with a regular straight stitch to mark the bar tack area, and backstitch back to the starting point. I found six machine stitches worked out to about ½" (1.3cm). This makes it easy to see where your bar tack is going to start and stop.

2 Without removing the fabric from the machine, change the machine settings to sew a narrow, dense zigzag, between 2mm–3mm wide and 0.3mm–0.5 mm long. Sew from the start point to the end point with the zigzag stitch.

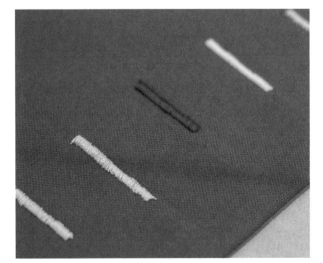

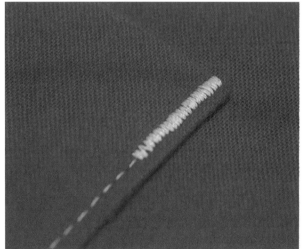

3 Make a few practice tacks on scrap fabric to be sure you're happy with the look and the length. Use a doubled thickness of fabric, so the scrap you're testing on is close to the thickness of your project. This is a good time to try out bar tacks in different colors if you're considering contrast stitching. Write down the stitch length and width so you remember what you've decided.

4 When you're ready to sew the real bar tack, sew the regular straight stitch first to mark the bar tack placement, switch to zigzag and sew the bar tack.

Turn over the work and gently pull the bobbin thread until you see the loop of the top thread. Insert a pin into this loop and pull the top thread to the back of your work. Tie both threads together in a knot to secure. Clip threads close to the knot. Press.

Basting

WHAT IS IT?

Basting is temporary stitching used to secure two or more layers of fabric together. It's used to line up the layers of fabric before sewing them permanently. Basting can be done by hand or by machine. Basting stitches also work well for marking on places like centerlines, fold lines or pocket placement lines.

Machine basting

Hand basting

WHEN DO YOU USE IT?

Basting is used anytime you want to sew two layers together with the option to remove the stitching later. Basting is also used for fitting. You can baste your seams together, try on the garment and adjust if needed before sewing the seams permanently. Basting hems in place makes them easier to sew. Baste along folded edges before pressing to hold them securely in place. Basting is a good way to test and check areas of the garment first, before sewing it in place permanently.

HOW DO YOU DECIDE WHEN TO BASTE BY HAND OR BY MACHINE?

Machine basting is faster, more even and slightly stronger due to the smaller stitches. Hand basting is looser and easier to remove. Hand basting gives you greater control over the fabric as you work and allows you to reposition the layers if they start to slip. Machine basting may leave needle holes when it's removed, while hand basting is less likely to leave any marks on the fabric.

Tips + Notes

Baste with contrast thread so it's easy to see and easy to remove.

Choose hand basting over machine basting whenever you have the time for more accuracy.

Keep a handsewing needle threaded in a bright color near your sewing station for quick and easy hand basting! Having the materials ready will make it feel less like a chore.

To remove basting stitches, gently slide the point of a seam ripper under a basting stitch and slice through the thread only. Be careful not to cut your fabric! Repeat every 2"–3" (5.1cm–7.6cm) along the length of the basting stitches. Pull out the basting threads between cuts, using the point of the seam ripper to lift the threads.

HOW TO BASTE BY MACHINE

1 Set your sewing machine to sew with a long stitch length, about 4mm. The longer the stitches, the looser your machine basting will be. Starting at one end of your work, machine stitch through all layers. Do not backstitch!

2 Remove the garment from the machine and trim the threads. Leave long tails so the basting does not come undone.

HOW TO BASTE BY HAND

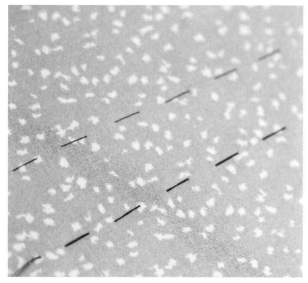

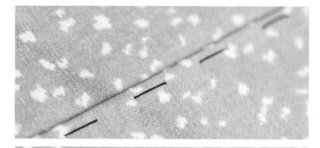

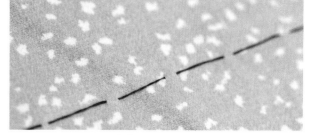

1 Thread a handsewing needle with thread and tie a knot in the end. If you're basting as a marking method, double the thread so it's easier to see. For all other types of basting, use a single thread. The top line of stitching uses a single thread; the bottom line uses a doubled thread.

2 Starting at one end of your work, sew in and out through all layers, making stitches and spaces approximately ½" (1.3cm) apart. For marking, you may want to sew longer stitches with shorter spaces in between (see second image above).

3 Tie a knot at the end of your basting threads or sew several stitches in place loosely.

Belt Loops

WHAT IS IT?

Belt loops, also called belt carriers, are loops placed at the waistline of a garment to hold your belt in place.

Topstitched belt loop on Robson Coat

Belt loop on Thurlow Trousers

▶ WHEN DO YOU USE IT?

Sew belt loops on skirts, dresses and trousers that are designed to wear with a belt. Coats and jackets may also feature belt loops to hold matching fabric belts. You can add belt loops to any garment that you want to wear belted. They're especially useful for garments that have a belt that might slip out of place if there were no loops. Belt loops are also very helpful to hold belts that are worn to cinch the garment to fit in the right place. The only disadvantage to sewing belt loops on your garment is that it may look unfinished to wear the garment without a belt.

HOW MANY BELT LOOPS TO ADD?

Two belt loops on a garment, placed at the side seams, is the absolute minimum. I wouldn't recommend that few, however, except on garments for which you want the loops out of the way and not visible from the front or back. At least four belt loops will keep a belt in place on the waistline. Place two on the front and two on the back. Five is a nice solid number of loops for trousers. Place the fifth loop at center back to keep the waistband from slipping down when you sit. You can even add six loops to a pair of trousers: two on the front, two at the sides and two near the middle of the back. It's completely up to you how many loops to add.

Tips + Notes

The folded belt loops are faster to sew, as turning the loops takes a little bit of time.

Double up belt loops for a design detail. Or place pairs of loops in an X formation.

Cut one extra belt loop in case of mistakes or so you can use only the loops with the neatest topstitching.

Short on fabric? Make belt loops in a contrasting fabric or choose a color that matches the belt you plan to wear.

HOW TO SEW BELT LOOPS, FOLDED METHOD

1 Belt loops are sewn first as one long piece and then are cut into multiple pieces to attach to the garment. Cut a strip of fabric approximately 1½" (3.8cm) wide by 16" (40.6cm) long. This will give you four belt loops. To make more, add 4" (10.2cm) to the length for each additional loop. Finish one long edge of this fabric piece with a serger or zigzag stitch.

2 Fold the strip in thirds lengthwise, right sides out, with the unfinished edge folded underneath.

3 Topstitch (page 218) along both edges of the loop. This type of loop is great for sewing into topstitched garments, like casual pants and jeans. Be sure to match your belt loop topstitching thread to the topstitching on the rest of the garment. Press. Cut into pieces for attaching to the garment (see page 22).

HOW TO SEW BELT LOOPS, TURNED METHOD

1 This method is just like sewing a strap. Take your belt loop piece and fold it in half lengthwise, right sides together. Sew along the long edge with a ¼" (6mm) seam allowance or use the seam allowance your pattern specifies. Trim seam allowances to ¼" (6mm) if using a wider seam allowance.

2 Turn right side out and press, positioning the seam in the center so it will be hidden on the underside of the belt loop. Topstitch edges if desired. You don't have to topstitch this type of loop, which makes this option suitable for dressy garments that have no topstitching anywhere else. Cut the length into pieces and attach them to your garment (see page 22).

HOW TO ATTACH BELT LOOPS

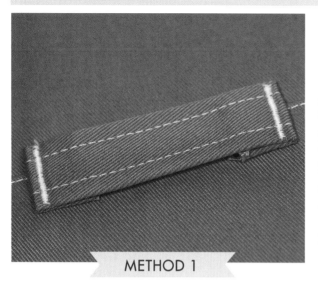

METHOD 1

The quickest method is to fold under the raw edges of each loop piece, place them at the waistline and edgestitch (page 69) or bar tack (page 16) across the folded ends of each loop.

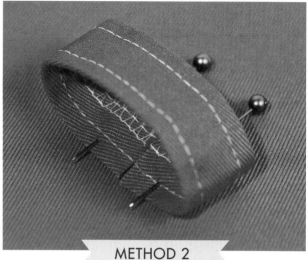

METHOD 2

Another method is to turn the raw edges of each loop piece under so that the raw edges meet in the middle. Zigzag across the raw edges of the loop, with the loop pulled out of the way. This will attach the loop to your garment, but there will be extra ease in the loop. Flatten the loop and bar tack (page 16) or edgestitch (page 69) to secure the other edge.

METHOD 3

With a garment that has a separate waistband, the loops will be the most secure if you enclose one end in the waistband seam. This will also hide one of the raw edges of the loop. Before attaching the waistband, pin the loop piece right side down to the garment's waistline and baste in place. Attach the waistband as usual (page 230). For belt loops that are wider than the waistband, stitch down inside the lower edge of the loop before attaching the top edge. Turn under the loose end of the loop, and line up the folded loop with the top of the waistband. Topstitch (page 218) or bar tack (page 16) in place. Press.

B Bias

WHAT IS IT?

Bias refers to the bias direction or the diagonal grain of the fabric. Just as the grain line (page 90) runs parallel to the selvedge, the bias runs at a 45° angle to the straight of grain. Sewing bias-cut garments is challenging, but practice will help you become familiar with the behavior of the bias and how to work with it. Fabric cut on the bias has stretch and more drape. Try pulling on your fabric along the length and then across the width. Unless it has spandex, it won't stretch very much. Now pull on your fabric diagonally; it will have a bit of stretch along the bias. Bias is most relevant for woven fabrics. Knit fabrics (page 109) stretch across the width and sometimes the length, so working with knits on the bias is uncommon.

Cinnamon Slip (Colette Patterns) on bias

Bias pockets on a straight-grain garment, Archer Shirt (Grainline Studio)

WHEN DO YOU USE IT?

You'll need to know where the bias is if you are instructed to cut fabric pieces on the bias. Making bias tape (page 25) starts with a cut on the bias. Bias tape is great for binding curves because the natural give of the bias allows it to form around curves without puckers. Pattern pieces may be cut on the bias to give them more drape and softness. An entire garment cut on the bias will drape and cling to the body, which makes gorgeous evening dresses and lingerie. Because the bias is the diagonal direction, it means that stripes and plaids cut on the bias will turn into diagonal patterns. This can be used as a design detail for yokes, pockets, cuffs or collars. As a bonus, you won't need to match up the lines on the bias section to the rest of the garment.

TIPS FOR SEWING ON THE BIAS

* Bias doesn't fray! If you look closely at the edges of bias, you'll see the woven fibers crossing each other at an angle. Try pulling on one of the threads. Unlike fabric that's cut on the cross grain or straight grain, where you can pull a thread across the whole edge, bias fabric will not fray.

* Cut pattern pieces on the bias through a single layer, as the bias is likely to shift and stretch. You might not notice if the underneath layer has moved until after the fabric is cut.

* When sewing bias seams, slightly stretch the fabric as it goes through the machine. Alternatively, you can sew bias seams with a narrow zigzag stitch to allow the seam to stretch naturally.

* When hemming bias garments, let them hang for at least twenty-four hours. You'll see this mentioned in pattern instructions. If you hem the garment right away, the bias sections of the hem may stretch out and hang lower than other parts of the hem and result in an uneven hemline (page 96). After the twenty-four-hour period, measure the hem up from the floor and trim off evenly.

* For bias garments, the best hems are narrow hems (page 123) or faced hems (page 94).

* You might want to cut wider seam allowances (page 170) on the bias, to allow for adjustments. This is especially helpful for delicate fabrics.

* Seam allowances on the bias don't need to be finished, as they will not fray. You can finish them if you like. A pinked seam finish (page 177) will lie flat without adding bulk. Serging bias seam allowances (page 179) can create a wavy, rippled edge, so it's not recommended.

CHANGING THE GRAIN LINE FROM STRAIGHT TO BIAS

You may want to change the direction of your pattern pieces to create a diagonal effect with plaid or striped fabric, or you may want a softer drape to your skirt. To change the grain line, simply draw in a new grain line that's 45° from the original grain line. See image, right, for how.

Be careful when you're changing the grain line. This is best to do on pieces that will not be affected by the change in drape, such as collars, cuffs, pocket pieces or waistbands. Changing major pieces of the garment from straight to bias grain will affect the fit, so proceed with caution.

Garments cut on the bias require more fabric, so if you've changed a garment to be cut on the bias, allow additional fabric. If you have the opportunity, take your adjusted pattern pieces to the fabric store and try them on the fabric, so you buy the right amount.

Don't be afraid to experiment with sewing on the bias. The best way to get familiar with grain lines and working with the bias is to practice.

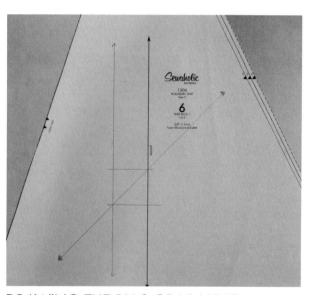

DRAWING THE BIAS GRAIN LINE

Draw a second grain line, parallel to the first one. Connect the lines to form a square. Now create a 45° diagonal line through the corners of the box. This diagonal line is your new grain line. Easy!

B Bias Tape

WHAT IS IT?

Bias tape is a continuous strip of fabric that's cut on the bias (page 23). You can buy prepackaged bias tape made from a cotton-polyester blend in a variety of solid colors. It's usually preshrunk so it can be used right away. You can make bias tape out of any flat fabric from printed cotton to polyester satin. The easiest fabrics to make bias tape from are tightly woven fabrics that press well, such as 100 percent cotton and cotton-polyester blends. Bias tape comes in two varieties: single-fold and double-fold. Single-fold bias tape has the edges pressed in toward center, and double-fold bias tape is single-fold tape that's been pressed in half.

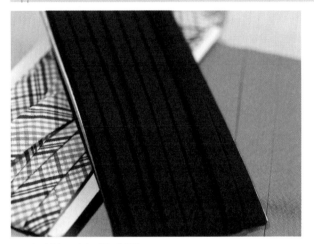

Single-fold and double-fold bias tape

Bias tape inside Robson Coat

WHEN DO YOU USE IT?

Bias tape is great for binding the edges of fabric, as the bias curves nicely around shaped edges without puckering. Bias tape is used for seam finishes such as bound seams (page 172) and seams with a Hong Kong finish (page 175). Bias tape can also be used for finishing the edges of hems or finishing inner edges of facings. You can even use bias tape instead of facings to finish necklines and armholes. Read the section on binding (page 28) to learn how to apply it to edges and how to finish garment openings. Bias tape has a bit of stretch, so you don't want to use it as a stabilizer like stay tape (page 204). Bias tape is also used to make covered piping (page 132).

Tips + Notes

Choose small prints rather than large prints for making bias tape, as large prints won't show up well on the narrow tape.

Stripes, plaid and gingham cut on the bias make neat bias tape!

When seaming the bias strips, save the shortest strips for the end and sew them one after another. That way you can start using the section with the least number of seams and save the part with several joins until the end of your project. Or cut from the end with many seams when you are using only small sections of tape.

You can turn double-fold bias tape into single-fold by pressing it open. Or turn single-fold into double-fold by pressing it in half.

Save the cardboard inserts from purchased bias tape to store your own tape. Wind the bias tape around the cardboard and secure the end with a straight pin or tuck it into the wound tape.

HOW TO MAKE YOUR OWN BIAS TAPE

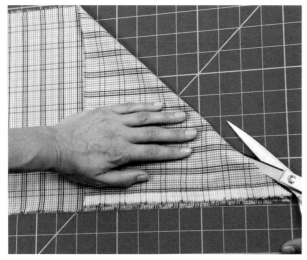

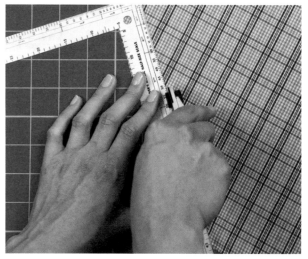

1 Prewash your fabric (page 157) and press it flat. To get an idea of how much fabric you'll need, 1 yard (0.9 meters) of 60"-wide (150cm) fabric will make over 45 yards (41 meters) of ½" (1.3cm) single-fold bias tape. Fold the selvedge of the fabric toward the cut edges to form a triangle. This 45° angle marks the bias direction. Cut along this line.

2 Draw a second line 1" (2.5cm) away from the first line. Cut along this line. Use a rotary cutter and cutting mat or chalk and scissors to measure off each new 1" (2.5cm) line and cut. Repeat until all of the fabric is cut into strips or until you have enough strips to make the length of bias tape you need.

3 Sew up the small strips into one continuous strip. To do this, trim the ends at a right angle. Form a right angle with two strips, and sew a seam from corner to corner with a ¼" (6mm) seam allowance where the two strips overlap. I find it easier to sew straight when I draw in the line before sewing. Repeat until all of the pieces are connected. Press the joining seams open.

4 Fold the edges in toward the center, ¼" (6mm) on both sides, and press. You can do this with your fingers, carefully, or use a bias tape maker. A bias tape maker is a helpful tool if you plan to make a lot of bias tape. It's a little gadget that folds the edges of the bias tape into the middle for you. The fabric goes in one end of the gadget as flat tape and comes out folded, so it's easy to press flat. Bias tape makers come in different widths, and the width noted on the package is for making single-fold bias tape. Divide the width in half for double-fold bias tape.

5 Once the strip is pressed, you've created single-fold bias tape!

If you're making long lengths of bias tape, start winding it onto a piece of cardboard as you go to keep it tidy. This will also help keep the folded edges in place.

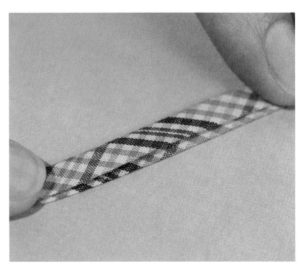

6 Press in half again for double-fold bias tape. Line up the edges so that one side is very slightly wider than the other. This will make it easier to sew later.

Binding

WHAT IS IT?

Binding refers to wrapping fabric around the edge of another piece of fabric to finish the edge. The binding is topstitched (page 218), edgestitched (page 69) or slipstitched (page 194) around the fabric, enclosing the raw edge. Binding is frequently cut on the bias (page 23) so it can be sewn along curved edges easily. Binding cut on the straight grain can only be used on straight edges. Binding cut on the bias can be used on straight or curved edges.

Binding around armhole on Pendrell Blouse

Binding inside Robson Coat

▶ WHEN DO YOU USE IT?

Binding is a way to finish edges and openings. Binding can be used instead of facings (page 74), as a seam finish (page 172) or even as a hem finish (page 96). Replacing facings with binding is a great idea for sheer and lightweight fabrics. Where the facing would show through, the binding is narrow and creates a more subtle finish. If you're concerned with stability around your edges, then a facing would be a better finish as it adds more support and strength. There are many different ways to apply binding. It can be sewn to your garments with visible topstitching (page 218) or invisible hand stitching (page 194).

Tips + Notes

Use hair clips or binder clips instead of pins to hold bias binding in place. These will keep the bias tape flat, whereas pins create bumps. Hand basting is an even more accurate method when the bias tape needs to be perfect.

Instead of hemming, why not bind your hems with bias binding? It's a great way to finish curved edges and add a nice border.

This is the most accurate method to sew on bias tape, but it is slower than the quick-and-easy Method 2 (page 30).

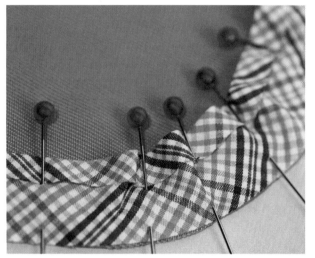

1 Unfold one side of the bias tape, and press that edge open. Pin the unfolded side of the bias tape to the raw edge of the piece that you want to bind, with the right sides together.

2 Sew in the groove of the unfolded part, where the fold was previously, about ¼" (6mm) from the edge.

3 Press the seam toward the binding. Fold the bias tape to the inside and line up the fold with the line of stitching you just sewed.

4 Pin or hand baste in place. If you're going around a curve, you may want to steam and press the bias tape as you pin it in place around the curves, so the tape fits the shape of the curve.

5 Edgestitch (page 69) close to the fold of the binding, and press.

HOW TO APPLY BIAS BINDING, METHOD 2

This is a fast and easy way to apply bias tape. If your fabric is slippery, or if you're concerned you will miss catching the other side of the tape with your stitching, choose Method 1 instead.

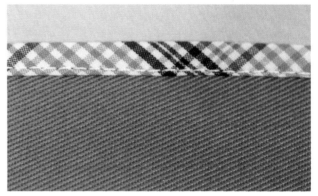

1 Press single-fold bias tape in half or use double-fold bias tape. Wrap the bias tape around the raw edge, while you push the fabric into the fold as far as it will go. Place the slightly wider side of the bias tape on the bottom. Pin in place. At this point you may want to lightly steam the binding so it forms around the curves.

2 Take your work to the sewing machine and edgestitch (page 69) close to the edge of the bias tape. When edgestitching, it's better to be a little farther away from the edge and to catch both sides of the tape than to be super close to the edge and risk going over the edge. Press.

BINDING AS A REPLACEMENT FOR FACINGS

It's easy to replace facings with binding. Trim off the full seam allowance around the neckline, and follow one of the two methods above to apply bias tape to the edge. This will result in a visible binding and is best used around the neckline or armholes.

When you sew hidden bias bindings in place of facings, the binding itself is invisible from the right side.

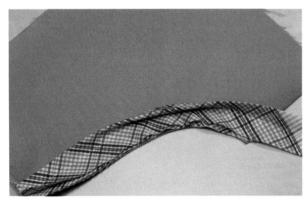

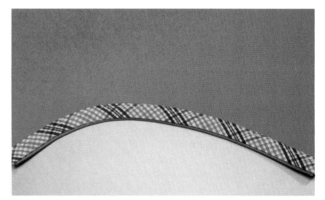

1 Press the bias binding flat. If you're applying the binding to a closed opening, sew the seam in the binding to form a loop. Otherwise leave the binding as one long piece. Press the binding in half lengthwise, with the wrong sides together.

Pin the binding to the edge of the opening, with the right side of the fabric up, and sew with a ⅝" (1.5cm) seam allowance.

2 Trim the seam allowance to ¼" (6mm) and clip curves (page 221). Press the folded binding all the way to the inside, so there is no binding showing on the right side. I like to press so there's a tiny ridge of the garment fabric pressed to the inside. Edgestitch (page 69) along the fold of the binding. Or slipstitch (page 194) the folded edge of the binding to the garment for an invisible finish.

B Blanket Stitch

WHAT IS IT?

Blanket stitch is a hand stitch used for finishing a raw edge. It's called blanket stitch because originally this type of stitch was used to finish the raw edges of a blanket. Blanket stitch is often done in contrast thread and adds a home-sewn, crafty look to your projects. It looks the same on both sides of the fabric, which makes it a good edge finish.

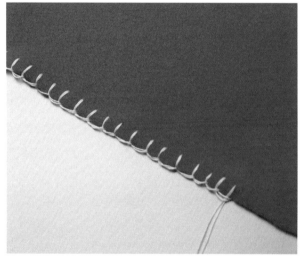

Blanket stitch around sample

Blanket stitch around appliqué

WHEN DO YOU USE IT?

You can use a blanket stitch to sew on appliqués (page 10), finish raw edges of blankets, make thread loops (page 216) or finish raw edges of seams. Choose a contrast thread color to make the blanket stitches show up, or choose a more subtle color so the stitches blend in. Use a blanket stitch when you want a home-sewn look on appliqué, patchwork or around visible edges.

Tips + Notes

To keep your stitches at an even distance from the fabric edge, mark a line up from the edge of the fabric to show where the blanket stitches will go.

Space stitches closer together to form a denser edge finish. Space stitches farther apart to make it faster to sew.

To blanket-stitch around corners, make the stitches closer together at the starting points and allow the loops to spread out around the edge like the spokes of a wheel.

Many modern sewing machines come with a blanket stitch function, also called an appliqué stitch. Check your machine's manual!

HOW TO BLANKET STITCH

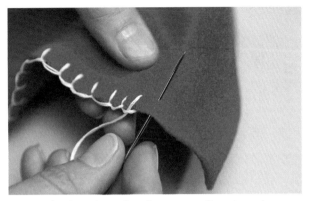

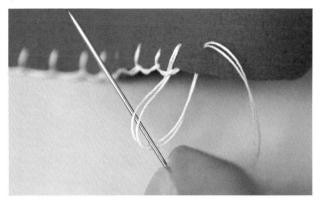

1 Start by threading a handsewing needle with single thread. You may want to use thicker thread if the stitching is meant to be seen as decorative stitching or for finishing the edges of a blanket. Arrange the fabric with the raw edge facing you and the right side up. Working from left to right, start with the needle through the fabric on the left side of the piece, coming up from the wrong side to the right side. Place the needle an equal distance above the raw edge and away from the last stitch.

2 Bring the needle out straight down toward you, looping the thread under the point of the needle.

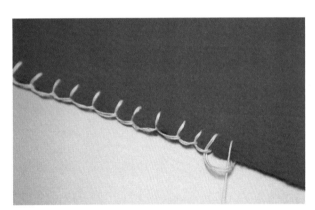

3 Do not pull the thread too tightly, just until the loop sits against the raw edge of the fabric. This forms the blanket stitch.

4 Repeat this stitch across the raw edge of the fabric. Keep the stitches equally spaced along the length of the fabric and an equal distance up from the raw edge. You are making a series of connected L-shaped stitches along the edge of the fabric.

B Boning

WHAT IS IT?

Boning is a narrow strip of plastic or metal sewn into seams or casings used to build structure and support into garments. It's called boning because years ago bones were used in place of plastic or metal. It's most commonly sold by the yard as hard plastic in a soft feltlike fabric casing or as thin flat plastic boning that you can sew through without a fabric casing. Metal boning is harder to find and may have to be ordered from specialty websites. Metal boning, also called spiral-steel boning, is more flexible, bends with the body and may be more comfortable to wear.

Boned bodice (Simplicity 4931)

Boned bodice, detail

WHEN DO YOU USE IT?

Boning is frequently seen in strapless dresses, halter tops, structured bodices, corsets, foundation garments and other tight-fitting garments. Boning helps smooth out the lines of a bodice. It holds the seams straight and keeps them from wrinkling. Boning is sewn along straight, vertical seams, including side seams, princess seams and center seams. Boning can be sewn on either side of a zipper for extra support. Sometimes you will even see boning sewn on an angle to help support the lines of the garment. You won't be able to see the boning from the right side of the garment, but you may see the topstitching lines of each casing. Sometimes the casings are sewn to the outside as a design feature, as seen in corsets or foundation garments.

Tips + Notes

You don't want to skip boning if your dress is strapless, especially if the pattern calls for boning. It's necessary to support the bodice and keep the dress from falling down.

You can buy metal boning by the yard or meter or in precut lengths. If you need to shorten metal boning, you'll need wire cutters. End caps cover the cut ends and are applied with pliers.

HOW TO SEW BONING INTO A BODICE

In this example, I'm using the type of boning that comes in the fabric casing. I am applying the boning to the lining of the bodice, so the casing seams are visible only inside the garment, not from the outside.

First, you'll construct the bodice lining. Sew all princess seams or darts, and sew side seams of bodice front and back. Leave the bodice open at the closure seam. In this case, the closure is a left side zipper. Press darts and press seam allowances open. Trim seam allowances to ¼" (6mm). Trimming (page 221) is optional, but it helps to reduce bulk, if necessary.

If the pattern calls for boning, it will indicate which seams require boning. If not, decide where you want to add the boning. At minimum, you'll want to add a piece of boning to each side seam. Those two pieces will add structure and help keep your dress up. Depending on the design, you may want to add boning to the vertical seams as well, along the vertical darts at the back or along center front or back. The more boning you add, the more structured your bodice will be.

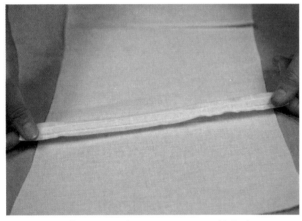

1 Measure the seams where you want to add the boning, and cut the boning to match the seam lines. You'll need one piece of boning in its casing for each seam.

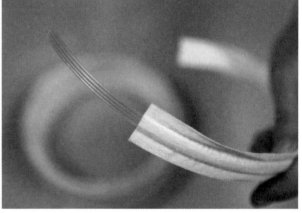

2 Take the boning out of its casings. You'll have curly plastic strips. To straighten out the boning pieces, fill a shallow dish with boiling water and drop the plastic pieces into the water. Leave the boning in the hot water for five to ten minutes, using a mug or dish to hold the pieces under water. Take the pieces out and press them flat under something heavy while they cool off. (If you're not able to soften the boning in hot water, alternate the direction of the curl as you insert each piece into its casing so that they don't curve the same way. Over time they should straighten out.)

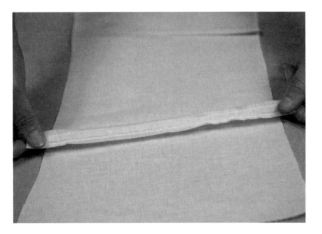

3 Center the casings along the seam lines or dart lines, and pin to the bodice. Pin all of the casings in place. Edgestitch (page 69) on either side of the casing, through the original casing stitch lines, with your sewing machine.

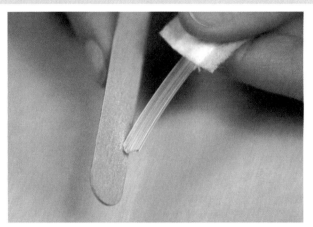

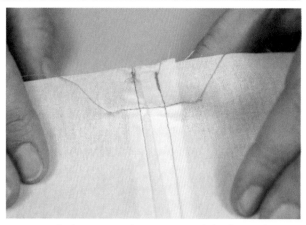

4 Before inserting the boning back into the casing, trim ¾" (1.9cm) off each end. You do this is to make sure you don't stitch through the boning when you sew your top and bottom seam allowances. Cut the ends in a slight curve to remove the corners. With a nail file, file the ends into a slight arc to smooth out any sharp points. Alternately you can melt the ends carefully with a match or lighter. The ends will form a hard knob without any sharp edges.

5 Insert the boning into the casings, and check to make sure each piece ends at least ⅝" (1.5cm) from the raw edge. Sew across each of the casing openings to keep the boning inside its casing.

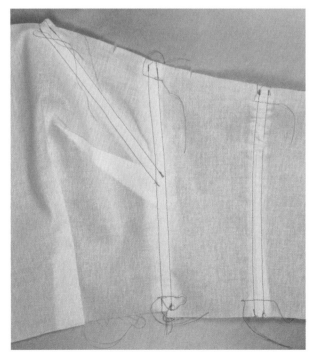

6 Voila! Your boned bodice is complete.

HOW TO SEW THE SEW-THROUGH TYPE OF BONING

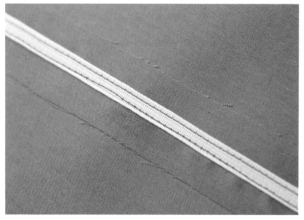

If you are using the sew-through type of boning, follow the same steps as above, cutting the boning pieces shorter than each seam by ¾" (1.9cm) on each end. Instead of sewing the fabric casings to the bodice, center the boning over the seam line, and edgestitch (page 69) along both edges right through the boning.

Border Print

WHAT IS IT?

Border print fabric is printed along one or both selvedges (page 187), along the border of the fabric. The border can be narrow or wide, or it can cover the entire width of the fabric. Some variations of a border print include ombré fabrics that fade from dark to light or color to color across the width of the fabric. Eyelet fabrics with scalloped edges can be treated as border print fabrics and work well in patterns designed for border prints.

Border print on Cambie Dress

WHEN DO YOU USE IT?

Border prints make great skirts and dresses! Full, gathered skirts work well in border prints. Place the border along the hemline for a traditional placement, or place the border at the top of the waist and have the pattern fade down the length of the skirt. When choosing a pattern for a border print fabric, look for patterns where the hemline is cut straight across the grain, not curved. You can use a pattern with a curved hemline, but you'll lose some of the border detail. There are sewing patterns designed specifically for border prints; look for these as a good choice for border print fabrics.

The hardest part about working with border prints is deciding where to place the print—the cutting and sewing is easy!

Border print on Cambie Dress Skirt

PLANNING PROJECTS WITH BORDER-PRINT FABRICS

* Analyze the border print fabric. Does the border print run along both selvedges or just one? How deep is the border? Does it cover most of the fabric, or is it decorating a narrow strip along the edge?

* Border prints with smaller borders are easier to lay out, as the majority of the fabric is solid.

* Border prints with wide borders are more challenging to lay out as the print needs to be considered for each pattern piece.

* Take the pattern pieces or the pattern piece diagram and look at the grain lines (page 90). That will determine where the border will fall on each piece. Look for straight edges parallel to the grain as ideas for where to place the border: Across a straight neckline? Along a straight hemline? On patch pockets?

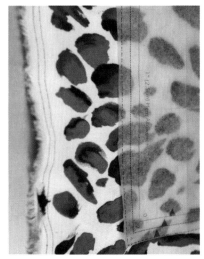  

1 Fold fabric lengthwise, with the selvedges together. You may want to fold your fabric wrong sides together to make it easier to see the border print as you work.

   Start with the largest pieces first. In the example, the largest pieces are the skirt front and back. As you place each piece, make sure to line up the border from piece to piece.

2 For example, on the skirt front and back, make sure the border matches across the side seams. If you place the pattern too high on one side and too low on the other, the seams will look sloppy. The example, left, shows a poorly matched side seam compared to the well-matched side seam, right. Measure up from the selvedge to ensure the seams will match.

3 Use the notches on the bodice pattern pieces to line up the pattern along the print. If there are no notches, line up the underarm seams.

Tips + Notes

You may have to change the grain line when working with border printed fabrics in order to get the print where you want it. It's OK to rotate the grain line 90°, but avoid changing it completely.

It's not necessary to match the actual print across the seams, but you may want to for large prints, stripes along the border or prints with distinct outlines. (See page 162 for more on matching prints.)

Buy extra fabric when working with a border print so you have room to work with the print and create your own cutting layout instead of following the pattern's layout. Do a trial layout before cutting.

If you are placing the border print along the hemline, make sure the garment is the correct length, as hemming it shorter once the garment is sewn may cut off part of the border.

To cut fabrics with finished borders, such as scalloped-edge lace, trim off the hem allowance and place the new hemline along the finished edge of the fabric.

B Bound Buttonhole

WHAT IS IT?

Bound buttonholes are buttonholes made with fabric strips. Instead of thread stitched around the opening, the opening is bound with fabric strips. These strips form the opening for buttons to pass through. They're durable, strong and give your sewing projects a professional look.

Garment with bound buttonholes (Simplicity 5928)

WHEN DO YOU USE IT?

Bound buttonholes work well for coats and outerwear and add an extra couture touch to blouses and dresses. I love how professional they look. You rarely see bound buttonholes on ready-to-wear clothing, unless it's a heavy coat. I also like that bound buttonholes are made at the beginning of a project, so you have a chance to get them right midproject instead of when it's all finished. (If the first attempt is not so great, you have an opportunity to recut the piece and start again!) Bound buttonholes are time-consuming but add a professional touch to your projects and have a great chance of success.

Regular buttonholes are done *after the garment is complete*, often the very last thing you do. Bound buttonholes are done *before sewing the garment*, as one of the first sewing steps.

Tips + Notes

Bound buttonholes work best when the back side is covered by a facing or another layer of fabric.

Use contrast fabric for the buttonholes, or cut the strips on the bias for striped or plaid fabrics to create a diagonal effect.

When making several bound buttonholes, sew the first step on all of the buttonholes, then proceed to the second step. It's more accurate and faster if you do it this way.

Bound buttonhole detail

HOW TO SEW BOUND BUTTONHOLES

This is my favorite method of making bound buttonholes. I've sewn bound buttonholes a few different ways, and this way always turns out the flattest and the most even.

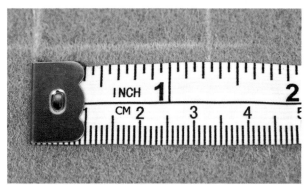

1 Before you begin, reinforce the buttonhole area with fusible interfacing (page 104), for strength, and so the cut edges don't fray as you sew. Pink around the edges of the interfacing before applying, so the edges don't show through to the right side. If your fabric is tightly woven, or if you have already fused interfacing to the entire piece, this may not be necessary.

2 Make sure the buttonhole placement is marked on the right side of your fabric piece. Draw a line down the middle of the buttonhole, and mark the ends. Measure the length of your buttonhole. You'll need to know how long the finished buttonhole should be so you can cut your bound buttonhole strips. In this example, the buttonhole length is 1¼" (3.2cm).

3 On a piece of your buttonhole fabric, draw a straight line. This line should be either parallel to your selvages or at a right angle. If you have a striped fabric, choose whether you want the stripes going across the buttonhole or along the length of the strip.
    Cut one strip for each half of the buttonhole, two strips per buttonhole. Here's how to calculate the size of each strip:

* For the length: Add 1" (2.5cm) to the buttonhole length. If your finished buttonhole should be 1¼" (3.2cm), cut each strip 2¼" (5.7 cm) long.

* For the width: Decide how wide you want the buttonhole welts to be when they're finished. Take that measurement and multiply it by 4. If you want your welts to be ¼" (6mm), then cut the strips 1" (2.5cm) wide.

4 Take each strip and press it in half lengthwise, wrong sides together. If your fabric is resistant to pressing, baste along the raw edges to keep them folded.

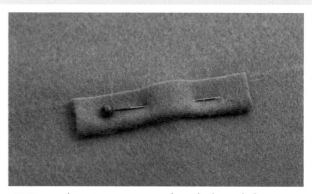

5 Line up the strip, centering it along the buttonhole placement line, raw edges in, and fold out. (This is very important! If you do it the other way around, you'll have some unpicking to do.)

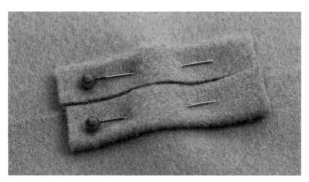

6 Take the other strip and line it up along the buttonhole placement marking the same way, with raw edges inward. The raw edges should meet along the buttonhole marking line.

7 Pin both fabric strips in place. Stitch right down the middle of each little strip. If it helps, mark the stitching line. Mark the starting and ending points as well. (Once you get it under your machine, it's a lot harder to see what's going on!)

Stitch from starting point to ending point, which is the length of your buttonhole as determined in step 2. There will be ½" (1.2cm) on either side of the stitching. Use a small stitch size for better accuracy. Basically you want to stop at the exact same spot on each side. Backstitch at both ends if you can do it without going farther than your start point. If you're worried you will backstitch too far, stitch in place for a few stitches instead to secure the ends.

8 Here's what it looks like on the opposite side. Check to see that both lines are the same length. If yours are a little off, go back in and make an extra stitch at the short end, so they match up.

9 This shows what's going to happen when you finish off this buttonhole. The welts that were facing outward are going to turn inward and fill in the hole. They'll meet in the middle because you sewed each strip exactly in half.

10 To turn the strips right side out, you'll need to cut the marked buttonhole. If you have a buttonhole knife and mini cutting mat, that's the best! Or you can fold the buttonhole in half and make a small snip, then use small scissors to cut the rest. I use the buttonhole slicer only to start the cutting, and I cut the rest with scissors.

11 Cut a Y shape into the corners between the two stitched lines. Use small scissors if you have them. Be careful not to cut the welts on the opposite side. You just want to cut through the bottom layer.

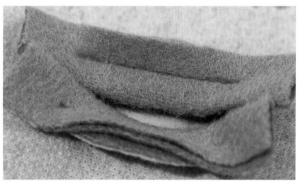

12 Turn the buttonhole welts to the inside. One at a time, turn each side of the buttonhole through the hole.

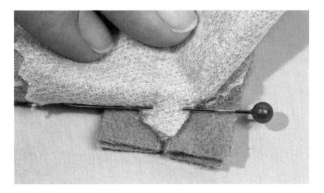

13 On the inside, arrange the buttonhole welts so they're flat and the little triangle from the Y cut is turned to line up with the buttonhole welts.

Before continuing, double-check that:

* The buttonhole welts are lined up with each other, and don't cross over each other.

* They meet in the middle of the opening.

* The triangle is turned to the inside.

* The triangle is centered over the place where the welts meet.

* The triangle is turned as far as it can go, so that the buttonhole forms a nice, clean rectangle.

14 Stitch down the triangles to form the shape of the buttonhole. Sewing these little triangles is the most important step in the bound buttonhole. It makes all the difference, so take your time! Stitch it down once, without backstitching. Be careful not to catch any of the garment fabric, just the triangle and the welt ends.

15 Check your work. Flip over your garment and check the right side of the buttonhole. Check to be sure it looks even, the corners are square to the edges of the buttonhole and there are no puckers at the corners.

If you're pleased with the appearance, run it under the machine back and forth about five times. That triangle's never coming undone. Repeat with the other side of the buttonhole, stitching down the triangle once, checking its position and stitching it securely.

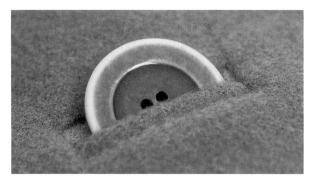

16 Voila! A pretty little bound buttonhole. Repeat with the rest of your buttonholes.

CHECKLIST FOR BOUND BUTTONHOLES

Keep this list in mind as you sew your bound buttonholes, and check the list again when your buttonholes are complete.

* Buttonholes are straight, either parallel or at perfect right angles to nearby garment edges.

* Buttonhole welts are equal thickness on both sides.

* The buttonhole mouth stays closed and doesn't gape open.

* There are no puckers at the corners.

HOW TO FINISH THE FACING SIDE OF A BOUND BUTTONHOLE

For the facing, you'll create little windows that will go around your bound buttonholes. This will cover the back of your buttonholes neatly and create an opening for the button to pass through.

You'll need fusible interfacing and the facing piece, interfaced and cut. Cut a square from the interfacing on the straight grain, approximately 1" (2.5cm) larger than the length of your buttonhole. In this example, the facing will be 2¼" (5.7cm) square. You can also use a piece of lining fabric, cut on the bias, in place of fusible interfacing.

1 To mark the facing placement, line up the buttonhole with the facing and poke pins through the four corners of the buttonhole on the right side of the garment. Draw a rectangle on the facing connecting these four points.

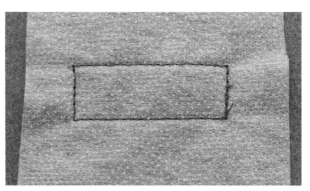

2 Place the fusible interfacing over the markings, sticky side up, and sew around the rectangle.

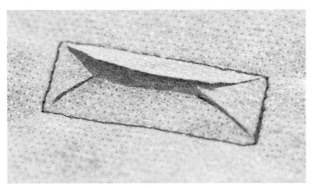

3 Cut in the middle of the rectangle, and cut outward in a Y shape toward the corners like you did with the bound buttonhole opening.

4 Turn the interfacing to the inside. Press to secure interfacing to the wrong side of the facing and the window is formed.

When the garment is nearly finished, slipstitch (page 194) around each facing window to secure the facing to the garment.

B Button Loops

WHAT IS IT?

Button loops are loops used to secure buttons, instead of buttonholes. These loops are often made of fabric but can also be made with purchased trim, cording or even elastic. Button loops can be sewn as individual loops, spaced along the opening, or continuous loops, with no space in between.

Button loops

Button loop detail

▶ WHEN DO YOU USE IT?

Button loops are sewn in place of buttonholes. Use them when you prefer the look of fabric loops over buttonholes on coats and jackets, blouses and dresses or as a single closure at the top of a placket (page 135). You'll see button loops placed along the back opening of bridal and evening wear as a decorative closure. Button loops can be a little tedious to undo and do up, so they aren't the best choice for hard-wearing garments. Unlike buttonholes, button loops are sewn before the opening edge is finished.

Tips + Notes

When sewing continuous loops, don't cut the long tube of fabric. Pin it in place as one long piece and bend the extra into the seam allowance.

On delicate and lightweight garments, thread loops (page 216) are a better choice, as they won't weigh down the opening.

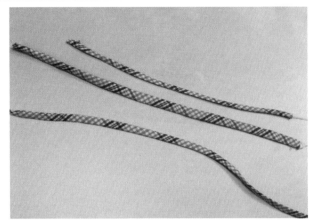

1 If using self fabric for the loops, cut bias strips (bias tape, page 25) and sew ⅛"-wide (3mm) tubes following the directions for sewing spaghetti straps (page 199). If your fabric is thicker, you may want to make wider fabric tubes. If using purchased trim or cording, make sure your machine can sew through it. Mark the seam line along the opening edge where the loops will go, ⅝" (1.5cm) from the raw edge unless the pattern specifies otherwise. You'll sew the loops to the edge before the facing is attached, so the loops are sewn in securely between the layers.

2 Mark the loop position along the seam line. Test the size by pushing the button through the loop—it should slip through fairly easily.

3 Cut and form the loops into position. If you are using fabric tubing, place the seam of the loops facing up, so when the facing is sewn and the loops are turned over, the seams will be hidden underneath. Machine baste along the seam line to secure the loops.

4 Sew the facing to the opening, right sides together with the loops sandwiched in between. Trim (page 221), turn right side out, understitch (page 228) the facing and press the loops.

Once the loops are finished, use the loops to mark the button positions on the other side of the opening. Overlap the edges where they will sit on the finished garment, and place a pin through the middle of the loop for each button marking. Sew buttons in place (page 50) to match the loops.

B Buttonholes

WHAT IS IT?

Buttonholes are reinforced openings worked in a garment to match up with the buttons. A button on one side of the garment slips through a buttonhole on the other to form the closure. There are three main types of buttonholes: machine buttonholes, hand-worked buttonholes and bound buttonholes. Machine-sewn buttonholes are the fastest and easiest. Hand-worked buttonholes are the slowest and require the most practice to sew successfully. Bound buttonholes (page 38) require a lot of sewing steps but are professional and durable. Buttonholes can be intimidating because they're usually the last thing you sew on your project. With a little practice, you can conquer the fear of buttonholes and make beautiful buttoned closures on your projects.

Machine-sewn buttonhole on Robson Coat

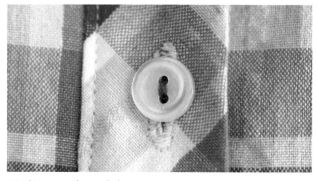

Machine-sewn buttonhole

▶ WHEN DO YOU USE IT?

Anytime you want to add functioning button and buttonhole closures to a garment, you'll need to make buttonholes. Even if the button is nonfunctional, you may want to sew buttonholes underneath the button so it looks more authentic. Buttons and buttonholes are seen on blouses, down the front of the placket and on the cuffs of long sleeves. They're used on the center front of coats, jackets and suits and at the waistband opening on skirts and trousers. They're used to close and secure pockets, flaps, tabs and epaulets. Buttonholes are used when there is an overlap at the opening so that the layers can cross over. (For more on button overlap, see page 49.)

HOW BIG SHOULD A BUTTONHOLE BE?

How do you decide how big to make your buttonhole if the buttonholes are not marked or if you're changing the size of the button? The buttonhole size is about the width of the button plus $1/8$" (3mm) for flat buttons. For rounded or textured buttons, it's the width plus the height. Here's an easy way to figure it out: Wrap a tape measure around the button and divide this measurement in half.

BUTTONHOLE POSITION

Horizontal buttonholes are the best as they are the most secure. The buttons are least likely to escape, and the buttonhole is strong on the grain of the fabric.

For narrow bands and plackets, position buttonholes vertically so they can fit on the band.

Diagonal buttonholes look neat, but they will stretch out on the bias. However, if you are sewing buttonholes on a bias garment (page 23), positioning them diagonally is a good idea because they'll be on the straight grain.

Once you've marked the buttonhole placement and determined the length of the buttonhole, it's time to sew it. All machines are set up slightly different, so take a look at the section on buttonholes in the manual for your sewing machine. Many machines, like mine, have a one-step buttonhole that will sew down the length of the buttonhole, make a few long tacks at the end and then sew in reverse up the other side of the buttonhole. Once it's set in place, all you need to do is keep your foot on the pedal!

1 Change the foot and adjust the settings for sewing the buttonhole. Make a practice buttonhole on scrap fabric using the same material as your project. If the buttonhole area is interfaced, interface your scrap fabric as well. It will give you the most accurate test. Place your fabric under the presser foot, with the right side up, starting at the back of the buttonhole and moving forward.

2 Cut the buttonhole using one of the three methods on page 48. Test the size by pushing the button through the cut hole. If it's too tight, adjust the length of the buttonhole and make another test. If the buttonhole is too loose, shorten the length of the buttonhole.

Once you're happy with the size of the test buttonhole, go ahead and sew the first buttonhole on the garment.

When the first buttonhole is finished, move on to the second buttonhole and so forth, if there are multiples. Make sure to position your presser foot the same distance from the edge for each buttonhole. Hold the thread tails as you sew the buttonhole so they don't get caught in the buttonhole stitching.

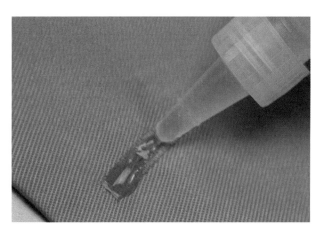

3 Once all of the buttonholes are sewn, apply Fray-Check to the buttonholes. This is a liquid that stiffens the fabric and makes the buttonholes easier to cut. Test the Fray-Check on your fabric scrap to be sure it won't stain or permanently darken your project. If it does, skip it.

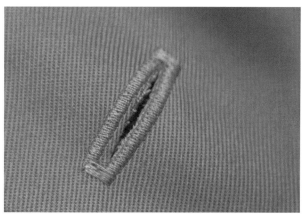

4 Let the Fray-Check dry. Cut open the buttonholes (see page 48). Trim the threads.

HOW TO CUT BUTTONHOLES

There are three ways to cut open buttonholes depending on which tools you have available. Method 2 is my favorite, but Method 3 will work if you don't have a buttonhole knife. Method 1 works only if you have a very sharp seam ripper.

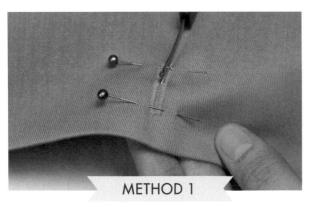

METHOD 1

This method uses a seam ripper, with pins at each end to ensure you don't cut too far. Place a pin at a right angle through each end of the buttonhole, just before the bar tack. Poke the seam ripper through the middle and slide it toward one end and then the other.

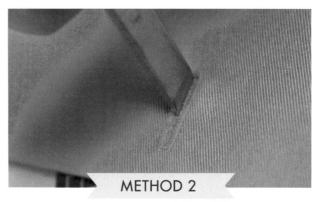

METHOD 2

This method requires a buttonhole knife and mat or wooden block. Place the mat or block underneath the buttonhole, and press hard with a buttonhole knife in the middle of the buttonhole. This will make a straight cut through the buttonhole. You can also use a sharp X-acto knife. Repeat the cutting step for larger buttonholes, moving the knife to get close to each end without cutting the bar tack stitching.

METHOD 3

You can also use a sharp pair of scissors. Fold the buttonhole in half, and snip the fold in the middle of the buttonhole with scissors to start. Open out the fold and insert the tip of the scissors to make a small snip toward each end.

Tips + Notes

Make a few test buttonholes and push your button through the test holes. Once you've determined the right size and machine settings, get a few nice ones turned out before making the buttonholes in your actual garment.

Make sure your bobbin is full! There's nothing more disappointing than sewing a buttonhole and running out of thread when it's 90 percent sewn.

Sew at an even speed. Speeding up and slowing down can result in the ends of the buttonhole not lining up.

Too-small buttonholes are bad, but avoid the inclination to overcompensate and make them too big. If your buttonholes are too big, the buttons will slip out and the garment won't stay closed.

You can sew buttonholes using contrast thread, but any mistakes or unevenness will be more obvious.

B *Button Overlap*

WHAT IS IT?

What if you want to add a button closure to a pattern that doesn't call for buttons? It's easy to modify zip-front styles by adding a button overlap to the pattern piece. The button overlap is an extension so that the layers can cross over each other, with a button sewn underneath each buttonhole.

Button overlap

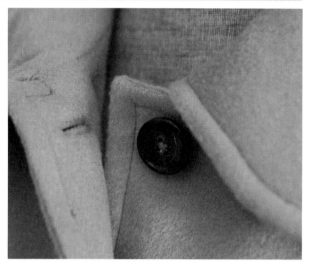

Button overlap

► WHEN DO YOU USE IT?

Anytime there are buttons and buttonholes, there has to be a button overlap added to each side of the opening. The only time that an overlap isn't required is when the buttons close through button loops (page 44) and the edges meet in the middle instead of overlapping. You may still want to have a button overlap with button loops on blouses or other garments where you want the fabric to cover the opening so no skin shows through.

HOW TO CALCULATE A BUTTON OVERLAP

1 The rule is that the overlap/extension should equal the width of the button being used. This ensures that the buttons sit nicely in the overlap and the overlap edge is proportional and pleasing to the eye.

2 From center front, measure the width of the button overlap from the top and from the bottom. Draw a line parallel to the center front line. This is your new overlap line! Connect the lines at the neckline and hem.

Buttons

WHAT IS IT?

Buttons form half of a two-part closure consisting of a button and buttonhole or button and button loop. The button slips through the buttonhole or loop, and since the button has to be turned to get through the buttonhole, the closure keeps the garment closed.

Buttons have two or four holes in the middle for sewing the button to the garment. Buttons may have a shank, a small loop underneath the button, for sewing it to the garment. This raises the button, making it a good choice for buttoning thick garments.

The majority of buttons are round, but they can also be square, oval, long and narrow or novelty shapes like hearts or leaves. Rounded buttons are the easiest to button and unbutton, which is why they are the most common shape.

Buttons can be made using a variety of different materials, including plastic, wood, metal, bone, horn, shell, leather, vegetable ivory (a type of nut), clay, fabric or glass. For more on fabric-covered buttons, see page 54.

Buttons

Wood and metal buttons

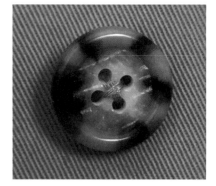

Button detail on Robson Coat

▶ WHEN DO YOU USE IT?

Buttons are used as closures on coats, blouses, dresses, jackets and suits. Buttons are a good choice when you want the closure to be a design feature or when you want a strong closure. If you lose a button, it's easy to replace it without taking apart the garment. Buttons are used to close pockets and secure cuffs, and they are often used as part of an adjustable feature; for example, dress straps with multiple buttons allow the straps to be tightened as needed without altering the garment. Buttons can be purely decorative; for instance, placed at necklines, waistlines and down the center of garments. Buttons can also decorate an opening that has a functioning zipper or snap placket as the real closure.

HOW TO CHOOSE BUTTONS

There are many factors to consider when choosing a button. Size is the most obvious, but you also want to consider the weight, washability, color and material. On lightweight garments, choose buttons that are both physically and visually light. Metal buttons may look out of place on a pale chiffon garment unless the contrast is part of the look you are after. Think about how easy the buttons are to button, especially on children's wear or on waistband closures. Novelty-shape buttons are fun but tricky for young children to manage on their own. When choosing buttons as a closure, make sure the garment doesn't fit too snugly, as the spaces between the buttons can gape and pull apart.

HOW TO MARK BUTTON PLACEMENT

Take your garment and line up the center fronts with the facing sides together, right sides outward. Line up the bottom edges, making the buttonhole side slightly longer than the button side. This will ensure your top layer is longer than the bottom layer at the center front. (Imagine how sloppy it would look the other way around, with the bottom layer hanging lower.)

Now pin your edges together to keep the edges aligned while you mark the button placement. You'll unpin these edges before sewing on the buttons. You might have a hard time pinning through all of these layers, so you could try using binder clips if that makes it easier.

Mark the button placement by sticking a pin through the buttonhole, through all layers of fabric, about ¹⁄₆" (3mm) from the edge of the buttonhole at the front edge. Repeat with each of the buttonholes.

These pins are marking the button placements. Because they might fall out as you work, mark where the pins come out with chalk or tailor's tacks (page 214). I chose chalk because it's faster than tailor's tacks, but it all depends on your fabric. If your fabric is light colored, you might want to use tailor's tacks. Mark an *X* over the pin spot. You'll find it easier to locate the exact right spot for the button if you use an *X* instead of a dot or circle.

HOW TO SEW ON A FLAT BUTTON

If the button is going to be used with a buttonhole, you don't want to sew the button completely flat to the garment. Leave space for the layer with the buttonholes to fit between the button and the bottom layer. Picture a button with a shank, like on the waistband of your jeans. You'll make a shank out of thread so the buttons button nicely without squishing that top layer.

To make the shank, stick something in your button stitches—a toothpick or straight pin—to keep the stitches loose. The longer you want the shank to be, the thicker the item you should use. For blouse buttons, a straight pin will be fine. For coat buttons on thick fabrics, a toothpick or skewer will work.

Thread a handsewing needle with doubled thread. To make the thread stronger and reduce tangles, run it through beeswax, pulling it through one of the slots from end to end. I like to press the waxed thread to make it much stronger and thicker. Press the thread between a folded piece of paper so you don't get wax on your iron or ironing board.

1 Take your needle and thread, knot the ends, and make a few stitches in the button placement spot, right through the X. The goal is to go just through the top layer, not through to the facing. It gives you a more professional look not to have little stitch marks on the inside of your garment. After you make two or three small stitches, poke your needle upward through any hole in the button.

 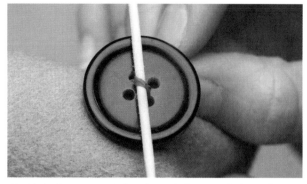

2 Take the thread and poke it back into the button's next hole. I like to make an X with my stitching on four-hole buttons. You can also make two parallel lines or a box around the four holes. On two-hole buttons, you simply sew from hole to hole. Before you pull the stitch tight, add the toothpick or straight pin to keep an even amount of extra space.

3 Make four more stitches through the same holes in the button. Turn the toothpick so you can make four more stitches through the opposite two holes for the X stitching.

 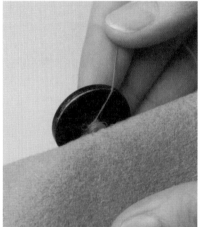 

4 Remove the toothpick. Push the button to the end of the stitches, so any extra space is under the button (not above the button).

5 Push up the button, so you're looking at the underside of the button and the stitch loops. Wrap your thread around the button threads, underneath the button, twenty or thirty times. Remember how many times you wrapped the thread on your first button so you can be consistent and do the same on all of your buttons.

6 Finish off your button by making a few small stitches at the base of your thread shank. I made about six or eight stitches, just to be sure it would stay put. These stitches take the place of a knot. Trim your thread.

HOW TO SEW ON A SHANK BUTTON

Thread your handsewing needle with doubled thread. Make a stitch in the button placement spot, right through the *X*. Again, the goal is to go just through the top layer, not through to the facing. After the thread is secured, sew the button in place. Place the button with the shank parallel to the buttonhole opening. Sew through the shank and garment several times. Finish off sewing the shank button by making a few small stitches at the base of the shank.

Shank button

HOW TO SEW REINFORCED BUTTONS

For hard-wearing, long-lasting buttons, add a reinforcing button. This is a small, flat button on the inside of the garment that will help strengthen the closure and reduce the possibility of the button stitching pulling out of the fabric. It's great for frequently worn coats and jackets.

Find a small, flat button and place it on the facing side of the garment. Sew through both buttons, following the steps above. It makes it easy if you choose a reinforcing button with the same number of holes as your garment button. Form the shank underneath the garment button.

Reinforced button

Tips + Notes

What side do the buttons go on? Here's the cheeky way I remember: "Women are always right!" This means that our buttonholes always go on the right side of the garment. The right always overlaps the left.

Choose buttons for your project before making the buttonholes, so you can try the buttons in your test buttonhole to make sure they fit.

Since decorative buttons are never going to be buttoned through a buttonhole, you don't need to leave space for a thread shank.

If you're adding decorative, nonfunctioning buttons, choose them once the garment is sewn. This gives you the chance to see how the buttons will look on the final project.

Buy one extra button and sew it to the inside of your garment seam allowances or in the side seam. If you lose a button later, it will be easy to replace it.

Some sewing machines have a function that will sew on buttons. Check your manual for settings and for which foot to use. This setting will sew a wide zigzag between the holes of the button, making stitches in place without pulling the fabric through the machine.

Choose contrasting thread to sew on your buttons for a pop of color.

Buttons, Covered

WHAT IS IT?

Covered buttons are buttons made from fabric—often the same fabric as the garment they will be sewed to. Using a covered button kit, fabric is wrapped around a metal or plastic dome to make matching buttons. Covered buttons look great and are easy to make!

Covered buttons

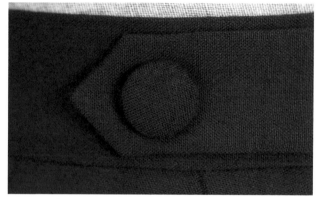

Covered button on Hollyburn Skirt

WHEN DO YOU USE IT?

Choose covered buttons when you prefer the look of matching fabric buttons, when you can't find suitable buttons to match your garment or when you want a round, smooth look to the buttons. Using the same fabric as your garment allows you to get a perfect match, which is great when you're sewing with unusual colors! If you're using contrast fabric for parts of your garment, covering buttons in the same contrast fabric can look quite smart. Covered buttons are elegant for evening wear in dressy fabrics like satin. Covered buttons are fairly inexpensive and can be replaced if the fabric starts to wear out. To sew covered buttons to your garments, follow the directions for sewing shank buttons on page 53.

Tips + Notes

Don't have the covered button kit, just the button forms? Run a gathering stitch along the outer edge of your fabric circle, place the button form on the circle and draw the threads up to cover the rounded part of the button. Press the backing onto the covered button form using your hands or a strong, flat object.

Make one extra button and save it in case you need to replace one later. Keep it in your button box, or sew it to the inside of your garment seam allowance. Sewing it to the inside of your garment means it will have been washed the same number of times as the rest of the buttons, so the color will have faded similarly.

If your fabric is sheer, double it or layer it with a piece of solid cotton or the lining fabric. This prevents show-through and makes the fabric on the covered button stronger.

If your fabric is thick, dampen it so it's easier to shape around the button form.

HOW TO MAKE COVERED BUTTONS

If you buy a kit, the instructions should be printed somewhere on the packaging, but here's a guide to making them just in case. In my example, the kit contains the button form, the button backing, a rubber cup and a plastic cap used to push the button together.

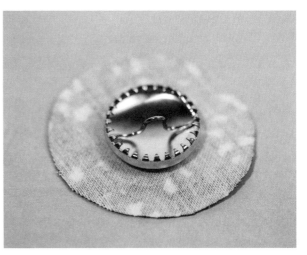

1 Cut a circle of fabric according to the template. If you've lost the template, cut a circle with a diameter that's twice the diameter of the button. For example, to cover a 1" (2.5cm) button, cut a circle that's 2" (5.1cm) across.

2 Place the button form on top of the fabric circle, with the wrong side of the fabric against the form.

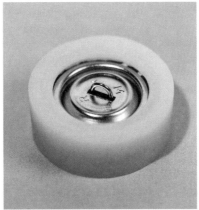

3 Push both pieces in the little rubber cup that comes with the kit.

4 Place the backing on using the plastic cap to push the backing into the form until it snaps in place.

5 Remove the covered button from the rubber cup.

Casing

WHAT IS IT?

A casing is basically a fabric tunnel that holds elastic, boning or a drawstring. It's created by either two lines of stitching or by a fold and a line of stitching. When the elastic or drawstring is pulled tight, the garment gathers in to fit the curves of the body. A drawstring or belt allows the opening to be tightened or loosened to fit the wearer; elastic allows the garment to stretch and move with the body.

Casings can be extensions of the pattern piece. For example, you can thread elastic through the sleeve hem to create a gathered cuff. Casings can also be created by sewing a separate piece to the garment, in the case of a waistband on a pair of drawstring pants. You can also make casings by sewing bias tape (page 25) to the back of a piece and leaving the ends open for inserting elastic or cord.

Casing with elastic on Saltspring Dress

Casing with drawstring and elastic on Tofino Pants

WHEN DO YOU USE IT?

You'll see casings on casual and athletic wear, sleepwear and lingerie. It's a great technique to use when you want to draw in fullness on a garment but want it to be adjustable or have stretch. Waistbands can be sewn with a casing, with elastic or with a drawstring inserted to hold up the pants. Casings are used on the hems of sleeves, blouses, pullovers and sweatshirts or around necklines, hoods and waistlines. Casings are cut longer than the desired length so the elastic or drawstring can gather it in and so the garment can stretch as needed. Whenever sewing a casing, leave an opening to insert the elastic or cord. Do this by leaving the ends open if the piece is flat or by leaving an opening if you sew the casing around a circular opening, like a waistline. For drawstrings and tie belts, sew buttonholes (page 46) on the right side of the garment to create an opening for the drawstring ends to come out.

Tips + Notes

For the most flexible and adjustable casing opening, consider adding both a drawstring *and* elastic. You can either thread both elastic and drawstring through the casing or sew fabric tie ends to a piece of elastic so the elastic is hidden in the casing and the tie ends are visible.

There are plenty of tools to help you thread drawstrings and elastic through casings. Plastic threading tools, bodkins and loop turners can make the process easier and faster.

HOW TO SEW AN EXTENDED CASING

  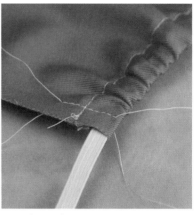

1 On the edge, turn under the seam allowance twice and press. Or finish the edge and press under once. Edgestitch (page 69) or topstitch (page 218) to form the casing. The casing should be slightly wider than your elastic—a good amount to add is ⅛"–¼" (3mm–6mm).

2 If the ends of the piece are open, proceed with threading the elastic through. If the casing is in a circle, leave an opening of about 4" (10.2cm) for threading the elastic. Thread elastic through the casing by pinning a safety pin to one end. Use your hands to work the safety pin through and to make sure the elastic hasn't twisted in the channel.

3 Edgestitch or topstitch the opening shut. Start and end in line with your previous stitching, if the casing is in a round opening. If the casing is in a flat piece, baste across the ends of the elastic to keep it in its casing.

HOW TO SEW A SEPARATE CASING

To add a separate casing to a garment edge, measure the opening and cut a straight piece to that length and to two times the width plus seam allowances. Pin one edge of the casing strip to the garment opening and sew. Turn under the seam allowance on the other edge of the casing strip, and line up the fold with the seam. Edgestitch (page 69) along the fold. If the casing is in a circle, leave an opening of about 4" (10.2cm) to insert the elastic or drawstring.

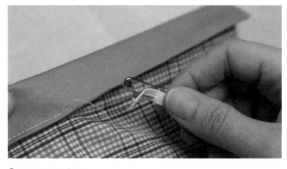

Separate casing

HOW TO SEW A BIAS TAPE CASING

Place the bias tape (page 25) along the wrong side of your fabric piece, and pin or baste (page 18) in place. Edgestitch (page 67) along the top and bottom of the bias tape, leaving an opening if the piece is applied in a circle. In this example, I'm using ½"-wide (1.3cm) bias tape to fit ¼" (6mm) elastic.

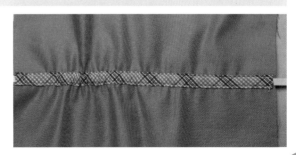

Bias tape casing

Catchstitch

WHAT IS IT?

A catchstitch is a hand stitch that's most frequently used for hemming (page 96) or catchstitching facings (page 74) to underlining (page 226). It's a lightweight, fairly fast hemming stitch with a little bit of stretch. This type of stitch is nearly invisible on the right side of your garment and will look like a series of little Xs on the inside of the hem. It's called "catchstitch" because you're "catching" just a thread or two of the fabric as you sew.

Catchstitched hem in contrasting thread

Catchstitch inside detail

WHEN DO YOU USE IT?

Use a catchstitch when hemming dresses, skirts and trousers. I use a catchstitch most often on hems that are turned once, with the hem edge finished. If you serge the raw edge (page 179) of your hem and catchstitch over it, the catchstitching will blend nicely into the serged stitching. Also, if your garment is underlined you can catchstitch your facings to the underlining to keep them from flipping to the right side.

Tips + Notes

As you sew your catchstitches, check the front of your work periodically to make sure your stitching is invisible. If you can see the dots of stitching, take smaller stitches and don't pull the thread as tightly.

Handsewing can seem slow, but it's a great way to sew nearly invisible hems. Relax and enjoy making tidy, invisible stitches while you think about how exciting it will be to wear your new dress!

1 If you are hemming a garment, finish the edge of the hem, press the hem allowance up and pin it in place. Thread a handsewing needle with a single thread, and tie a knot in the end. Start by going under the hem with the needle and coming out on the top of the hem about ¼" (6mm) away from the edge, so the knotted end is hidden.

2 Working from left to right, catch just a thread or two of the main fabric with the needle tip pointing to the left.

3 Next move your needle about ¼" (6mm) to the right along the hemline and catch a thread or two of the hem fabric, again with the needle tip pointing to the left.

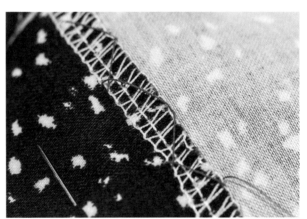

4 Repeat these steps until the hem is sewn. Press the hem.

Cuff

WHAT IS IT?

A cuff is a band of fabric used to finish the hemlines of sleeves or pant legs. Cuffs can be elasticized with a casing (page 56) or interfaced (page 104) and flat. Cuffs are often cut smaller than the opening, or they can be cut the same width as the sleeve or pant. Cuffs on tailored dress shirts are often sewn with a placket opening (page 135) so the shirt can be released to put it on and buttoned tightly around the wrist. Cuffs on sleeves that end above the elbow are usually wide enough to fit over the hand and won't need a placket, but you may want a placket as a design detail or so the sleeves can be rolled up.

Buttoned cuff on a blouse

Cuff on Thurlow Shorts

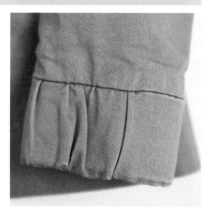
Elastic cuff on Minoru Jacket

WHEN DO YOU USE IT?

Cuffs add an elegant touch to shirts and blouses and look more polished than a plain hem. Add cuffs to trousers or shorts when you want to draw attention to the hems or when you want the option of taking down the cuffs and adding length later on. For athletic wear or casual garments, elasticized cuffs add movement and comfort. Cuffs may be a single rectangular piece folded at the edge or cut from two pieces, an outer cuff and a facing. Having a facing (page 74) on your cuff allows you to use contrast fabric on the inside, to shape the cuff or to insert lace or trim along the cuff edge.

Tips + Notes

For elastic cuffs, follow the directions for making a casing on page 56.

Test the fit of the cuff by making a muslin sample. Make sure the cuff is not too tight on your wrist or arm. If it is, add width to the cuff and reduce the pleats or gathers in the sleeve to match, or add to the sleeve seam.

To sew a French cuff, cut your cuff piece twice as long and fold it back to form a double cuff. Instead of sewing buttons, make four buttonholes on the cuff and attach cuff links through the buttonholes. This is a nice detail on dress shirts. If you can't find cuff links, sew two buttons together with a long thread loop (page 216) in between and use them to secure the French cuff.

HOW TO SEW A CUFF WITH PLACKET

Prepare the sleeve for the cuff by making the placket opening (page 135) in the sleeve and sewing and finishing the sleeve seams. If there are pleats (page 141) or gathers (page 86) where the sleeve meets the cuff, sew the pleats or gathering stitches. You can either sew the cuff to the sleeve before sewing the sleeve into the garment, or you can apply the cuff to the attached sleeve.

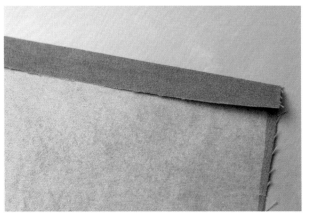

1 Cut the cuff piece from your fabric, mark the fold line and apply interfacing (page 104). Turn under the seam allowance on the long side of the cuff that is not going to be sewn to the sleeve, and press. Usually this side has no notches and is called the "unnotched" side of the cuff. Trim this seam allowance down to ¼" (6mm), if you like, to reduce bulk.

2 Fold the cuff along the fold line, with the right sides together, and sew along the short sides of the cuff.

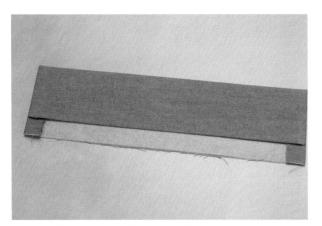

3 Trim the corners and turn the cuff right side out. Press. You may want to sew the buttonhole (page 46) at this point, while the cuff is still flat.

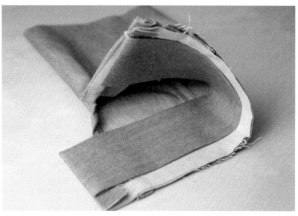

4 Pin the right side of the cuff to the wrong side of the sleeve, matching notches, remembering that there will be an extension on one side of the placket for the closure. I find this easiest to do with the sleeve turned right side out and the cuff pinned to the inside. Sew the cuff to the sleeve, while pulling the folded edge out of the way.

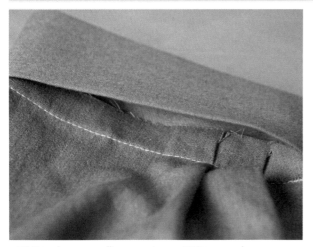

5 Trim the seam allowance (page 170), press the seam allowance toward the cuff and line up the folded edge of the cuff along the seam line, tucking the seam allowance into the cuff at the corners. Baste (page 18) or pin the folded edge in place.

6 Edgestitch (page 69) across the cuff seam first to close up the cuff, then continue edgestitching around the entire cuff. Topstitch (page 218) a second row of stitching parallel to the edgestitching if desired.

Make a buttonhole on the overlap (page 49) if you didn't make it in the previous step. Mark the button placement and sew a button (page 50) on the underlap to finish the cuff.

HOW TO SEW CUFFS ON TROUSERS AND SHORTS

Decide how wide of a cuff you want to add and add enough length to the hemline of your garment to cover twice the desired cuff width. Mark a line up from the hem that's the cuff width plus the hem allowance. This will be the fold line for the hem. Finish the edge of the hem. Press up the hem along the fold line, and sew in place. Press up the cuff along the cuff fold line, and tack in place at side seams and inner leg seams.

Cuff on Thurlow Shorts

D Darts

WHAT IS IT?

A dart is a wedge section of fabric that's folded and stitched in place. From the right side of the garment, a dart will look like a straight line with no visible stitching. From the inside of the garment, darts will look like triangles, curved triangles or narrow diamond shapes. The angled lines of the dart are called "dart legs."

Darts on bodice (Simplicity 3965)

Darts on Cambie Dress

▶ WHEN DO YOU USE IT?

Darts are used to shape flat fabric into three-dimensional forms around curves. Darts add shaping over the bust, at the waistline and over the hips. Anytime you want to remove excess fabric, a dart is a good way to do it. Darts can be placed in pairs or multiples for added shaping or as a design detail.

TYPES OF DARTS

* Single-pointed darts. You'll see these at the side of a bodice pointing toward the bust, placed vertically from the waistline toward the bust, or at the waist of skirts and trousers, taking fullness out toward the waistband. These darts can be shaped, with curves inward or outward, or sewn perfectly straight.

* Double-pointed darts. These have points at each end, shaped like a diamond. You'll see these darts used to shape the waistline on dresses, blouses, jackets and coats. Again, these darts can be either curved or straight, depending on the desired fit.

Tips + Notes

Mark the dart stitching line for greater accuracy. This is more important for curved darts than for straight darts.

Use a tailor's ham (page 212) to press darts.

For darts in thick or heavy fabrics, slash along the fold line, stopping about 1" (2.5cm) short of the tip and press open. Press the dart tip to one side.

You may see darts sewn with the wrong sides together, so the dart wedge is on the outside of the garment. This works best with small darts. If you plan to add this feature, make sure your dart stitching is very even and accurate. Instead of backstitching at the tip, pull the threads to the inside and tie in a knot.

HOW TO SEW SINGLE-POINTED DARTS

1 Transfer markings from the pattern to the fabric. With right sides together, fold the dart along the fold line. If the fold line is not marked, fold so that the dart points meet up with each other. Pin the dart in place. I like to poke the pins right through the fold line so I can sew toward each pinhole.

2 Sew the dart from the wide point to the narrow point. Secure (see sidebar) and trim the thread ends.

HOW TO SEW DOUBLE-POINTED DARTS

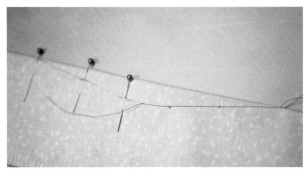 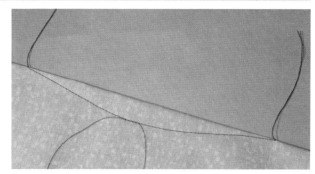

1 Transfer markings from the pattern to the fabric, just like the single-pointed dart. With right sides together, fold the dart along the fold line, and pin the dart in place. Start in the middle of the dart, at the widest point, and sew toward one end.

2 Turn the garment piece upside down. Start again in the middle of the dart, face the other point and start sewing about five stitches over the previous stitching. Sew toward the end. Secure (see sidebar) and trim the thread ends.

Four Ways to Secure the End of a Dart

1. Tie a knot in the tails. Tie the knot and hold your finger over the tip of the dart when you pull the thread tails so the knot tightens as close to the dart stitching as possible.

2. Backstitch the dart. This isn't recommended unless you can backstitch over the stitching perfectly without crossing into the body. Backstitching also adds bulk and stiffness to the dart.

3. Before snipping the threads from the machine, lift your presser foot and slide the fabric piece down. Re-place the machine needle through the fold of the dart, about 1" (2.5cm) below the tip, and sew a few stitches to secure. Trim the threads.

4. Begin and end stitching with a shortened stitch length.

Ease

WHAT IS IT?

Ease is extra room built into a pattern. There are two types of ease: wearing ease and design ease.

Wearing ease refers to ease needed for movement. Your clothing needs to be larger than you are so you can lift your arms and sit. It may be tempting to choose the size with little to no ease, but that will be uncomfortable and the seams may tear over time. On the other hand, too much ease will result in clothing that is too large for you.

Design ease refers to extra ease added by the designer to create a specific silhouette. For example, a gathered skirt may have more ease than you need to move around through the hips as part of the design. An oversize jacket has generous amounts of ease added to create a slouchy, relaxed silhouette.

Most of the time when I refer to ease it's the measurement larger than the body, or positive ease. Negative ease happens when the pattern and the garment are smaller than the body. In this case, the garment has to stretch to fit. Formfitting knit garments are often designed with negative ease so they hug the curves of the body. Lingerie and swimwear also may be designed with negative ease.

Cambie Skirt with positive ease

▶ WHEN DO YOU USE IT?

When you're choosing a pattern, look for the finished measurements. Sometimes these are printed on the outside of the envelope; sometimes they are printed right on the pattern pieces. The difference between the body measurement and the finished garment measurements is the amount of ease. Keep in mind that your preferred amount of ease may be different from the designer's vision.

How much ease is in a garment? At the waistline, pinch the garment fabric until the garment is tight against your body. This pinched amount is the ease. To determine how much ease you like in your clothing, try on your favorite dress and pinch the ease at the bustline, the waist and the hips. This will give you an idea how much ease is in your garment and how much ease to look for when planning a sewing project.

Renfrew Top with negative ease

HOW TO WORK WITH EASE

What kind of fabric are you sewing? The more stretch and give in the fabric, the less ease is needed. Stretch knits can fit with little or no ease; workout wear and swimwear fit snugly with negative ease. On the same note, the stiffer the fabric, the more ease is required so that your body can move. In general, natural fibers have more give than synthetic fibers. Knits have more elasticity than wovens because of the way they're constructed.

What type of garment are you making? Clothing for relaxing is more comfortable if the fit is loose. This is why elastic waistlines, loose fits and draped silhouettes are popular for loungewear. Fitted garments are suited for formal occasions, where you don't need to stretch and bend but want to show off your figure. Skirts need to have enough ease to sit down, and if you're making a skirt for work, make sure it's comfortable to sit in all day. You may find that modern sewing patterns have more ease than vintage sewing patterns, as modern women are more active, and women wore more restrictive foundation garments in the past.

Don't forget to consider what you will wear with the finished garment. If you like to tuck in your blouses, make sure there's enough room in the waistline of your skirt for your blouse. If you are making a blazer and love to wear them layered over sweaters, make sure there is enough ease to accommodate the thickness of the sweater. To check that there is enough ease in a garment, bend your elbows and reach your arms in front of you to give an imaginary hug. If the garment is too tight, it will strain at the seams and eventually tear. You should be able to bend and reach easily without the garment holding you back.

Personal taste is an important factor, too. Do you like fitted tops or blousy silhouettes? If you don't feel comfortable when the waistline is fitted against your body, add more ease to make it suit your preferences. If you like your clothing to look relaxed, choose a size up or add more ease. That's the beauty of sewing your own clothing—you can customize the garment ease and final fit!

Positive ease in a blouse

Patterns from different eras

Ease allows this Robson Coat to fit over a sweater

Easestitch

WHAT IS IT?

Easestitching is a technique used to sew a seam smoothly without puckers or gathers when you have one longer edge and one shorter edge to join.

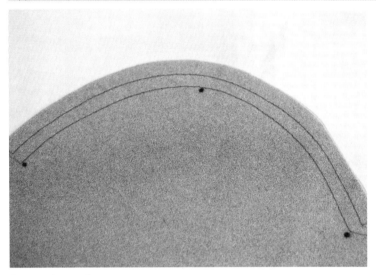

Easestitching a sleeve

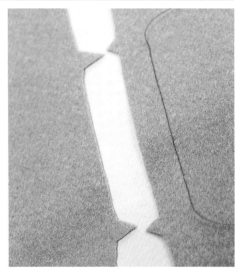

Edges to be joined with easetitching

▶ WHEN DO YOU USE IT?

Easestitching works when there is only a little extra fullness to work into the smaller edge. If there is a lot of fullness, you will want to gather it (page 86), pleat it (page 141) or take it out with a dart (page 63). Easestitching is used when joining skirts to waistbands and when sewing sleeve seams over the elbow and anywhere that a little bit of fullness has been added but needs to be smoothed out. Easestitching with machine basting (page 18) is similar to gathering except that with easestitching the goal is a smooth seam, as opposed to gathering, which produces small pleats on one side.

HOW TO EASESTITCH WITH MACHINE BASTING

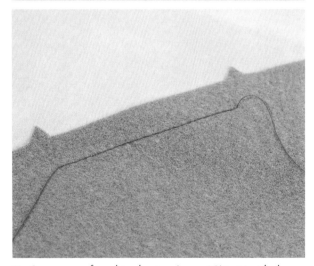

1 Sew a row of machine basting (page 18) just inside the seam line on the longer edge. For very curved areas, like the top of a sleeve cap, sew a second row in between the seam line and the raw edge.

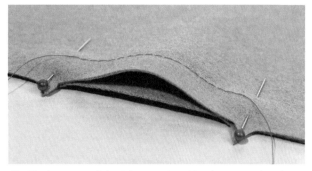

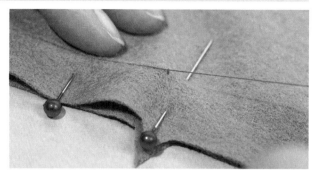

2 Pin the seam, right sides together. Match start and end points of the section to be eased, with a few points pinned in the middle.

3 Pull up the machine basted thread very slightly to fit the shorter side.

4 Sew the seam with the shorter side on top. Check that there are no puckers, and press.

HOW TO EASESTITCH WITH STRETCHING

This is best on natural fibers like cotton and wool or fabrics with a bit of give. Wool is great as it can be stretched, shrunk and shaped with steam. On delicate fabrics, easestitch with machine basting instead of stretching.

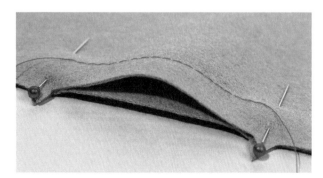

1 Pin the seam, right sides together, matching start and end points of the section to be eased with a few pins in between.

2 Sew the seam with the shorter side on top. As you sew, stretch the shorter side to match the longer side. Sew slowly and check for puckers as you go. Press, steaming slightly to shrink out any fullness.

Edgestitch

WHAT IS IT?

Edgestitching is a type of topstitching (page 218) that is sewn very close to the edge.

Edgestitched pocket

Edgestitched cuff

▶ WHEN DO YOU USE IT?

Edgestitching is used around collars, on waistbands, around patch pocket edges (page 69) and anywhere a very close topstitch would look good. Edgestitch to attach bias tape (page 25) or binding (page 28) or to sew appliqués (page 10) by machine. Edgestitching is also used to secure waistbands to skirts and pants or to close an opening that was used to turn something right side out. For example, a tie belt requires an opening left to turn it right side out. You can slipstitch (see page 194) or you can edgestitch to close the opening.

HOW TO EDGESTITCH

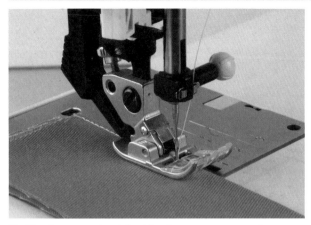

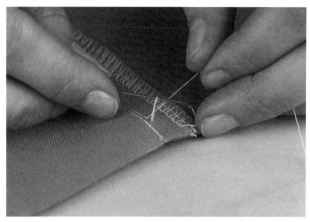

1 Simply sew on the right side of your garment, getting your stitching as close to the edge as you can maintain without crossing over the edge. Press after edgestitching.

If you're finding it difficult to sew close to the edge without falling off, try switching to a zipper foot with the needle on the right side of the foot. This way more of the fabric is under the foot, making it easier to sew.

2 Depending on where the start and end points of your edgestitching fall, you may want to backstitch (page 14) or you may not want to. I usually backstitch if the end point is going to be hidden or covered by another seam. If the end point is going to be visible, then stitch in place to secure the end or pull the threads to the back and tie them in a knot.

HOW TO EDGESTITCH A SEAM

To edgestitch a seam, work from the right side of the garment. Pull the seam apart gently with your fingers and stitch as close as you can to the seam line without crossing over. Sew from top to bottom, following the seam line as you go.

Edgestitch an opening closed

HOW TO EDGESTITCH AN OPENING CLOSED

When the instructions ask you to slipstitch (page 194) an opening closed, you may be able to replace the slipstitching with edgestitching. This works well if the stitching blends into the fabric or if the opening is in a hidden place. Depending on what part of the garment you are working on, you may want to continue the edgestitching all around the piece. For example, if you are edgestitching a waistband, you may want to edgestitch all the way around the waistband so that the stitching looks intentional.

To edgestitch an opening closed, press it in place, turning the seam allowances in evenly with the rest of the seam. Start at the end of the opening, backstitch, and sew to the other end, getting as close to the fold as you can without falling off the edge.

Elastic

WHAT IS IT?

Elastic is stretchy strips of rubber, poly, nylon or cotton that are used to draw in fullness of garments while keeping them stretchy and moveable. Elastic can be applied so it's visible or hidden. Stretch lace works as visible elastic, for example, as wide lace bands on underwear. Elastic thread can be used in the bobbin of a sewing machine to sew stretchy rows of stitching. Several rows of elastic stitching sewn across parts of a garment are called shirring. Elastic comes in white or black in a variety of widths. You may also find colored elastic, clear elastic and even novelty elastic with metallic thread.

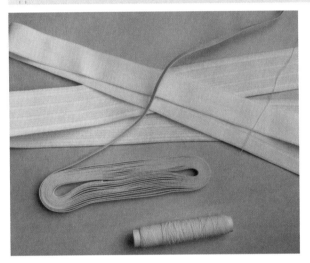

Elastic and elastic thread

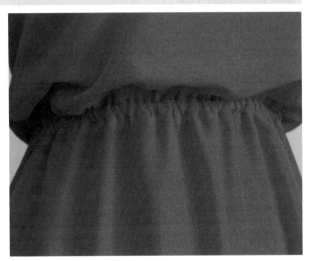

Elastic waistline in Saltspring Dress

► WHEN DO YOU USE IT?

Elastic works well in waistlines and waistbands, cuffs and necklines, and in stretch apparel like swimwear and lingerie. Add elastic to garments to fit narrow parts of the body, while still allowing the garment to stretch to its full width. For garments that are cut much wider than the body, the elastic draws the fabric closer.

Elastic is used to add shaping to waistlines on dresses and jackets, or to add movement and stretch in cuffs, the top edges of garments, necklines and waistbands on skirts and pants. Casings (page 56) are used to hide elastic and to protect skin from the rubber. You can also intentionally leave the elastic visible.

Fold-over elastic (referred to as FOE) can be used to finish the edges of a garment while still allowing the edges to stretch. This type of elastic is softer against the skin and comes in a variety of colors.

HOW TO SEW EXPOSED ELASTIC TO AN OPENING

This is an easy way to apply elastic to a garment opening, for example
on sleeve hems and wide necklines, or on swimwear and lingerie.

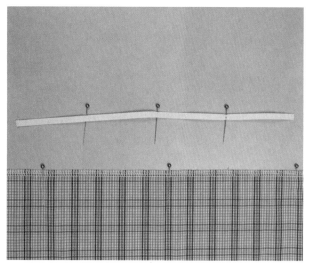

1 Finish the top edge of the fabric opening, and divide the
opening into quarters. For placing elastic in the middle of a
garment, such as the waistline, mark the elastic placement line
and divide it into quarters.

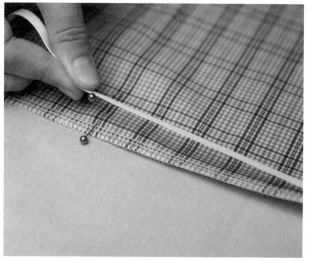

2 Match the elastic dividing points to the fabric dividing
points. If there is too much space between the pins, divide
the points between the pins in half, and match the halfway
points of the fabric and elastic.

3 Zigzag the elastic to the fabric with the elastic side up,
and stretch the elastic as you sew. Place one hand in front
of the needle and one hand behind, and stretch the elastic as
much as it will stretch.

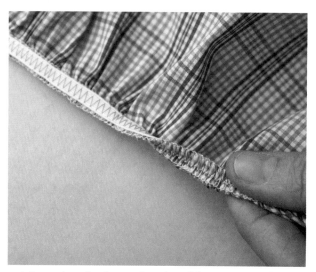

4 For a clean finish, turn the edge of the garment to the
inside along the edge of the elastic, and zigzag to hold it
in place.

HOW TO SEW FOLD-OVER ELASTIC (FOE)

To apply fold-over elastic, you don't need to finish the edge of the garment. The elastic will cover the raw edge completely. Divide the fabric edge into quarters, and divide the elastic into quarters, as well. Match the dividing points of the elastic and fabric, and wrap the fold-over elastic over the edge, pinning or basting (page 18) it in place. Sew with a stretch stitch or zigzag, stretching slightly as you sew.

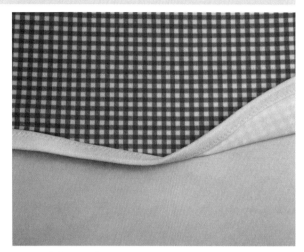

Sewing fold-over elastic

HOW TO SEW WITH ELASTIC THREAD

Before you begin, check your machine's manual as requirements may vary. In many cases, you will wind the elastic thread around a bobbin by hand, stretching it very slightly, and use regular thread in the top of the machine. Sew several rows of stitching, equally spaced, with the right side of the fabric up. Without touching the iron to the fabric, steam above the elastic stitching. The piece will shrink! Sew rows over an entire piece of fabric to create a stretchy, elasticized piece. This is called shirring. This technique is great for children's wear and sundresses or for creating a snug fit on many garments.

Tips + Notes

When sewing elastic, always sew with a zigzag or other stretchy stitch. The exception is when you're sewing elastic into a circle and sewing over the overlapping ends.

See page 56 for sewing elastic in a casing.

Elastic can break down over time or with repeated washing and wearing. You may find that the elastic is no longer stretchy and the opening has grown as the elastic has worn out. If it's in a casing, it's easy to replace by removing the old elastic and threading new elastic through.

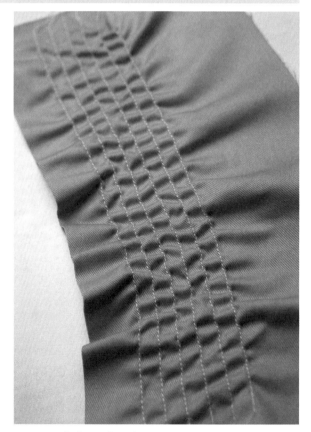

Sewing with elastic thread

Facing

WHAT IS IT?

A facing is a layer of fabric sewn on the inside of garment openings, such as armholes, necklines or waistlines. Facings can be cut from the garment fabric or a different fabric. Unless they are topstitched (page 218) or edgestitched (page 69), facings are invisible from the right side of the garment. Facings finish the edge of the opening and add structure and support. They are usually interfaced (page 104) for strength but don't have to be. Sometimes facings can be drafted as extensions to the pattern piece, if the edge is straight. If the edge is curved, a separate piece of fabric is applied. Facings may be sewn on the right side of the garment as a design detail.

Facing inside Robson Coat

Facing inside dress

WHEN DO YOU USE IT?

Facings are used to finish garment openings in place of waistbands, collars and sleeves. They can be cut to an even width all around the opening, or they can be shaped. Skirts and trousers with facings instead of waistbands are generally more comfortable to wear, as no tight band digs into the waistline. Facings also allow for a little more wiggle room in the fit, as the skirt can slip up or down the waist to a place that's comfortable.

CHOOSING FACING FABRIC AND FINISH

If the garment fabric is opaque and a facing won't show through to the right side, use self-fabric (the same fabric as your garment) for the facing. If your garment fabric is sheer, or sheer enough that the design will show through to the right side, choose a matching solid-colored fabric to use for facings. If your garment fabric is thick or textured, use a solid, medium-weight fabric instead for facings.

If there is no lining sewn to the facing, then the outer edge of the facing needs to be finished. You can simply sew around the edges with a zigzag stitch (page 183) or with a serger (page 179). You could turn the edge under and stitch it or pink the edges. A pinked finish (page 177) is best for tightly woven fabric that won't fray. For unlined coats and jackets, bind the edges with bias tape (page 25) for a professional look. Doing so creates bulk, so it's best used for garments in thick fabrics where the edges won't show through.

HOW TO SEW A FACING

Assemble the area of the garment where the facing will be sewn, so the opening is ready for the facing to be attached. Press seams open. Fuse or sew interfacing (page 104) to facing pieces. Assemble the facing by sewing the side seams, and finish the long outer edge of the facing, the one that isn't going to be sewn to the opening.

1 With right sides together, pin the facing to the opening. Match up the seams of the facing to the garment seams, and sew around the facing with a regular ⅝" (1.5cm) seam allowance.

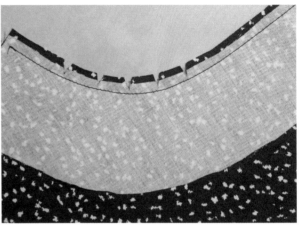

2 Trim the seam allowance to ¼" (6mm), or trim the seam allowance in half. If the edge is curved, clip and notch curves. See page 221 for more on trimming and clipping curves.

3 Understitch (page 228) the facing. If you are stitching toward an enclosed area, where it may be hard to reach by machine, such as a corner, understitch as far into the corner as you can and then backstitch (page 14) to secure the stitching. Press the facing to the inside of the garment. The understitching will help the facing roll to the inside; pressing it will keep it in place.

4 If desired, tack the facing to the garment at the seams. This helps keep the facing from flipping out to the right side. You can do this by hand, taking a few hand stitches through both layers. Or stitch in the ditch of the seam (page 206) and clip threads close to the stitching.

HOW TO MAKE A PATTERN FOR A FACING

If you want to add a facing to a pattern, it's quite easy to do!

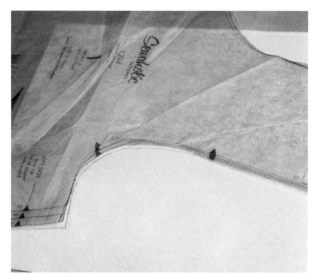

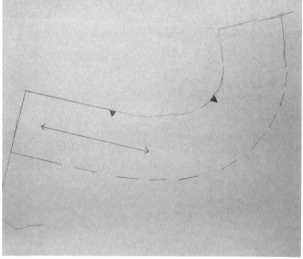

1 Once you've decided where to add the facing, fold out any darts or pleats from the pattern piece that will affect the facing area. Then lay the pattern piece on scrap paper and trace around the outer edges. This is the start of your new pattern piece.

2 Measure out from the opening about 2" (5.1cm) all along the edge, and draw in the facing line parallel to the opening edge. Depending on where the facing is located, you may want a narrower facing or a deeper one. Remember, you can always cut off the facing if it seems too deep. Mark the grain line to match the grain of your original pattern piece, and transfer any notches from the original pattern piece so it's easy to sew the facing to the opening. If the piece was cut on the fold, mark the cut on the fold side. Before cutting out the new pattern piece, use a ruler to redraw the straight lines.

Tips + Notes

Facings need to be deep enough to stay hidden, but not too deep to be bulky.

Trimming and clipping facings (page 221) is important to reduce bulk and ensure curved necklines and armholes can turn all the way right side out and maintain their curves.

If your garment has an underlining, catchstitch (page 58) your facings to the underlining to keep them in place. See page 226 for more on underlining.

You may want to stabilize a faced opening with stay tape (page 204), if it's an area that may stretch out over time.

Flat-Felled Seam

WHAT IS IT?

A flat-felled seam is a strong, topstitched (page 218) seam where the raw edges are enclosed. It's also referred to as a felled seam or a flat fell seam. A true flat-felled seam will be cleanly finished on both sides of the garment. You may also see mock flat-felled seams, which have the appearance of flat-felled seams but are less work to sew. For flat-felled seams, you can choose to have the fell on the right side of your garment, which will have two lines of stitching, or on the inside of your garment, where only one line of stitching will show.

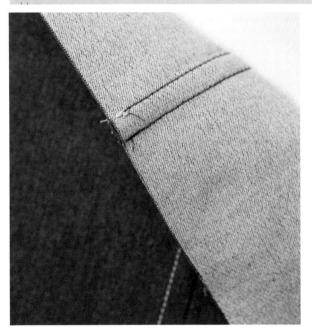

Inside of flat-felled seam

Mock flat-felled seam

▶ WHEN DO YOU USE IT?

Use a flat-felled seam on heavy-duty clothing, such as work wear and jeans. It's also great on tailored shirts that will be frequently washed or dry-cleaned. It would be an excellent seam finish on reversible garments and unlined garments, as it looks great from both sides. This type of seam finish is best on straight or mostly straight seam lines, as it's a bit harder to sew flat-felled seams around curves. Keep it in mind for menswear, as there are more straight seams than curved ones.

HOW TO SEW A FLAT-FELLED SEAM

1 Sew the seam with a ⅝" (1.5cm) seam allowance. If you want the fell to show with two lines of stitching, sew the seam with the wrong sides together. If you want only one line of stitching on your garment, sew the seam with the right sides together. Choose the side where you want the flat-fell stitching to go, and press the seams to that side.

2 Trim the seam allowance that's on the bottom of the two to about ¼" (6mm).

3 Turn under the edge on the top seam allowance about ¼" (6mm) and press. Pin this edge in place, and edgestitch (page 69) along the folded edge.

HOW TO SEW A MOCK FLAT-FELLED SEAM

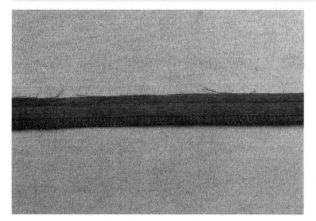
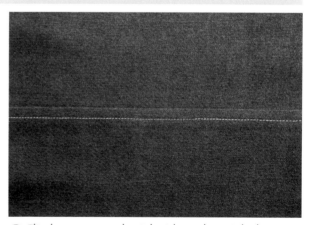

1 Sew the seam right sides together with a ⅝" (1.5cm) seam allowance. This type of seam will only work with the one line of stitching showing, with the mock fell on the inside. Serge (page 179), zigzag (page 183) or pink (page 177) the edge of one seam allowance. Press the seams to one side, with the finished side on top.

   Trim the seam allowance that's on the bottom to about ¼" (6mm).

2 Flip the garment to the right side, and topstitch about ⅜" (1cm) from the seam line, to hold down the finished edge.

Fly Closure

WHAT IS IT?

A fly closure is a type of placket (page 135) with an overlapping opening and either a button or zipper closure, usually at the center front of a garment. Fly closures can be cut as an extension of the front or as separate pieces sewn to the opening. An extension inside the fly opening protects your skin from the zipper teeth. This type of closure is strong and sturdy, so it works well on pants and jeans. On the outside of the garment, a topstitching line (page 218) outlines the fly closure.

Fly closure

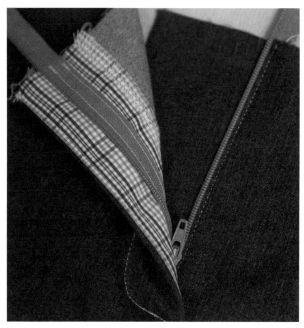

Inside of fly closure

▶ WHEN DO YOU USE IT?

Fly closures are most often seen on trousers, jeans, pants, suit pants and shorts. You may see fly closures on jean-style skirts, but they tend to be reserved for pants and shorts. The fly is sewn while the front and back pieces are flat, and afterward, the crotch seam is sewn. On men's garments, the fly laps with the left side over the right, and on women's garments, the fly laps with the right side over the left. However, on jeans and casual pants, you may see the left side of the fly on top, as they were originally designed for men. Either side is fine. You may be used to unzipping your pants with the left side on top if you wear jeans often, so that might feel the most natural to you.

Tips + Notes

Shorten your zipper from the top, not the bottom. It's easy to trim off the top of the zipper tape after the waistband is sewn to the top edge. Just be sure to wait to zip up the zipper until the top ends are enclosed in the waistband.

For a more subtle look, sew only one row of fly topstitching. For a more obvious look, or if the rest of the garment has two rows of topstitching, sew two rows of fly topstitching.

HOW TO SEW A FLY

There are many different ways to sew a fly closure, but this is my favorite method. In this example, the fly extension as well as the fly facing are cut as separate pieces. I find this gives a nicer result to the fly opening. The fly facing is interfaced but the fly extension is not. On the left side of the front, the seam allowance should have a ³/₈" (1 cm) extension, so the zipper is sewn well inside the fly opening and won't peek out. You'll need to have a notch on the front opening where the fly closure is to stop on both sides of the front. You'll also need two notches at the top edge of the right front showing where the fly extension is going to fall: one at the seam allowance and one ³/₈" (1cm) in from the seam allowance. Sew the crotch seam up to the notch for the fly opening, leaving it open above the notch, and finish the seam allowances separately.

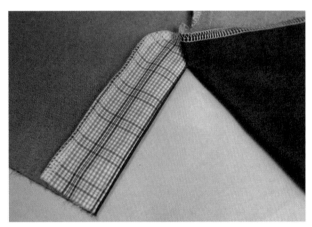

1 Interface (page 104) and finish the long curved edge of the fly facing. Finish the edge with bias binding (page 28) if desired. Sew the fly facing to the right front of the garment, right sides together, starting at the top edge and stopping at the notch. Ideally this stitching will stop right at the start of the crotch seam with no space in between. Understitch (page 228) the fly facing, trim seam allowances and press.

2 Fold the fly extension along the fold line, right sides together, and sew across the lower edge. Trim seam allowances, turn right side out and press. Finish the long raw edges together.

3 Sew the zipper to the fly extension, face up, lining up the closed end of the zipper with the notch. Let any extra zipper extend over the top edge, and do not trim until zipper is enclosed in the waistband seam.

4 Sew the fly extension to the left front using a zipper foot, stopping at the notch. Turn and edgestitch (page 69) close to the fold with a zipper foot.

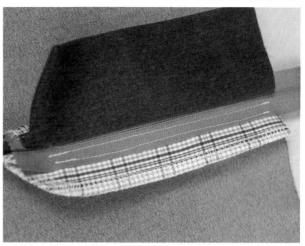

5 If the zipper is open, close the zipper. From the inside, line up the fly facing seam line on the right front with the second notch (the one that's farther away) on the left front. Pin through the fly facing and zipper without catching the fly extension or front of the garment.

6 Flip over and pin the remainder of the zipper tape to the fly facing. Sew two rows of stitching through the zipper tape, using a zipper foot.

7 On the right side, draw in the fly stitching line with chalk or a marking pen. Start below the zipper stop and curve up toward the waist, drawing the straight line 1½" (4 cm) from the center. Topstitch (page 218) through the front and facing only.

8 On the inside, tack the fly extension to the fly facing by stitching back and forth through both layers. You could also sew a bar tack (page 16) at the curve of the fly topstitching, through all the layers.

F French Seam

WHAT IS IT?

A French seam is a narrow, fully enclosed seam. In France, it's called an English seam! The seam is sewn with the right sides out first, then turned to the inside and sewn, enclosing the seam allowances within the seam. The result is tidy and clean without requiring a lot of work to finish the seams.

French seam

French seam

▶ WHEN DO YOU USE IT?

French seams are perfect for sheer fabric, fabrics that fray or anywhere you want a clean finish. It's best on straight seams or nearly straight seams. French seams can be done on curved seams but need clipping for them to lie flat, which may not be best for sheer fabrics or fabrics that fray easily. French seams are tidy and professional. Plus, there's no need to worry about matching your serger thread! If you plan to use French seams, you need to decide before sewing any of the garment seams, as they are sewn differently starting from the first step.

Tips + Notes

Trim evenly, especially if your fabric is sheer. You'll be able to see the trimmed edge enclosed in the French seam, so make sure it looks tidy!

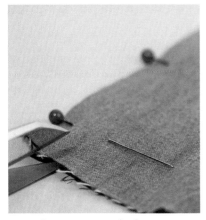

1 Make a tiny snip in both pieces at the top edge of the seam, indicating your seam allowance. My snip is ⅝" (1.5cm) away from the raw edges. This will help you sew the final seam accurately.

2 Pin your fabric pieces together along the seam line, *wrong sides together*. The right side of your fabric is facing you. This is going to feel wrong, but it will result in a lovely finished edge. Trust me! Pin the whole seam line from top to bottom.

3 Sew the seam with a ¼" (6mm) seam allowance. Backstitch at both ends. Trim seam allowance to ⅛" (3mm), or if it's easier to think of it this way, trim the seam allowance in half.

4 Press your tiny seam allowance to one side. To make sure you didn't press any ridges into your seam, turn the seam over and press the other side, too. Make sure the seam allowance is pressed as flat as it can be. You may find it easier to press the seam allowance first, and then trim it in half. It's up to you!

5 Pinch your seam allowance along the fold, as shown. The seam line should be at the exact center of your fold, not rolling to one side or the other. Press this fold flat, rolling it out as you go.

6 Stitch ¼" (6mm) from the fold, using the clipped notch at the top of the seam to ensure you're taking the proper seam allowance.

Your French seam is done! Press this seam toward the back or as directed in your pattern instructions.

French Tack

WHAT IS IT?

A French tack is a thread chain that connects layers of fabric together loosely, usually at the hemline of a garment. The tack is made of regular sewing thread that's hand crocheted to form the chain and attached between the garment and its lining.

French tack under hem of dress

▶ WHEN DO YOU USE IT?

Use a French tack to keep the lining from separating from your garment. It's used when the lining and the garment are hemmed separately, so the layers are completely free from each other. If you skip the French tack, you'll be able to separate the layers and iron each one individually, so that's one reason not to sew the tacks. In the end it's up to you. You can always add them later if you find the lining moves too much. French tacks are sewn at the very end, once the garment and lining are both sewn and hemmed.

For a lined garment, two French tacks placed at the side seams are all you need.

HOW TO SEW A FRENCH TACK

1 Thread a handsewing needle with doubled thread. Start the tack by taking a few stitches in the garment to secure the end, about ¾" (1.9cm) above the fold of the hem. Take another stitch, but don't pull the thread all the way through. Leave a loop of thread big enough for your fingers to fit through, about 3" (7.6cm).

2 Hold the loop open with the forefinger and thumb of one hand; if you are right-handed, use your left hand. With your other hand, grab the thread through the original loop, pulling the original loop tight. This is the beginning of your hand-crocheted chain!

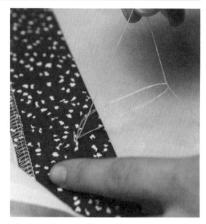

3 Continue pulling a new loop through each loop you make.

4 Stop once the thread chain is ¼"–¾" (1.3cm–1.9cm) long. You don't want to make too long of a tack or the layers will separate. Too short of a tack won't allow the lining to move freely.

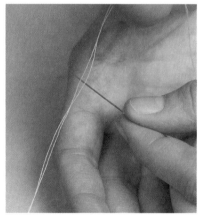

5 When the tack is the right length, pass the needle through the open loop and pull it tight to form a knot.

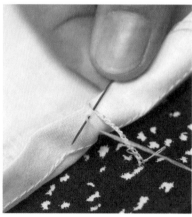

6 Make sure the lining is smooth from the top of the garment. Usually the lining is hemmed shorter than the main fabric, so make sure you're aligning the lining to the garment correctly. Sew a few stitches through the lining to secure the tack. Knot the end and trim the thread tails.

Gathering

WHAT IS IT?

Gathering is a technique that adds fullness to a garment by joining a large piece of fabric to a smaller piece with tiny uneven pleats. Gathering is most frequently done by machine, although you can gather by hand, as well. Gathering stitches are sewn to pull up the fabric, and the gathered fabric is sewn permanently in place.

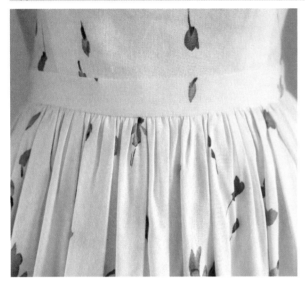

Gathered skirt on Cambie Dress

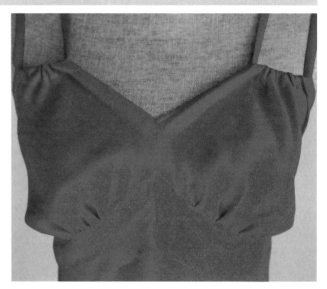

Gathered bust on Cinnamon Slip (Colette Patterns)

▶ WHEN DO YOU USE IT?

Use gathers when sewing skirts and dresses, especially those with very full skirts. One place where you will see gathers used is on ruffles. A ruffle is simply a gathered piece of fabric. (More on ruffles on page 166.) Gathering adds fullness and dimension, so you may see it as part of the garment's structure, for example, on puffed sleeves that are shaped with gathers at the top of the sleeve or at the bustline or neckline.

You can also change pleats to gathers, for example, on a pleated skirt or pleated bodice. Simply disregard the pleat lines and gather the edges instead. Or eliminate darts by replacing them with gathers. This will create a softer look with less structure than darts. Again, simply ignore the dart markings and sew gathering stitches between the dart lines. You may need to sew about 1" (2.5cm) past the dart markings to gather the area evenly.

HOW TO GATHER

Determine where you need to gather. Sometimes it will be between two notches or two small circles; other times you will be gathering the entire length of a piece. Make sure you know where you're starting and where you're stopping before you begin.

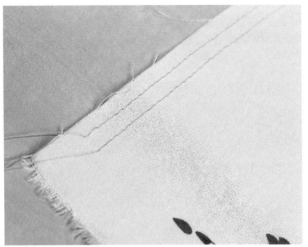

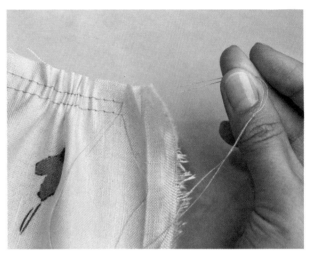

1 Sew one row of long machine stitches from the start point to the end point. Usually stitch size 4 is used for gathering. Sew this first row just inside your seam line. If your seam allowances are ⅝" (1.5cm), make your stitch line ½" (1.3cm) from the edge. Do not backstitch or trim the threads.

Sew a second row of stitching ¼" (6mm) from the edge. Or aim to center the second row between the first row of stitching and the raw edge.

2 Separate the top two threads from the bottom two threads. Tie the two bobbin threads together in a knot. I do this for two reasons. One, it will help you easily find the right threads to pull and keep them separate from the top threads. Two, it will help you pull each row of gathering evenly. If you pull one thread more than the other, your gathering may be uneven.

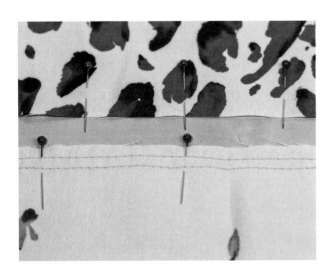

3 If you are gathering a long section, make sure the gathers are distributed evenly. Divide both sections in half and mark the halfway point on both pieces. Repeat by dividing these two sections in half, then in half again.

4 Hold the bottom threads in your right hand, and use your left hand to slide the fabric along the length of the gathering stitches. Pull with your right hand, and slide the fabric down the bottom threads. You're going to end up with a very long tail of threads in your right hand.

Keep pulling the gathers until they match the opposite edge. Pin your gathers to the straight edge and adjust them to fit. You can redistribute the fullness of the gathers if it's more gathered in one place and less gathered in other spots. Just use your fingers to smooth the fullness into place.

If you're not going to sew the seam right away, secure the gathering stitches by placing a pin at each end and wrapping the long thread tails around the pin in a figure-eight pattern.

Baste (page 18) the seam, then check to see if the gathers are even. Look for large tucks or ungathered sections. Regather these sections and baste in place. Sew the seam permanently. Once the seam is sewn permanently, remove the gathering stitches. Or, instead, carefully unpick any gathering stitches that are visible from the right side.

Tips + Notes

You can turn gathers into pleats (page 141), but it's much easier to go the other way and turn pleats into gathers! If you really want to turn a gathered section into pleats, decide how many pleats you want, mark them evenly and sew the pleats. Baste and check your work to make sure you are happy with the effect of the pleats.

For gathering thicker fabrics, try stitching with a zigzag stitch over heavy thread or dental floss, then pulling the thicker thread to form the gathers.

Loosen the tension on the top thread slightly before sewing your rows of gathers. This makes the bobbin thread easier to pull.

Start both rows in line with each other. If you have the same number of gathering stitches in each row, your gathers will be even. This is more important when gathering smaller sections of fabric.

Gather in a contrast thread color so it's easy to remove the stitches. This also saves your matching thread for permanent sewing only.

Godet

WHAT IS IT?

A godet, pronounced go-DAY, is a triangular insert at the edge of a garment. Godets are used to add volume to a garment at the hemline. On narrow garments, for example a slim skirt, godets are added to allow movement. On already wide garments, godets are added as decorative elements, as a place to insert other fabrics or to add even more volume. Godets can be small triangles or as big as quarter or half circles!

Godet detail

▶ WHEN DO YOU USE IT?

Add godets to a straight skirt to add flare, to add room to move or to add volume. Sewing godets in a narrow skirt will change the silhouette from straight to flared. If your garment has a center back seam, that is a natural place to add a godet in place of a slit. Make godets in the same fabric as your garment, in contrast fabric or even sheer or lace fabrics. Set godets into a seam, slash or cutout of the garment.

HOW TO SEW A GODET

1 On the godet, make a mark at the top of the triangle where the seam allowances intersect. Sew the seam above the godet, leaving open where the godet will be attached. Pin the godet to the seam allowance: line up the marking on the godet piece with the start of the seam, and sew with the garment side on top from the hemline to the start of the previous seam stitching. Press the seam allowances toward the garment.

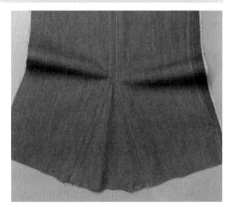

2 To add topstitching (page 218), topstitch the godet on the garment side, not the godet side, and continue the line of stitching on either side of the seam line above the godet.

Grain Line

WHAT IS IT?

The grain line is a printed line on pattern pieces that marks the lengthwise grain, also called the straight of goods or straight grain. It's usually marked with an arrow. This line is used to help align your pattern pieces on your fabric so that they are cut on grain. The grain is the lengthwise direction of your fabric, running parallel to the selvage. Think of a vertically striped fabric, where the stripes go up and down the fabric. That's what the grain line would look like if you could see it.

Opposite to the lengthwise grain is the crosswise grain. The crosswise grain runs across the width—that's an easy way to remember the difference.

Garments cut on grain will hang straight along the lines of the body, while garments cut off grain may twist around your body or hang unevenly. Sometimes the grain line will appear as a "cut on fold" marking on the pattern piece. This marking is directing you to fold the fabric on the straight grain and then line up the edge of this piece along the fold of the fabric. When you cut it out, you'll end up with a mirrored piece with the centerline aligned with the lengthwise grain.

Pattern placed on grain line

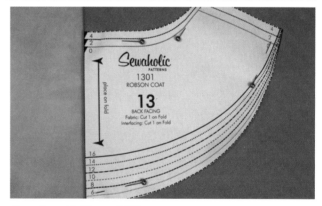

Grain line with "Cut on fold"

▶ WHEN DO YOU USE IT?

You'll use the grain line every time you cut out pattern pieces from fabric. Every pattern piece is marked with a grain line or a cut on fold marking. The grain line is also helpful when placing pieces on the bias (page 23). If you are cutting striped (page 208) or plaid (page 138) fabric, the grain line will help you to line up the stripe and plaid lines.

Take a look at the striped fabric above. Striped, plaid and other vertically printed or textured fabrics make it easy to see where the grain line

is. See how the grain line arrow is parallel to the direction of the stripes?

When you see diagonal stripes or plaids, it usually means the fabric is cut on the bias. True bias refers to a 45° angle from the grain line—exactly halfway between the lengthwise grain and the crosswise grain. See page 23 for more on the bias. On your pattern pieces, the grain line will be marked with a diagonal line to indicate cutting on the bias.

HOW TO LAY OUT FABRIC ACCORDING TO THE GRAIN LINE

Look at the fabric-cutting diagram and find the one for the garment you're making. Sometimes there will be one fold; sometimes there will be two folds with the selvedges folded into the middle. Or sometimes there are both types of cutting layouts for a single view.

1 Fold the fabric in half according to the cutting layout. Line up the selvedges (page 187) so they are even, and smooth out any wrinkles.

2 Place your pattern on the fabric. Rotate the pattern piece until the grain line is parallel to the selvedge or to the fold. Don't worry about having it exactly parallel yet; you'll fix that in the next step.

4 Measure from the opposite end of the grain line arrow toward the same fold or selvedge. You want this measurement to be exactly the same. If it is, then your garment piece is cut on grain. Rotate the pattern piece until the measurement is the same at both ends of the arrow.

With these two points pinned at each end of the grain line arrow, the pattern piece is aligned with the lengthwise grain of the fabric and you're ready to pin the rest of the piece in place.

3 Starting at one end of the grain line arrow, measure from the arrow to the fold or selvedge, whichever is closer. Note this measurement. Pin the pattern in place next to the grain line arrow.

Hair Canvas

WHAT IS IT?

Hair canvas is a type of interfacing (page 104) that is springy, strong and resilient. In the past it was made from horsehair or goat's hair, but these days most hair canvas is made from synthetic materials. It's used for tailoring and creating shaping in a tailored garment. It's a bit expensive, so it's traditionally used sparingly in the most important parts of a garment: collars, lapels and hems. When you fold hair canvas, it forms a soft roll instead of a crease, making it perfect for collars, lapels and other tailoring applications. It usually comes in one color: a natural grayish beige.

Hair canvas

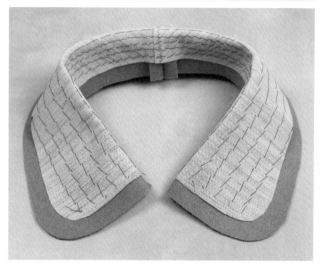

Padstitching on hair canvas

WHEN DO YOU USE IT?

Tailoring sometimes makes use of hair canvas on collars, lapels, roll lines, hems and even larger jobs like the entire jacket front, if the design requires extra support. To apply hair canvas, you can either padstitch (page 126) it to the garment fabric to keep its shape or follow machine-tailoring methods to apply it by machine. Hair canvas works for wide waistbands on skirts and trousers. It's impossible to flatten seams in hair canvas, so the seam allowances need to be trimmed from hair canvas interfacing pieces before you apply it to the garment fabric.

Tips + Notes

Layer hair canvas for extra stiffness.

HOW TO WORK WITH HAIR CANVAS

Preshrink hair canvas by spraying it with water and pressing it dry.

SEWING SEAMS IN HAIR CANVAS

To sew seams in hair canvas, use abutted seams (page 8) or lap the edges and zigzag, then trim off the extra seam allowances.

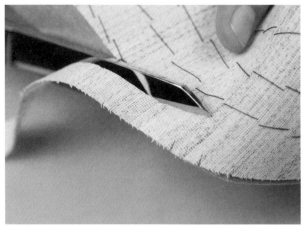

PADSTITCHING

If you are padstitching (page 126) the hair canvas, cut a piece of hair canvas using the pattern piece, including the seam allowances. Padstitch the canvas to the garment fabric, and trim away the seam allowances after the padstitching is complete. Make sure the interfacing doesn't shrink up as you stitch it to the garment fabric.

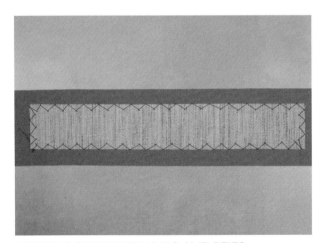

APPLYING TO WAISTBANDS AND BELTS

For other garment pieces, such as a wide waistband or fabric belt, cut a piece of hair canvas using the pattern piece, but trim off all seam allowances. Center the hair canvas in the middle of the fabric piece and catchstitch (page 58) around the edges of the hair canvas. If you're using thick fabric, cut the hair canvas piece a little smaller so there's room for the interfacing to lie flat inside the garment piece without puckering.

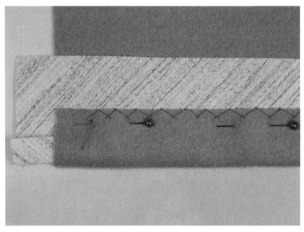

APPLYING TO HEMLINES

To apply hair canvas to hemlines, cut a bias strip (page 23) of hair canvas. Extend the canvas into the fold of the hem about ½" (1.3cm) for a softer fold, and extend it about 1" (2.5cm) higher than the hem allowance so the hem can be stitched to the interfacing.

Hem Facing

WHAT IS IT?

A hem facing is a facing (page 74) sewn to the hemline of a garment. Great for curved hems and full skirts, it adds weight to the garment and adds structure to the hemline. A hem facing is cut from a separate piece of fabric and sewn along the edge of the garment, instead of having extra length that is folded up and sewn. This allows you to cut the hem facing from a different fabric if you desire.

Hem facing

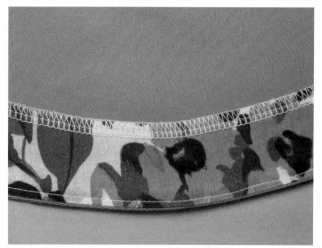

Contrast hem facing

▶ WHEN DO YOU USE IT?

Hem facings work wonders when you are low on fabric, want to lengthen a too-short skirt or want to add structure and weight to the hemline. A hem facing is a good choice for a very thick or heavy fabric that won't fold up into a hem easily. You can even add a surprise pop of color by sewing your hem facing in a contrast color. Just like regular facings, consider whether the pattern on the fabric will show through if used as a facing. You may want to choose a coordinating solid fabric for your hem facing. Interface the hem facing for even more support and structure. Sew the garment normally and when it comes time to sew the hem, that's when you will attach the hem facing.

Tips + Notes

Hem facings are great for underlined garments (page 226). You can hem the facing to the underlining instead of the garment fabric, thereby making it completely invisible.

If you are trying to get as much length as possible out of a too-short garment, sew your hem facing with a small seam allowance, as narrow as ¼" (6mm).

HOW TO DRAFT A HEM FACING

First, if there is a hem allowance on your pattern and you want to keep the same length, reduce this hem allowance to ⅝" (1.5cm). (See page 170 for how to adjust seam allowances.) Lay the pattern piece on scrap paper, and trace around the hem at least 3" (7.6cm) up the sides. This is the start of your new pattern piece. On the new pattern piece, measure up from the hem edge about 2" (5.1cm), and draw in the facing line parallel to the hemline edge. You can make it wider if you like; the wider the hem facing the more structured and stiff the hem will be. Mark the grain line (page 90) to match the grain of your original pattern piece. If the piece was cut on the fold, mark the cut on the fold side.

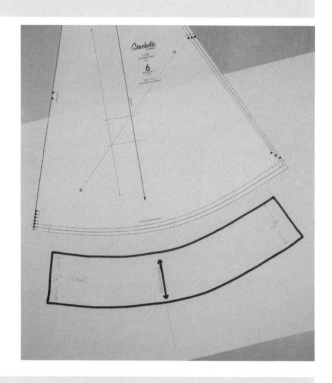

HOW TO SEW A HEM FACING

A hem facing is constructed and sewn the same way as a regular facing (page 74) except that it is sewn on last, once the garment is fully constructed. Assemble the garment but leave it unhemmed. Press seams open. Fuse interfacing to facing pieces, if desired. Assemble the facing, sew all seams and finish the upper edge of the facing that isn't going to be sewn to the hem.

1 With right sides together, pin the facing to the hem. Match up any seams in the facing to the seams of the garment, and sew along the hem edge with a regular ⅝" (1.5cm) seam allowance. Clip and notch curves. Trim seam allowance to ¼" (6mm), or trim the seam allowance in half.

2 Understitch (page 228) the facing. Press the facing to the inside of the garment. The understitching will help the facing roll to the inside; pressing it will keep it in place.

3 Catchstitch (page 58) the hem facing to the garment fabric. Tack the facing securely to the garment at the seams. You can do this by hand, sewing a few hand stitches through both layers. I usually do it as I pass by each seam with my catchstitching.

Hemming

WHAT IS IT?

Hemming is a method of finishing the raw edges of garments. Hems are sewn on the lower edges of skirts and trousers, blouses and sleeves, or on parts of a garment like ruffles, flounces and pocket edges. The raw edge is turned to the inside of the garment and sewn in place. You can either sew the hem by hand or by machine. Machine-stitched hems will be visible unless you use a special blind hem stitch. Hand-stitched hems will be nearly invisible.

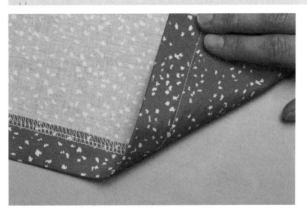

Once-turned hem

Twice-turned hem

WHEN DO YOU USE IT?

You'll sew hems on all types of garments or when mending or altering clothing. From skirts to blouses, all edges need to be finished with some type of hem unless you're deliberately choosing a raw edge finish. Even home décor sewing requires hems on curtains and napkins. Hems are usually sewn at the end of the construction process, once the garment is complete. Some hems, for example sleeve hems, may be sewn when that section of the garment is constructed.

WHAT'S A HEM ALLOWANCE?

A hem allowance is the length included in the pattern for the hem. You must account for this when choosing the length of your garments. The hem allowance is often noted right on the pattern pieces; if not, it will be mentioned in the pattern instructions. Hem allowances can be very narrow, just a regular seam allowance, or very wide, up to 6" (15.2cm).

Tips + Notes

It's easier to shorten garments at the hemline than it is to lengthen them! When in doubt, add extra length to the hemline.

Lining is always hemmed to hang shorter than the main fabric. The general rule is to hem the lining 1" (2.5cm) shorter.

When hemming in a circle, for example on a sleeve hem, overlap the stitching by four or five stitches when you reach the start point, instead of backstitching, for a subtle look.

HOW TO SEW A HEM

If your hemline is on the bias (page 23), if the whole garment is cut on the bias or if bias sections fall along the curve of the hemline, allow your garment to hang on a hanger for at least twenty-four hours before hemming. If you're not sure, you may want to let your garment hang just to be safe. This gives the bias part of the hem time to grow and stretch to its natural length.

1 Measure up from the floor and trim off the excess evenly. It's easiest to do this with a friend to do the measuring or with the garment on a dress form. If you do adjust the hem using a dress form, try it on yourself as well to ensure that the hemline is still even when it's on your body.

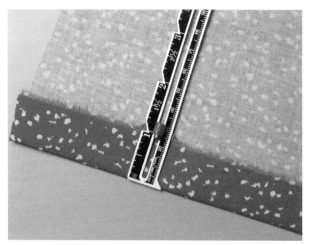

2 Press up the hem allowance. Try on the garment and ensure you are happy with the length. You can shorten it at this time or take a very narrow hem if needed to keep as much length as possible.

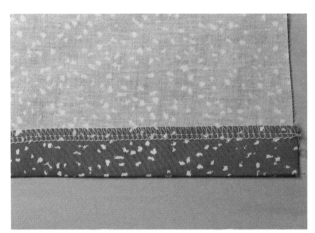

3 Finish the raw edge of the hem. You can do this by turning under the raw edge and pressing it, by serging (page 179), zigzagging (page 183), pinking (page 177), binding it (page 172) or by applying lace tape. All of these methods will ensure that the raw edge doesn't unravel.

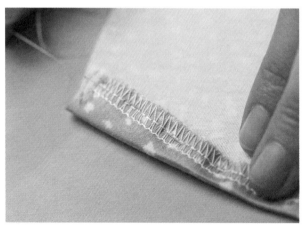

4 If the hem edge is wider than the garment, ease in the fullness. You can do this by sewing a line of hand basting along the raw edge and pulling the threads until the hemline fits the garment.

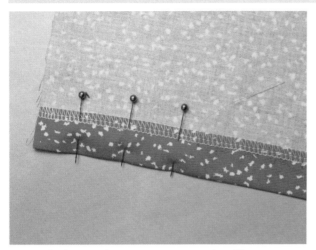

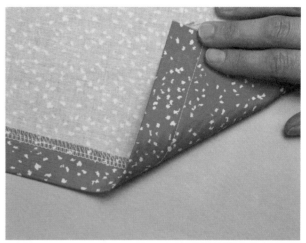

5 Pin the hem in place. You may want to hand baste (page 18) the hem as well, if you are sewing it by machine.

6 Sew the hem in place. For finished edges that have been serged or zigzagged, sew with a catchstitch (page 58) or topstitch (page 218). If the edges have been turned under, you can slipstitch (page 194) the folded edge to the garment for an invisible hem or edgestitch (page 69) along the fold for visible stitch lines. If you're sewing by hand, sew loosely and don't pull the thread too tightly or dimples will show on the right side.

HOW TO CHOOSE THE HEM WIDTH

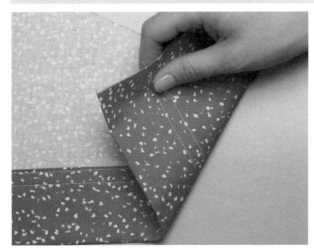

WIDE HEM
Wide hems add weight to the garment and are best for straight edges.

If you want a wide hem on a curved edge, consider adding a hem facing (page 94). This will allow you to sew a wide hem on a curved edge without having to ease in a lot of fullness.

NARROW HEM
Narrow hems are lightweight and best used for curved edges, but they work great on straight edges as well.

For a very narrow hem that looks great from both sides, see page 123. This hem is turned under twice and is best used for lighter weight fabrics rather than bulkier fabrics.

Hook and Eye, Hook and Bar

WHAT IS IT?

This is a two-part closure consisting of a hook on one side and either an eye or a bar on the other. These are usually made of metal, although thread bars and thread eyes can be used in place of the metal eyes or bars. In ready-to-wear garments, hook and bars are applied by machine before the waistband is constructed, but in home sewing, they are sewn on by hand. I prefer the handsewn type because they are easy to replace if they come apart; the factory-applied hooks and bars leave a hole and can't be reattached once the waistband is sewn.

Hook-and-eye closure

Hook-and-bar closure

▶ WHEN DO YOU USE IT?

Hook-and-eye closures are used as a fastening where edges meet, for example, at the top of a zippered opening or at the top of a neckline. You'll also see hook-and-eye closures used as extra support, say at the waistline or where the opening is likely to gap, such as in between buttons.

Hook-and-bar closures are used in places where the edges overlap. Hook-and-bar closures are strong and can be used on waistbands of skirts and trousers in place of a button. The advantage of using a hook-and-bar closure, instead of a button, is that the closure is completely hidden for a clean look.

Tips + Notes

Cover metal hooks and eyes with thread so they blend in. Use blanket stitches (page 31) to cover each piece with thread before sewing them to the garment.

Place a hook and thread eye (page 216) at the waistline of your dresses to reduce the stress on the zipper.

Does your zipper not reach the top of the opening, leaving a gap? Add a hook-and-eye closure to the top of the opening to bring those edges together.

Hate sewing hooks and eyes? If you extend your zipper to reach the top of the opening, a hook and eye isn't necessary.

For wider waistbands, sew two hooks and bars to the opening for a stronger closure.

HOW TO SEW A HOOK-AND-EYE CLOSURE

 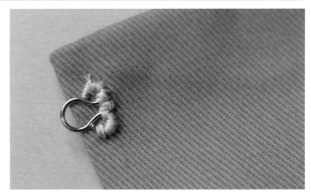

1 Thread a handsewing needle with single thread. With the hook-and-eye closure closed, place the closure behind the opening on the inside of the garment. Make sure that the opening edges are meeting in the middle. Sew the hook first so that you can move the eye, if needed, to ensure the edges are fully closed. Place the hook so the tip of the hook is flush with the opening edge. Sew through the hook's loops with whipstitches (page 233) or blanket stitches (page 31) and cover the entire loop with stitches. Make sure the hook stays straight and doesn't tilt to one side.

2 Hook the eye through the hook and pull it until the opening edges meet. Stick a pin through the center of the loops to mark the placement, and unhook the closure. Sew around the eye's loops in the same manner as the hook.

HOW TO SEW A HOOK-AND-BAR CLOSURE

 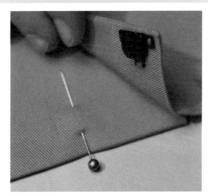 

1 Follow step 1 above for sewing the hook. If it's on a waistband or tab, center the hook in the middle of the band. Start your thread under the hook so the knot is hidden and sew through all of the attachment holes. Sew through the inner layer of fabric only so your stitches are not visible from the right side.

2 Try on the garment and decide where the overlap needs to be for the best fit. Mark the overlap line with a pin placed parallel to the overlap.

3 Hook the bar through the hook, and line up the overlap so the top edge of the overlap lines up with the pin. Mark the placement of the bar and unhook the closure. Sew through the bar attachment holes in the same manner as the hook.

Horsehair Braid

WHAT IS IT?

This stiff plastic meshlike trim made of nylon thread was formerly made of horsehair. Horsehair braid can be white or black, and it comes in many colors as well. It's available in different widths; wider ones will have a thread running along one side to help ease it into a curved shape.

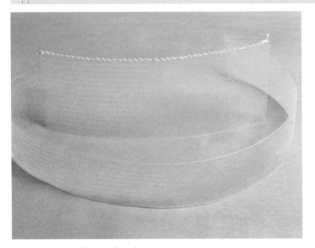

Horsehair braid trim detail

WHEN DO YOU USE IT?

Horsehair braid adds structure to the hemline of garments. Use it anytime you want to stiffen a hem. It's especially effective for circle skirts, as it helps to define the shape of the hemline. You can add it to curved hems as well as straight hems.

Skirt without horsehair braid

Tips + Notes

As an alternative, adding a hem facing (see page 94) or interfacing (page 104) to the hem allowance will also stiffen the hemline and add structure.

The wider the braid, the more your hem will stand out.

Skirt with horsehair braid

HOW TO SEW HORSEHAIR BRAID

Here are two ways to apply horsehair braid. The first method is best if you don't mind the trim showing on the inside; the second method covers the trim completely.

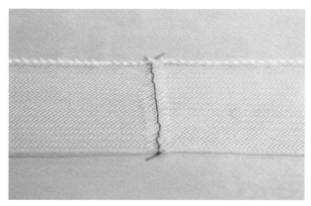

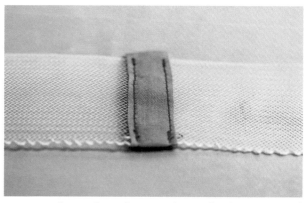

1 Measure the hem of your garment. Cut the horsehair braid the length of your hem plus two seam allowances. Overlap the ends of the horsehair braid and sew across the ends.

2 Cover the overlapped seam with seam binding or strips of fabric, and edgestitch (page 69) the binding in place. The cut ends of horsehair braid are scratchy, so covering them will make it more comfortable to wear.

METHOD 1

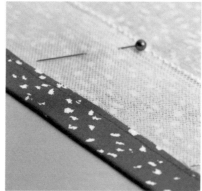

1 Reduce the hem allowance to ½" (1.3cm) if it's wider than that, and trim off the excess. With the wrong side of your garment up, overlap the hem ¼" (6mm) on top of the horsehair braid and pin it in place. Edgestitch (page 69) the horsehair braid all around the hemline.

2 Turn the braid to the inside, folding the hem ½" (1.3cm) toward the inside of the garment so it's not visible from the right side, and press. If the hemline is curved, pull up the threads on the upper edge of the horsehair braid trim, easing the trim to fit the garment. The braid will curve inward at the upper edge.

3 Slipstitch (page 194) the upper edge of the braid to the fabric or underlining.

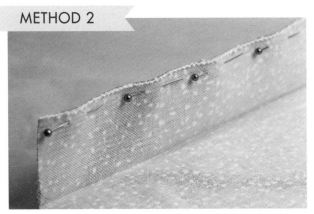

1 For this method, choose a horsehair braid that's the same width as the hem allowance. Or change the hem allowance on your pattern to match the width of braid you'd like to use. Press up the hem allowance on the garment. Tuck the horsehair braid trim into the fold of the hem, and pin or hand baste (page 18) in place.

2 Finish the horsehair braid trim together with the hem edge. Seam binding or bias tape finishes this type of hem nicely. (See page 172 for bound seam finish.)

3 Topstitch (page 218) or slipstitch (page 194) the hem in place. Topstitching by machine can be a nice way to show off the curved hem, but it will be visible on the right side. Slipstitching by hand produces a nearly invisible hem.

Interfacing

WHAT IS IT?

Interfacing is a support fabric applied to garments to add structure and stability. It prevents areas of the garment from stretching out, as most interfacings do not stretch or stretch very little. Interfacing can be sewn into the garment (sew-in interfacing) or glued or "fused" to the fabric with an iron-on adhesive (fusible interfacing). Interfacing may also be called "fusing," in reference to the fusible type. If you have interfacing and aren't sure if it's the fusible type, look for shiny little dots on one side of the interfacing. Those dots are the glue that bonds to the fabric when ironed. Hair canvas (page 92) is a type of interfacing that's extremely stiff and springy. Fusible and sew-in interfacings come in black and white, though often the black option will be more of a gray or charcoal.

Fusible and sew-in interfacings

Interfaced collar and epaulette on Robson Coat

Interfacing applied to fabric

▶ WHEN DO YOU USE IT?

Sewing patterns will indicate when to use interfacing and which pieces to apply the interfacing to. They will also specify whether to use fusible or sew-in interfacing. Keep in mind that older sewing patterns will ask for sew-in interfacing, as fusible interfacings weren't available in the past. You're not forced to follow the pattern directions if you prefer another type. Fusible interfacing is fast and easy to use, but it may come unglued over time. Sew-in interfacing is slower to work with, but because it's never glued in place, it won't change after washing or wearing.

Interfacing is applied to collars, cuffs, waistbands, plackets, facings and any other part of the garment that needs structure or stiffness. In tailored jackets, often the entire garment front is interfaced to give it a defined, crisp shape. Choose white interfacing for light- and medium-colored fabrics; choose black for dark colors. Match the weight of your garment fabric to the weight of the interfacing: lightweight fabric with lightweight interfacing, heavy fabrics with a more substantial interfacing.

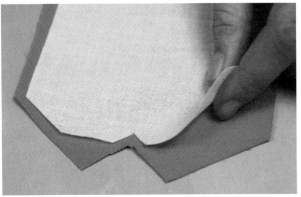

2 Place the interfacing on the fabric, with the sticky side of the interfacing on top of the wrong side of the fabric piece. I like to apply my interfacing with the interfacing side up. It's easy to position the interfacing on the piece that way, especially when it's cut smaller than the main fabric. Make sure your fabric piece is pressed flat and there are no bumps or ripples under the interfacing.

1 Cut out the piece to be interfaced from fusible interfacing. If you're cutting a single layer piece, make sure the sticky side of the interfacing matches the wrong side of the fabric piece. Trim ⅛" (3mm) around the interfacing edges to help reduce bulk. You can skip this step if you want, but it makes for neater facings and collars. If your piece has corners or points that will be enclosed, trim diagonally across the corners of the interfacing so the corners are easier to turn.

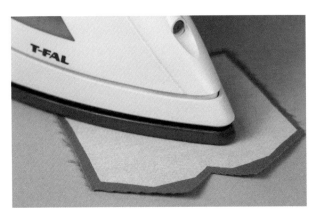

3 To apply fusible interfacing, you need three things: heat, steam and pressure. Press with an iron; lift up the iron to move it instead of sliding it along the fabric. Your interfacing may come with instructions printed on paper or plastic and rolled up into the bolt. Follow these directions for the best results. Generally I set the iron to the right setting for my fabric, keep the iron in the same place for ten to fifteen seconds, then lift and move it to a new position. I repeat this action until the whole piece has been fused. Use a press cloth (page 153) to protect your iron from the adhesive.

Tips + Notes

Check the label on the interfacing bolt at the store to see if your interfacing is preshrunk.

For stretch fabrics, stretch interfacings are best. Even if the area of the garment isn't meant to stretch when worn (for example, collars or cuffs), if the fabric does stretch, it can pull apart from the fused interfacing. Look for lightweight knit or mesh interfacings.

Test different types of fusible interfacing on scrap pieces of your garment fabric. To choose the best interfacing, look for bubbles or ripples, and fold and bend the interfaced sample to feel how stiff it will be. Try to peel off the fused interfacing at the edges and see how well it's adhered to the fabric.

Did you accidentally fuse interfacing to the wrong side of the fabric piece? Depending on the interfacing, you may be able to remove it without damaging the fabric. Carefully peel off the interfacing. Cut a fresh piece of interfacing and apply it to the correct side.

HOW TO APPLY SEW-IN INTERFACING

Cut out the piece to be interfaced from the sew-in interfacing. Trim $^1/_8$" (3mm) around the interfacing edges to help reduce bulk. You can skip this step if you want, but it makes for neater facings and collars. If your piece has corners that will be enclosed, trim diagonally across the corners of the interfacing so the corners are easier to turn.

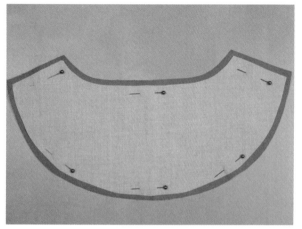

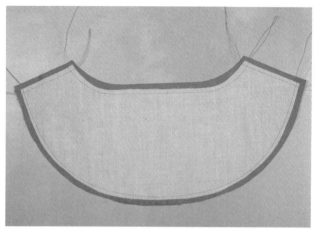

1 Place the interfacing on the fabric, with the interfacing facing the wrong side of the fabric piece. Pin the interfacing to the fabric around the edges.

2 Machine baste or hand baste (page 18) around the edges of the interfacing. Keep the basting stitches inside the seam allowance.

ALTERNATIVES

Need interfacing and can't get to the fabric store? Cotton muslin, plain cotton broadcloth or your garment fabric cut double can all serve as interfacing. Make sure the substitute fabric is prewashed before using. Cotton alternatives make great interfacing solutions for summer clothing, as the cotton is breathable.

Tips + Notes

Be careful not to glue lint or threads in between your fusible interfacing and fabric. It looks funny to have bright-colored threads trapped under white interfacing, and it's hard to remove without peeling off the interfacing. Give your fabric piece a quick cleaning with a lint roller or brush to remove any loose threads or fluff before placing the interfacing on top.

Iron fusible interfacing to your pattern pieces to make them last longer. Make sure to turn off the steam and use low heat. Place the interfacing sticky side up under the tissue. Fuse the interfacing to the tissue, using a press cloth (page 153) to avoid getting sticky residue on your iron. Apply the interfacing before the pattern pieces are cut, then cut both the interfacing and pattern piece along the cutting lines.

Store fusible interfacings carefully with as few folds as possible—you can't press out the wrinkles. Sew-in interfacing can be pressed flat if it gets creased.

Interlining

WHAT IS IT?

Interlining is a layer of fabric placed between the lining and main fabric to provide extra warmth. This layer is completely hidden from the outside and the inside of the garment. Lambswool is the most luxurious interlining as it's light, soft and warm. It may be hard to find, though, and it is quite expensive. Cotton flannel is an easy-to-find interlining fabric that's affordable and easy to work with.

Interlining fabrics

▶ WHEN DO YOU USE IT?

Interline winter coats to make them extra warm. You might also add interlining to a winter suit jacket. The interlining is applied to the lining fabric before the lining is constructed, right after the pieces are cut out.

Interlined lining

Tips + Notes

Remember to allow enough room for interlining when fitting the coat, especially if you're using a bulky material such as lambswool.

You can also look for warmer lining fabrics as an alternative to interlining. Kasha lining is a thick polyester lining with a soft flannel backing. It's warmer, thicker and, as a bonus, it's easier to sew than thinner lining fabrics.

HOW TO ADD INTERLINING TO A COAT

Using your lining pieces as a guide, cut the same pieces from the interlining as you did for the lining. If the back lining is cut with a pleat, eliminate the pleat from the interlining. Sew the back pleat in the lining before adding the interlining layer.

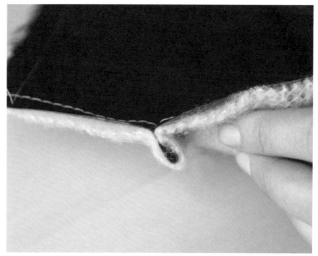

1 Pin each interlining piece to its corresponding lining piece, matching the wrong side of the lining to the interlining. Baste (page 18) all around each piece to secure the layers together.

2 If there are darts (page 63) or tucks (page 224), make the darts and tucks in the lining and interlining as if it were a single layer.

For the sleeves, if you have two-piece sleeves, interline only the upper sleeve. The best-fitting coat sleeves are two-piece sleeves, as they follow the shape of the arm. But if you have a one-piece sleeve, decide whether to add interlining to the whole sleeve or to skip interlining the sleeves altogether.

Treat the lining and interlining as a single layer from this point forward. Sew the shoulder seams and side seams and follow the pattern instructions to insert this double-layer of extra warmth into your coat.

HOW TO QUILT INTERLINING

Quilt your lining to the interlining for a luxurious touch. Cut out both pieces, draw your quilting lines with chalk, pin the layers together between the lines and sew along lines through both layers. Work from one side to the other, smoothing out the layers so there aren't any bumps or wrinkles.

Knit Fabric

WHAT IS IT?

Knit fabric is a type of fabric that's made by knitting instead of weaving. The yarns are looped around each other to form the fabric, and these loops make knit fabric stretchy. On the other hand, woven fabric does not stretch on the straight grain (page 90), only on the bias (page 23) unless it contains spandex. Knit fabrics allow for closer-fitting garments with less construction details, making them comfortable to wear. Knit fabrics resist wrinkles, which makes them great for travel. Knit fabrics may stretch in one direction, across the width (two-way stretch) or stretch both across the width and length of the fabric (four-way stretch.)

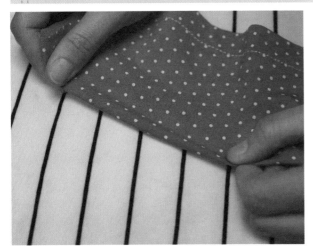

Knit fabric

Renfrew top in knit fabric

▶ WHEN DO YOU USE IT?

Knit fabrics are perfect for casual clothing, athletic and workout wear, swimwear and lingerie and body-hugging designs. Look for sewing patterns designed specifically for knit fabrics. These patterns have less ease (page 65) and have accounted for the stretch when it comes to bindings, cuffs and other garment pieces. Look for a guide on the back of the envelope showing how much stretch is required. Knit garments are quick to sew as they often have fewer seams and design details. With knit garments you can often eliminate the need for closures such as buttons or zippers. They stretch when you put them on and fit the body comfortably. Using knit fabrics also allows you to use negative ease (page 65) to get a snug fit. Knits are more forgiving when it comes to fitting, as they will stretch to fit your body.

HOW TO CUT KNIT FABRIC

When cutting knit fabric, it's important to cut it straight on grain. Otherwise the side seams will twist around the body. Look closely at the surface of your knit fabric and you'll see ribbed lines running along the length of the fabric. This indicates the grain line (page 90). Use these ribbed lines to line up the pattern pieces to ensure your pieces are on grain.

You may find it easier and more accurate to cut knit pieces on a single layer of fabric. Just remember to flip over the second piece so it's a mirror image, not a duplicate!

HOW TO SEW WITH KNIT FABRIC

There are a few differences between sewing with knit fabric and sewing with woven fabrics.

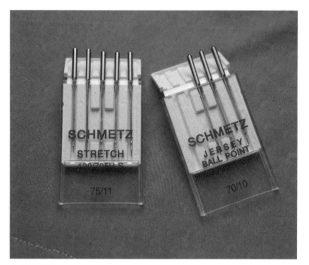

NEEDLE

First, you'll want to choose the right needle. Look for stretch or ballpoint needles, which have slightly rounded tips instead of sharp points. They're designed so the needle doesn't pierce the threads of the knit fabric and create holes; instead they penetrate between the fabric threads, pushing them aside. Test your needle on a scrap of your knit fabric to select the best needle for your project.

STITCH TYPE

Use a stretch stitch so the seams can stretch with the rest of the garment and the threads won't break. Some machines have a variety of stretch stitches to choose from. If not, use a narrow zigzag stitch. Test your stitch on scrap fabric: stretch the seam to make sure the stitch is stretchy enough for your fabric.

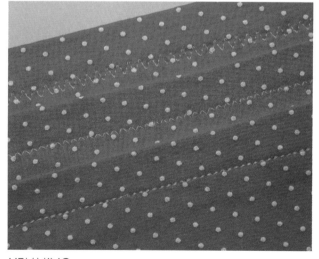

SERGING

A serger will sew stretchy seams and finish the edges at the same time. However, you don't need to finish the seam allowances of knit fabric because it will not fray like woven fabric. You may want to neaten the insides, however.

HEMMING

Sew hems with a stretch stitch as well, otherwise they won't stretch with the garment and the thread will snap. Here are three different options for stretchy hems: (from top to bottom) three-step zigzag, standard zigzag and stretch stitch.

Lapped Seam

WHAT IS IT?

A lapped seam is a type of seam that's sewn with one side overlapping the other. Instead of sewing the two sides right sides together and pressing them open, one side is turned under and pressed and then lapped over the unpressed side. The seam is then either slipstitched (page 194) or topstitched (page 218) to close the seam.

Lapped seam detail

Lapped seam on Crescent Skirt

▶ WHEN DO YOU USE IT?

Use a lapped seam when a regular seam would be tricky to sew and turn, for example on corners, curved edges and yokes (page 234). It's challenging to sew seams with very pointed lines, so a lapped seam allows you to press under the points of the corner exactly and then overlap it on top of the other side for perfect corners. If you're adding design lines to a garment across the body, and the lines are curved or shaped, a lapped seam is a good solution to achieving the right shape.

Tips + Notes

Lapped seams are hard to alter after they're sewn, so make sure the fit is right before sewing them. Make a muslin test garment first (page 118) to check the fit.

Change regular garment seams to lapped seams if you are having trouble turning a tidy corner or curve.

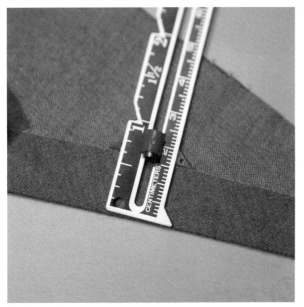

1 Turn under the seam allowance on the side that's going to be on top. Choose the side that has the corners and points as your top side. You want the side with any outward curves to be on top to reduce the amount you have to clip into the seam allowance.

2 Overlap the turned edge on top of the flat side and line up the raw edges. Pin in place. For extra hold, hand baste (page 18) along the fold.

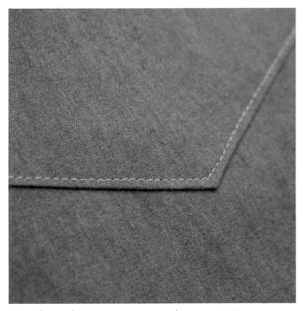

3 Edgestitch (page 69) or topstitch (page 218) an even distance from the fold. Press.

Lining

WHAT IS IT?

Lining is the inner fabric of a garment. Lining can cover the full interior of a garment; garments with a full lining covering all of the inner workings are called "fully lined." Garments can have a partial lining, including half linings that cover the upper back shoulders or sleeves. Lining is often a thin, slippery, silky fabric, which makes it easy to slip garments on and off. Lining can be made using cotton, polyester, rayon, acetate, flannel or even cotton jersey. Quilted lining fabrics and flannel-backed linings are available for adding extra warmth to winter garments.

Lining fabrics

Lining in Cambie Dress

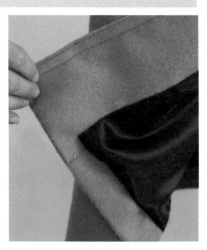

Lining in a coat

WHEN DO YOU USE IT?

Use lining when a pattern calls for it. Sometimes pattern instructions will suggest specific lining fabrics; other times they will simply state "lining fabrics." Fabric stores often have their lining fabrics labeled or set aside in a separate section, so it's easy to find. The lining is sewn separately from the main garment, so it's almost like sewing an entire second garment in lining. The garment and the lining are then joined around the edges, with the wrong sides facing each other so all of the inner construction is hidden. If your pattern doesn't include lining, you can still add it if you desire. For simple styles like skirts with waistbands, you can simply cut a second set of pieces from lining fabric and sew both layers into the waistband.

Tips + Notes

Don't limit yourself to fabric labeled as lining in the fabric store. Polyester satin prints, silks and cotton batiste are all suitable lining fabrics that may not be sold specifically as lining.

Choose cotton linings, such as voile, lawn or batiste, when breathability is important, for example, when sewing summer clothing.

When sewing winter dresses and skirts, a slippery lining will ensure the lining doesn't stick to your tights.

For pockets made of lining fabric, sew the seam around the pocket bag twice. This is often the first place where the lining seams tear.

If you make alterations to your garment, be sure to make the same changes to the lining, too.

HOW TO SEW LINING

Your pattern instructions will likely cover how to sew in the lining, as the construction will be different depending on the design of the pattern. The basic steps follow below.

When it's time to add the lining, you will have the shell of your garment sewn and the lining pieces cut out. Sew the lining in the same way you sewed the shell. Sew all darts and pleats, then sew the side seams and shoulder seams, and if it's a jacket or coat, set in the sleeves, so that the lining is fully constructed.

If the lining is enclosed, you don't have to finish the seams. Press seam allowances open, or press lining-facing seam allowances toward the lining and leave them unfinished. If the lining is free hanging, then seam finish (see pages 172–184) if desired. Consider finishing the seams if the lining will be visible. Remember, finishing the seams adds bulk.

1 If there is a facing, sew the lining to the facing. This will give you two nearly complete garments, one made of your main fabric, and one made of lining with facings at the edges. Here's an example of a piece of lining, with a facing along the top edge, and the garment piece it will be lining. Press the seam toward the lining.

Join the constructed lining to the garment shell around the outer edges. Sew, trim and understitch (page 228) where possible, then turn right side out and press.

2 Hem (page 96) the lining separately. The lining should be about 1" (2.5cm) shorter than the garment when the lining is left hanging freely. Either cut the lining shorter when you cut out the pattern or trim the lining after it is sewn. To prevent fraying, enclose the raw edge of the lining inside the hem by turning it under twice and topstitching.

If the lining is hanging free, attach it to the garment shell with French tacks (page 84).

3 For sleeves, turn under the seam allowance on the lower edge of the lining, and line up the raw edges of the lining to the raw edges of the sleeve hem. Slipstitch the lining to the sleeve cuffs. An extra bubble of fabric above the slipstitched hem allows movement within the sleeve. You can press this bubble flat as a pleat or leave it loose.

Measuring

WHAT IS IT?

Measure yourself to determine the proper size to start with and any immediate adjustments to make. You may know your size for ready-to-wear clothing, but pattern sizing is completely different!

Measuring high bust

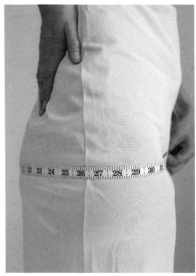

Measuring hips

▶ WHEN DO YOU USE IT?

Measure yourself when starting a new project. Measure the person that you're sewing for, when sewing for someone other than yourself. You'll need a measuring tape, a mirror, notepaper and pencil, and a friend to help you, if there's someone around who's willing!

There is no alternative to measuring yourself! Sure, you might not want to get out the tape measure. But it's the only way to figure out which size to make. Sewing pattern sizes aren't the same as store-bought clothing sizes, and sizing can vary between pattern companies.

Wear the undergarments that you plan to wear under the finished garment. If your dress requires a special bra or foundation garments, measure yourself wearing that bra and undergarments.

Tips + Notes

If possible, get a friend to help you measure yourself. It's a lot easier to have help!

Don't pull the tape measure too tightly. You should be able to take a breath in and out.

Don't be tempted to cheat on your measurements. They're only numbers, and accuracy is important to getting the right fit. Write down the real measurements from the tape measure, no matter what they are—even if they've increased since the last time you measured. You'll only be cheating yourself—and making it harder to fit—if you don't use accurate measurements.

If you already have your measurements recorded, but it's been a while since the last time you measured yourself, measure again. Even if it seems like nothing has changed, your measurements may have changed slightly.

To learn how to measure a sewing pattern to determine a garment's finished measurements, see page 129.

HOW TO MEASURE YOURSELF

Wear underwear or a slip or other snug-fitting clothing. Don't measure over your
regular clothes or your measurements will end up much larger than you need.

BUST

The first measurement will be the bust. Measure this around
the widest part of your bustline, making sure the tape is
straight around the back. (This is where having a mirror
comes in handy!) If it dips down, your measurement will end
up larger than your actual body.

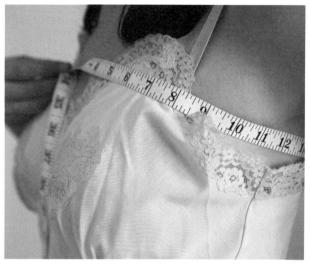

HIGH BUST

While working on your top half, also measure your high
bust. If you are especially busty, you may want to choose the
pattern size for your high bust size and adjust for a full bust.
This picture demonstrates the high bust position. You want
to loop the tape measure above the bust in front and under
the shoulder blades in the back, where your bra sits. The
tape measure is not straight for this measurement but angled
upward at the front.

WAIST

Measure your natural waistline, not where you wear your
pants. Bend at the side, and the string or ribbon around your
waist will slip into your natural waistline. That's where you
want to measure.

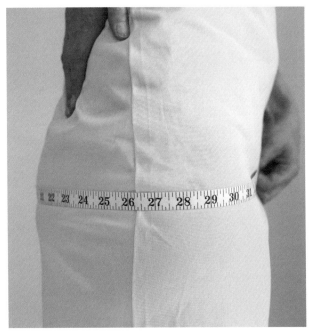

HIPS

Loop the tape measure around the widest part of your hips. Make sure it's straight around your rear end, not dipping down or pulling upward. Again, it helps to use the mirror as a guide, to make sure the tape is straight.

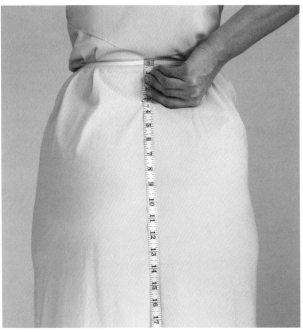

LENGTH

For skirts, measure from your waistline to the desired skirt length. You may want to measure a skirt from your wardrobe that is a length you like. For trousers, measure the inseam from the crotch to the floor while wearing the shoes you plan to wear. Compare this measurement against the inseam of a pair of trousers that you like.

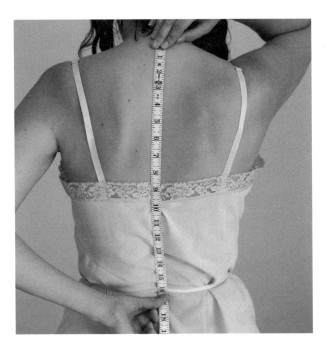

BACK WAIST

For dresses and blouses, measure from the bump at the nape of your neck to your waist for the back waist length. This measurement is often noted on patterns so you can adjust above the waist if needed.

Muslin

WHAT IS IT?

Muslin is a woven cotton fabric, either bleached or unbleached. The unbleached is more common and usually less expensive. "A muslin" refers to a test garment, often made using muslin fabric, that's sewn to test a pattern in order to work out any fitting changes before cutting into the project fabric. In the UK, a muslin used for fitting purposes is called a "toile."

Muslin fabric

Muslin test garment

WHEN DO YOU USE IT?

Muslin fabric is used for making test garments, as well as for interfacings (see page 104), underlining (see page 226) and support fabrics. A muslin test garment is used to test the fit of a new pattern or to test the fit before sewing with very expensive fabrics. You can also use muslin to mock up challenging parts of the pattern before sewing with your real fabric. Some people will make a muslin for every new pattern they use.

WHEN SHOULD YOU MAKE A MUSLIN?

If you always, always make pattern adjustments, then you'll probably want to make a muslin each and every time you make something for yourself.

Depending on the adjustment, you may be able to make a partial muslin (just the bodice) to check the fit. Just don't forget to consider how the rest of the garment will affect the fit. A heavy full skirt, for instance, will affect the way a bodice fits.

If the pattern is very fitted, it's best to make a muslin. Loose-fitting and relaxed-fit patterns have more room built in for wearing ease (page 65), so it's less important to check the fit first.

If you won't be able to fit as you go, I recommend making a muslin. Some patterns make it easy to adjust the fit as you sew. Some make it really hard because of the order of construction. Read through the pattern instructions and see if there is an opportunity to try on and fit the pattern before it's completely sewn up.

Your fabric choice may also determine whether you need to make a muslin. If you are limited on fabric, it's a good time to sew a muslin, as you won't be able to recut pieces if needed. If your fabric is particularly expensive or irreplaceable, making a muslin ensures the final garment will fit just right.

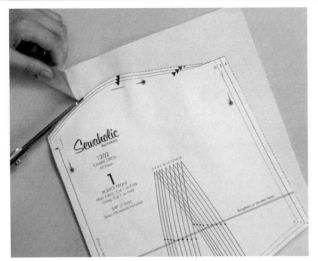

1 Cut your pattern pieces from muslin. You can skip facings, pockets and anything that does not make up the structure of the garment. If you'd like to test something specific that doesn't affect the fit, such as the pocket placement, then include that piece in the muslin garment as well.

2 Label each muslin piece with the pattern name, number, size and description of the pattern piece. Mark darts, pleats and other internal markings. I like to write with a ballpoint pen, because it's permanent and won't disappear as you fit the muslin.

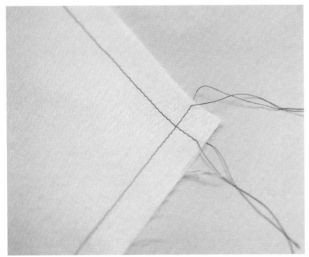

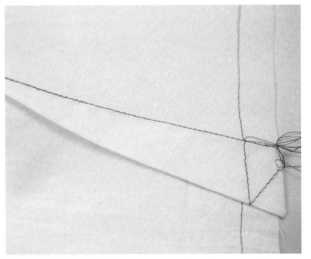

3 Machine baste (page 18) along the seam lines, tracing out all edges and any darts. I do this so that sewing the muslin can be like sewing with the tissue pattern pieces. Everything is marked and labeled, and the seam lines are super clear. Any changes you make will be easy to apply to the pattern pieces this way. Run your stitching off the edges of the fabric; don't pivot at the corners. If you need to let out the seams, or to take them in, you'll have a clear idea of how far the new seam lines are from the original stitched seam lines.

4 Make all of the darts (page 63), pleats (page 141) or tucks (page 224) in the bodice. This should be easy because you've stitched the pleat/tuck/dart lines with machine stitching, which is easy to follow. Press the darts, tucks or pleats toward the center or down, as you would on the real bodice.

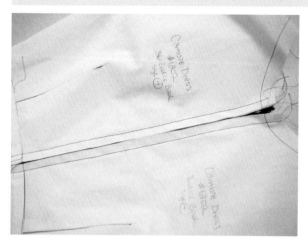
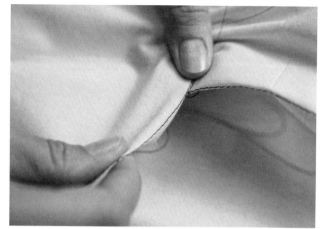

5 Figure out where the closure is going to be and leave the seam with the closure open. Sew up the pattern according to the sewing instructions. Accuracy is important because if the seams aren't sewn to the correct seam allowance, the fit will be off, and that's the whole point of making this test garment!

Pin a zipper along the closure opening. Baste it into place. Even if you're only making a muslin of the bodice, pin the correct-length zipper into your muslin bodice so that you're able to unzip it properly and try it on. If your garment has buttons and an overlap (page 49), mark center front so you know how far to overlap the edges.

6 Clip curves (page 221) along the garment edges, and fold in your seam allowances. This will give you a better idea of where the neckline will sit and where the outer edges of your garment will be. Press under the clipped seam allowances. If you prefer, you can cut and sew facings to finish the edges instead of clipping.

Try on the muslin garment, and make adjustments as needed. Remember to wear the same undergarments you plan to wear under the finished garment.

Tips + Notes

For knit fabrics, use a knit fabric with similar stretch for the muslin if you plan to test the pattern first. For heavy garments such as coats, use a heavier fabric for the test garment.

N Nap

Nap refers to the direction of napped fabrics, which are fabrics with a brushed or raised surface and hairs or fibers that lie smoothly in one direction. Fabrics that may have nap include velvet, corduroy, faux fur and velveteen. Fur is the most obvious napped fabric and demonstrates the concept of nap well. The hairs of fur fall directionally and feel smooth if stroked in one direction but not the other. Velvet and other napped fabrics work the same way on a smaller scale, but the fibers are not as tall, which makes it harder to see the nap in action. Fabric looks different going up and down with the nap; it may look darker or lighter depending on which way the nap is facing. Less obvious napped fabrics include wool and cashmere. You may not be able to see it, but there's a very slight difference to the way the fabric feels when you run your hand up or down the length of the bolt.

Some fabrics don't have a napped surface but are treated the same way, such as one-way designs or directional printed fabrics.

Nap of faux fur

Nap of corduroy and wool coating

▶ WHEN DO YOU USE IT?

If your fabric has a napped surface, you'll want to follow a cutting layout for napped fabric. In the pattern instructions, the cutting layouts will specify with or without nap. Use the with nap layout for napped fabrics as well as one-way designs. These cutting layouts will have the top of all your pattern pieces facing the same way, which uses more fabric. All pieces need to face the same way or one panel might look lighter or darker than the rest. Layouts without nap will sometimes turn pieces upside down if needed for a better fit.

WHICH IS THE RIGHT DIRECTION?

For directional prints, it's the direction where the people are not standing on their heads. With faux fur, the right direction is when the fur pile is facing down. Brush your hand down the fabric; if it feels soft, that is the direction of nap. It should feel rough or coarse when you brush your hand in the opposite direction.

Directional prints that should be treated like napped fabrics

Tips + Notes

If you cut the nap upside down, your garment may attract more lint and dust! This is yet another reason to ensure the nap is going in the right direction.

No pattern layout for napped fabrics? Simply arrange the pattern pieces on your fabric so that the top of each piece (the top of where it would fall on your body, so shoulders of blouses, waistlines on skirts) is at one end. Pattern pieces are usually labeled so the label is readable with the top of the piece facing up.

If you make a mistake cutting the first piece and have the nap facing up instead of down, switch all of the pieces to match this direction. It's better to have the nap facing the wrong way than to have varying nap directions from piece to piece.

Narrow Hem

WHAT IS IT?

A narrow hem is a thin hem that's turned twice and stitched in place. Also referred to as a rolled hem, it's subtle and small, hardly noticeable on the garment. Narrow hems don't add weight to the hemline, making them suitable for sheer and lightweight garments. They're tidy, neat and professional and look good on both the right and wrong sides of the fabric.

Narrow hem detail

A slightly wider narrow hem

▶ WHEN DO YOU USE IT?

Narrow hems are best on lightweight fabrics. Narrow hems can be used on sleeves, ruffles and flounces and hems of blouses, skirts and dresses. Because only a small amount is folded and stitched, it's a great hem finish for sheer fabrics and for curved edges, as folding and sewing a large amount of fabric is hard to do on a curve. You'll see narrow hems on napkins, tablecloths and bed linens. Narrow hems work well on bias garments because they're easy to manage and don't weigh down the lower edge. Because they look good on both sides of the fabric, they're a good choice when the wrong side of the garment will be visible. Use narrow hems when you want to preserve as much length as possible.

Tips + Notes

Measure and shorten the length of your garment, if necessary, before starting the narrow hem.

Sew narrow hems in contrast thread or metallic thread for a decorative effect.

Your machine may have a special foot for sewing rolled hems or narrow hems. Check your owner's manual for how to set it up.

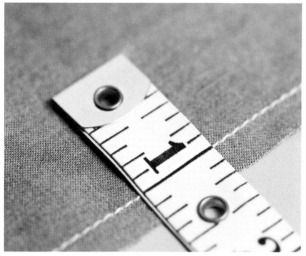

1 To prepare the edge for a narrow hem, reduce the hem allowance to ⅝" (1.5cm). If your pattern piece has a wider hem allowance than that, trim off the extra all along the hemline. Stitch ¼" (6mm) along the edge to be hemmed. I like to use the edge of my presser foot as a guide.

2 Press the stitched edge under so the stitching is just barely rolled to the inside, approximately ¹⁄₁₆" (1mm–2mm) from the fold. Trim the seam allowance as close as possible to the line of stitching.

3 Fold the edge in again, along the trimmed edge, and press. You should have a very narrow pressed hem, approximately ⅛" (3mm).

4 Edgestitch (page 69) along the fold. Hold onto the thread tails when you start, so the machine doesn't eat your hem edge. Here's a close-up of the narrow hem. The goal is to have it look nice from both sides!

Overcast Stitch

WHAT IS IT?

Overcasting is handsewing stitches over the edge of the fabric. It's a very simple hand sewn stitch, consisting of slanting stitches wrapping around the raw edge. Some sewing machines have an overcast stitch function, as well, that looks similar.

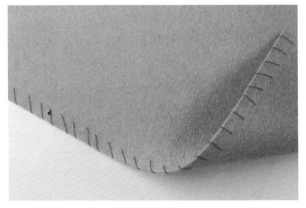

Overcast stitches

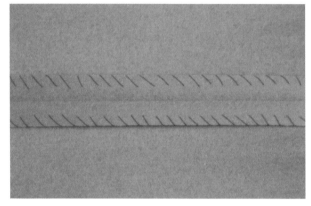

Overcasting on seam allowance

▶ WHEN DO YOU USE IT?

Overcast to finish seam allowances or raw edges by hand and to stop the fabric from fraying. Compared to other methods, this is a slow seam finish, but it can come in handy when you want to finish seams that are hard to get to by machine. If you've forgotten to finish a seam allowance, it's easy to go back in later on and overcast the edges by hand.

HOW TO OVERCAST

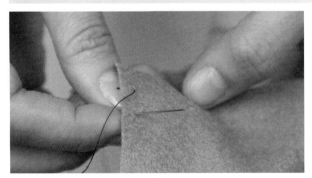

1 Thread a handsewing needle with single thread. Starting at one end of the fabric edge, go up from the wrong side and place the needle above the starting point, coming back up from the wrong side.

2 Repeat along the edge of the fabric, placing the stitches close enough to keep the fabric from fraying, about ¼" (6mm) apart. Don't pull the stitches too tightly; leave them loosely wrapped around the edge.

Padstitch

WHAT IS IT?

Padstitching is permanent hand stitching that is used to secure interfacing to the fabric and to give shape to pieces. When padstitching, you have two layers of fabric—the garment fabric and the hair canvas (page 92). Normally when you apply interfacing, you fuse or baste it to the fabric piece flat. With hair canvas and padstitching, the piece is curved or rolled into shape and padstitches are sewn through both layers to keep them in shape. It's a way of turning flat pieces of fabric into permanently shaped three-dimensional forms.

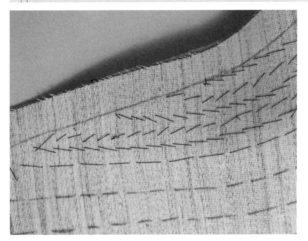

Padstitching

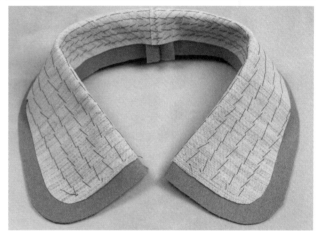

Padstitching on coat collar

WHEN DO YOU USE IT?

Padstitch collars and lapels in tailored jackets to add shape and to form permanent curves and rolls but only when using hair canvas. You can't padstitch with fusible interfacing. The padstitching is done on the undercollar and inner layer of the lapel, so that the stitching won't show through on the upper surface. Padstitching is traditionally done with silk thread, but you can get the same effect using all-purpose polyester thread if silk thread is hard to find. Silk thread is slippery, so it passes through the hair canvas easily and won't leave impressions on your fabric from the basting. It's also strong, which is great for creating structure with padstitching. The ability to mold, shape and form garments is just another way to add quality to your sewn garments. Padstitching a collar, for example, adds quality to tailored garments and makes them look less homemade.

Tips + Notes

Practice makes perfect! It's OK for your stitches to be uneven when you start padstitching.

Padstitching works best on thicker wool fabrics, so the stitches are hidden in the thickness.

Only padstitch the undercollar. Leave the upper collar as is or apply a light fusible interfacing.

Wear a thimble to protect the tip of your finger. Use the tip of the thimble to push the needle through, instead of the soft pads of your fingers.

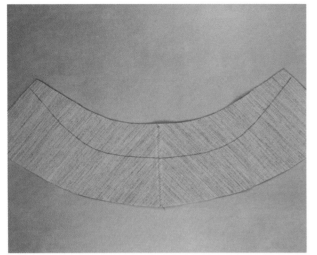

1 Cut a layer of hair canvas (page 92) using your pattern piece. In this example I padstitch a coat collar, creating a roll where I want the fold of the collar to fall. If your undercollar is two pieces, sew the seam with an abutted seam (page 8) or overlap the edges and zigzag and then trim the excess seam allowance. To decide where to place the padstitching, you'll need to have the roll line marked on your hair canvas. This line may be marked on your pattern piece.

2 If not, use your muslin (page 118) to determine the roll line. Pin the garment closed at the center front, let the collar fold over naturally, and mark the line where the collar rolls over. Transfer this line with a marking pen onto the hair canvas.

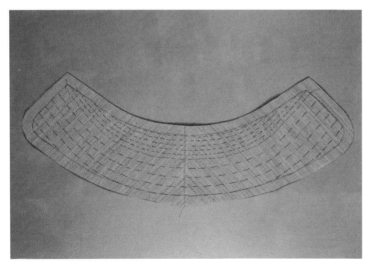

3 Once you have the roll line marked on the hair canvas piece, draw in the padstitching lines. For the collar stand, draw lines parallel to the roll line about ¼" (6mm) apart. On the collar itself, draw lines ½" (1.3cm) apart. Do not draw the lines into the seam allowances but leave a ⅝" (1.5cm) border all around the edges. Lay the undercollar on your table, with the wrong side facing up, and layer the hair canvas interfacing on top. Thread a handsewing needle with thread, and baste (page 18) all along the roll line, with uneven stitches, through both layers. Make long stitches on the surface, with small stitches through the collar fabric. This will keep the layers together in the right place when you fold it.

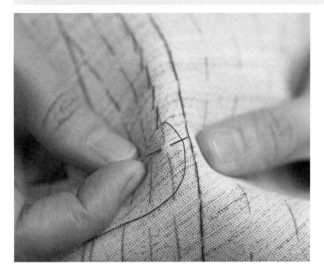

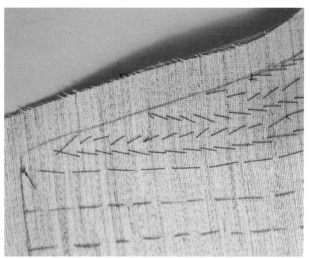

4 Start your padstitching on the collar stand. Roll the collar along the roll line, keeping your opposite hand under the collar to hold the shape. Starting at one side, make a series of diagonal stitching lines between the roll line and the first marked line, stopping before you reach the seam allowances. Make each stitch about ¼" (6mm) long, catching just a thread or two of the collar fabric without going through.

5 On your second row, alternate the angle of the stitches so they make a row of Vs with the first row. Continue until the collar stand is covered with stitches.

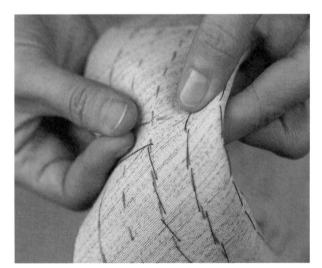

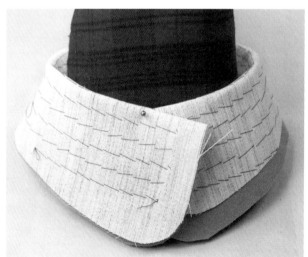

6 With the hair canvas side up, rotate the piece so the collar stand is away from you and the collar itself is facing you. Fold the collar along the roll line, and hold the collar in this position as you sew, making another row of diagonal lines on the first ½" (1.3cm) line after the roll line. Continue to sew rows of padstitching. Make the stitches in this section about ½" (1.3cm) long. After a couple of rows, the collar will start to keep its shape. Keep going until the collar is covered with stitches. It will now hold the rolled shape all on its own.

7 Wrap the collar around a tailor's ham (page 212) and pin it in place. Steam to shape the collar, and leave it overnight to dry. Once it's dry, trim off the hair canvas seam allowance ⅝" (1.5cm) around the edges. Measure the distance to trim from the collar fabric, not from the hair canvas, so there is an even ⅝" (1.5cm) all around the hair canvas piece.

Pattern Measurements

WHAT IS IT?

Pattern measurements, or flat pattern measurements, refer to the process of measuring out the flat pattern pieces to determine the finished garment measurements. You can determine the dimensions of any part of the garment simply by measuring off the flat pattern.

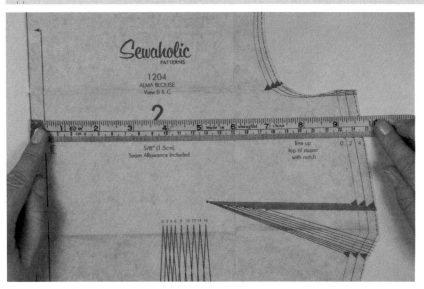

Measuring a flat pattern

▶ WHEN DO YOU USE IT?

Finished garment measurements are usually provided somewhere in each sewing pattern. They may be on the outside of the envelope, printed on the pattern tissue or located somewhere in the instructions. If you can't find them, or if there is something else you wish to check against your own measurements, measure the pattern pieces. Sometimes you may want to know the finished dimensions of a part of the pattern that isn't listed, for example, the shoulder width or across the thighs. Measuring the pattern pieces will give you that answer!

Measuring the pattern can also save time. For some patterns, you may be able to measure the pattern pieces and compare that to your body measurements (page 115), thereby skipping the making of a test garment (page 118). If you're making a very flared skirt, the only measurement you need to worry about is the waist. You'll be able to measure the waistband, compare that measurement to your own waistline and know if it will fit.

Tips + Notes

For sleeve length, measure from shoulder to elbow and elbow to hem. If the elbow is not marked, measure from the shoulder to the hem.

For trouser length, measure from the waist to crotch, crotch to knee and knee to hem. If knee is not indicated, measure from crotch to hem.

For skirt length, measure from waist to hip and hip to hem. If hipline is not indicated, measure from waist to hem.

HOW TO MEASURE THE PATTERN

Determine how much seam allowance is provided in the pattern; a standard seam allowance is ⅝" (1.5cm). Choose the size you plan to measure. Gather all of the pieces that make up the complete front, back and sleeve or skirt front and back. Skip any pieces that don't affect the shape of the garment, for example, the pockets.

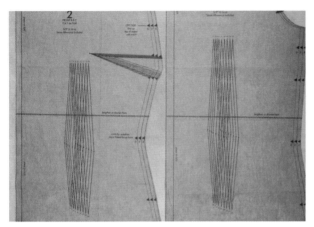

1 Arrange the pieces so the seam lines are next to each other as they would be sewn. Match side seams to side seams. If there are vertical or horizontal seams to complete the garment, place these next to each other as well.

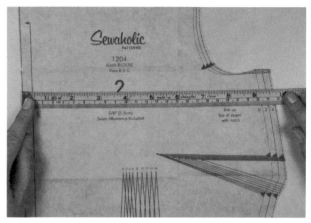

2 Measure the bust of the pattern piece from seam line to seam line, 1" (2.5cm) below the armhole. Skip darts and seams; skip overlaps and openings. You're measuring the space on the pattern pieces that doesn't get sewn into seams, darts or openings. If it helps, measure each section and note it on a scrap paper, then add them up at the end to arrive at the total bust measurement.

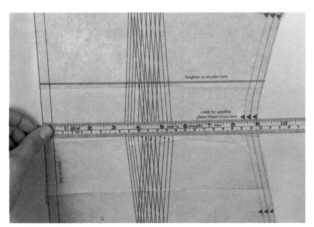

3 Repeat this step for the waist, hip and other horizontal measurements.

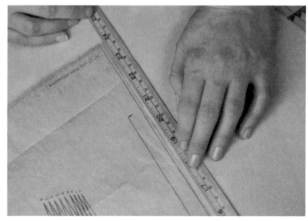

4 When measuring the length of pattern pieces, measure from back neck to waistline, then waistline to hem. The hem allowance amount is usually printed on the lower edge of the pattern piece, but it may be noted in the instruction sheet as well.

Pinking

WHAT IS IT?

Pinking is simply cutting with pinking shears, which are special scissors that cut in a zigzag pattern.

Pinked fabric

WHEN DO YOU USE IT?

Pinking is a quick and simple way to finish seams (page 177). It's best for fabrics that are firmly woven and won't fray. You can also pink to reduce bulk in enclosed seams. When applying fusible interfacing (page 104), pinking the edges ensures you won't have a visible line where the interfacing starts.

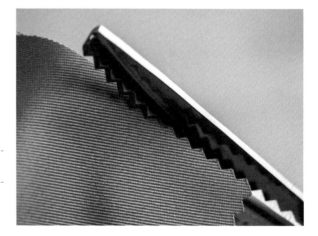

Tips + Notes

Pink the edges of fusible interfacing (page 104) when you don't want to see a sharp line where the interfacing is attached. This works best when applying interfacing to a portion of a fabric piece, for example to the area behind bound buttonholes (page 38). Trim all around the edges with pinking shears.

Pinking shears can be sharpened by a professional; talk to your local sewing shop or sewing machine repair center for recommendations. You can also sharpen pinking shears by cutting through doubled aluminum foil. Repeat several times until the shears are sharp. This might not work for all pinking shears, so do it as a last resort!

HOW TO PINK AS A SEAM FINISH

Simply trim the edges of your seam allowance with pinking shears, opening the blades wide and cutting all the way through until the shears are fully closed. For lightweight fabrics, pink both edges at once. For medium-weight and heavier fabrics, pink each edge separately.

When making the second cut, line up the blades with the pinked edges of the fabric. If you're having trouble pinking the edges evenly, draw a chalk line first with a ruler, then pink along the chalk line.

Piping

WHAT IS IT?

Piping is a decorative trim made from folded bias strips of fabric. It's often filled with cord to give it a rounded look. Piping adds emphasis and outlines areas of the garment, adds a touch of contrast color and adds structure to seams. You can buy premade piping in solid colors, or you can make your own!

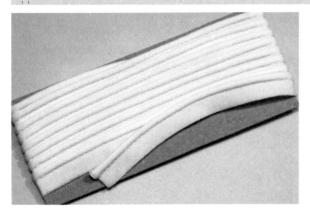

Piping

Piping on Tofino Pants

WHEN DO YOU USE IT?

Piping can be added to just about any seam! You can insert it along seam lines or along edges. Piping looks great added to a waistline seam, across the neckline, around collars and lapels, inserted between the facing and lining, around cuffs, in between a ruffle and a skirt on a hemline and along princess seams. Piping can be tonal and match the garment, or it can be a contrast color. Adding solid piping is a nice way to outline a printed garment. Piping is sewn to the garment pieces before the seam is sewn or before the facing is attached.

Tips + Notes

Striped or plaid bias tape will make neat diagonal striped piping!

Piping can make seams a little stiffer, so keep that in mind when adding piping to your garments. Stiffness is good for waistlines and necklines, but not so good for seams that cross the body, as it will restrict your movement.

HOW TO MAKE YOUR OWN PIPING

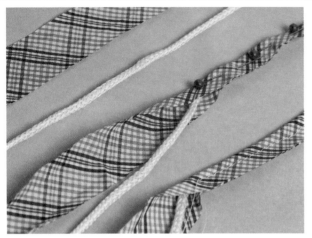

CORDED PIPING

Start with a length of bias tape. (See page 25 for instructions on making your own bias tape.) Cut a length of cording to match the bias tape. Look for cording that's ⅛"–¼" (3mm–6mm) wide. Fold bias tape around the cording with the wrong sides together. Line up the raw edges.

Baste close to the cording with a zipper foot.

FLAT PIPING

You can skip the cording step to make flat piping, if you prefer the look. To make flat piping, fold bias tape in half lengthwise, wrong sides together, and press. Baste along raw edges.

HOW TO SEW PIPING INTO SEAMS

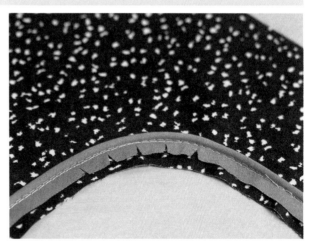

1 Baste piping to one side of the seam, with the right side facing up. Place the piping along the stitching line, so that when you sew a ⅝" (1.5cm) seam, you are sewing as close as you can to the piping. This may mean the raw edges of the piping are not in line with the fabric's raw edges. If you are sewing piping between a gathered and straight edge, baste the piping to the straight edge.

2 If you are sewing piping to a curved seam, clip or notch (page 221) the piping so that it can curve around the corner without puckers. For inside curves, notch the piping seam allowance to reduce bulk and eliminate the chance of puckers.

3 For outside curves, clip the piping seam allowance around the curved area so it can form around the corner.

4 When sewing piping around a corner, clip into the seam allowance at the corner point and bend the piping at a 90° angle.

5 Place the other side of the seam on top of the side with the piping attached, right sides together, with the piping sandwiched in between the two layers.

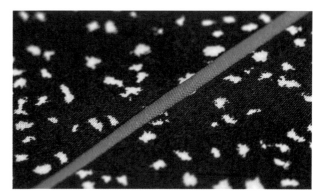

6 Sew close to the piping using a zipper foot or a piping foot, if you have one.

7 Trim the piping to ⅛" (3mm) between the seam allowances. Trim or finish seams as desired.

HOW TO END A PIPED SEAM

If you are sewing piping in a circle, for example around a neckline or a cuff, overlap the ends and curve them toward the seam allowance.

If you are sewing toward an edge that will be enclosed in another seam, curve the piping toward the seam allowance just before the seam line of the crossing seam.

Piping curved toward seam allowance

Placket

WHAT IS IT?

A placket is a finished opening that allows garments to fit over the body. Plackets are commonly used at the cuff and at the front or back neckline. Plackets can be fairly simple or more elaborate, visible or hidden, made in contrast fabric as a design feature or self-fabric to blend in. They may sit open or close up with buttons or a zipper.

Placket on a shirt

Continuous bound placket

▶ WHEN DO YOU USE IT?

Plackets are used when the garment needs to open more than the current opening allows. For example, you'll see plackets used on polo shirts, because the neck opening with the collar alone isn't large enough to get over the head. If your neck opening is too tight on a blouse or dress, consider adding a small placket at the center back neck for extra ease (page 65). Also, if you want to add a zipper in a garment where there is no seam, a slashed placket gives you an opening to insert the zipper. Plackets can be set in a seam, added to a seam or sewn to a slash in the garment.

Tips + Notes

If your fabric is sheer or slippery, consider using a stable fabric for your plackets.

HOW TO SEW A FACED PLACKET

This is the easiest type of placket to sew. Use it for cuffs or at the neckline, or for zipper openings where there is no seam to insert a zipper. The placket will reduce the top edge of the garment by ½" (1.3cm), so make sure there is enough fullness to account for this amount. If not, add it back to the side of the piece.

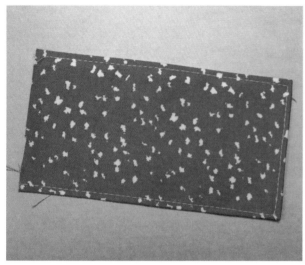

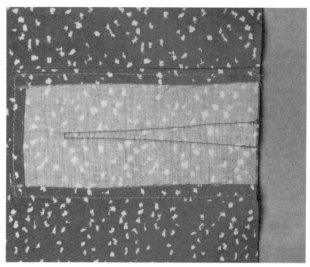

1 Cut a piece of facing that's at least 1" (2.5cm) longer than the opening and 3" (7.6cm) wide. Interface (page 104) the placket if desired. Finish the edges of the placket by serging the edges (page 179), turning them under and stitching (page 181) or zigzagging (page 183).

2 Lay the placket piece on the garment piece, right sides together, line up the raw edges and center the placket where you want the opening to be. Pin or baste (page 18) the placket in place. Draw a line straight down the center of the placket. Stop 1" (2.5cm) above the end of the placket. Sew ¼" (6mm) on one side of the marked stitching line, sew one or two stitches across the bottom, and sew ¼" (6mm) up the other side of the stitching line.

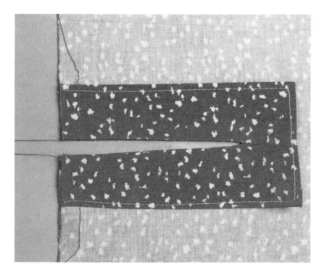

3 Slash along the marked line, then turn the placket to the inside of the garment, and press. Baste across the top edge to hold the facing in place.

HOW TO SEW A CONTINUOUS BOUND PLACKET

This is a fairly simple placket used for cuff openings. It's set into a slash opening. You'll need a strip of fabric 1½" (3.8cm) wide, cut on the bias and double the length of the placket.

1 Staystitch (page 202) about ⅛" (3mm) outside the slash opening on either side before cutting it open, using small stitches at the top of the slash to reinforce (page 165) the opening. Cut along the opening, right up to the stitching line at the top, without cutting through the stitches.

2 Press under ¼" (6mm) on one long side of the fabric strip. Pin the unpressed edge of the strip to the slashed opening with a ¼" (6mm) seam allowance. Spread the cut opening open so you can sew in a straight line. Sew with the garment side up. The slashed opening will not meet the raw edge of the placket in the center, as shown.

3 Press the seam toward the fabric strip. Turn the folded edge of the strip to meet the stitching line and edgestitch (page 69) or slipstitch (page 194). Fold the placket in half so the raw edges line up, and stitch across the corner of the placket at a 45° angle two or three times to keep the fold in place.

Plaid

WHAT IS IT?

Plaid is a type of fabric with stripes running both lengthwise and horizontally, intersecting and overlapping. Plaids are usually yarn dyed, meaning the yarn is dyed and then woven together, but sometimes the plaid is actually a print on the surface of the fabric. If the plaid looks the same on both sides, then it's likely yarn dyed. Plaids are classified as even plaids or uneven plaids. Even plaids have a mirror-image pattern where, if you fold back the corner, the lines of the plaid meet and continue the pattern. The stripe order repeats itself symmetrically across the fabric and may go in a pattern like this: 1 2 3 4 3 2 1 2 3 4. Uneven plaids will not match up if you fold back the corner and have a more irregular striping pattern. An uneven plaid may have a stripe pattern like this: 1 2 3 4 1 2 3 4 1 2 3 4. Plaids woven from wool fabric are also called tartans, originally used for traditional Scottish kilts and highland dress. Gingham and checked fabrics are types of plaid.

Even plaids

Uneven plaid

Printed plaid

WHEN DO YOU USE IT?

Plaid fabric is popular for all kinds of garments, from dressy to casual. Woolen plaids are great for sewing warm winter apparel—coats, jackets, skirts and dresses, even trousers! Plaid flannel shirts are cozy for casual wear; lightweight cotton plaid shirts are often styled with curved yokes (page 234) and called western shirts. In summer, look for lightweight plaid shirting for blouses, dresses and skirts. Plaid fabrics are best for confident beginners, as it takes work to match up the plaids.

HOW TO PLACE PLAIDS ON GARMENTS

Just like stripes (page 208) and border print fabrics (page 36), plaid fabrics require careful planning and cutting. You'll want to figure out where you want the plaid to go on every piece before cutting it out. In addition, you will want to match the plaid lines at the seam lines, so the lines travel across the body.

Placing pieces on the bias (page 23) for a diagonal effect is a great alternative to matching the plaids, for example, on patch pockets, yokes, waistbands, midriff bands and trim.

PLANNING A PLAID GARMENT

* Buy a little extra fabric. You know how they say, "Allow extra fabric to match stripes or plaids"? Make sure you do! Allow at least 25 percent more than the pattern calls for and more if you have a very large plaid.

* Pick a pattern with not too many pieces. If you pick a coat with a lot of seaming and panels, you're creating a lot of work for yourself. Either the seaming will be lost in the plaid, if the plaid is perfectly matched, or there will be plenty of opportunities for less-than-perfect matching to be seen!

* Think about where you want the plaid lines to be placed. This could be at the hemline, on the collar or over certain areas of your body. I'd never want a wide band of plaid around my hips! (But I might over my bustline for extra attention.) Think about which lines you want at the hemline, especially if it's curved.

HOW TO MATCH PLAIDS

Matching plaid is all about the cutting. The good news is that once the cutting is done, the sewing part is easy. Laying out your fabric and matching the plaids is a tedious process, but I feel it's worth it to sew professional-looking garments.

Decide where you are going to match the plaids. It's critical to match plaids at center front and center back. After that, the rest is up to you and depends on the pattern and the scale of your plaid.

Lay out your fabric on your table or floor, folding it according to the pattern's cutting diagram. Now you will line up every plaid intersection and pin them together. Tedious and time-consuming? You bet. But it's the best way to ensure perfectly matching plaids through both layers.

Alternately you could cut the fabric open and cut each pattern piece twice. That would mean less matching of plaid intersections but more marking plaid lines on pattern pieces. For uneven plaids especially, this may be the best solution.

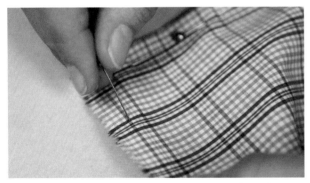

1 Start at one end of the fold edge. Stick a pin through one of the intersections—this will be easiest if you always use the same place on the pattern. Flip over your fabric and look at where the pin went through on the other side. Your goal is to get the pin poking through the exact same place on the plaid pattern. If the intersection doesn't line up, reposition the pin so it's through the right spot and then smooth the fabric around the pin.

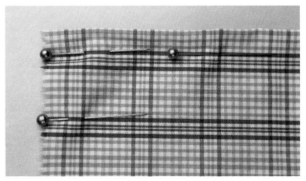

2 Secure the pin through both layers of fabric. I find it helps to always pin in the same direction. Repeat with the next intersection. Stick the pin through the intersection, check and reposition the other side and secure the pin. Once the fold has been matched, work your way toward the selvedges.

For large-scale plaids, pin every intersection. On smaller plaids, like this one, pinning every second intersection is probably enough.

When it comes time to place the pattern pieces, it helps if you already know where you want your plaid lines to fall. Think about where the dominant lines are going to fall on the pattern piece as you place each one.

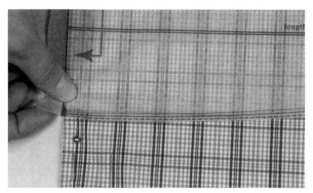
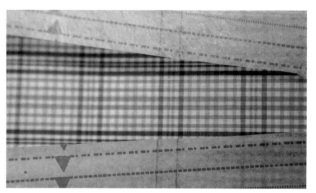

3 Line up the most important part of the piece first and then continue pinning along the fold of the piece. Pin all around the piece, smoothing out the tissue. Now you're almost ready to cut. Before you cut, mark the main plaid lines onto the pattern piece, using a ruler. I'm doing this on the side seams, so I can match the front side seam plaid to the back side seam plaid lines. Draw the lines approximately 2" (5.1 cm) onto the pattern piece. That's all you need, as the lines may not meet in a straight line. You'll have a slight V where the plaids meet on the side seam. The important part is to know where the plaid lines cross the seam line.

Repeat the markings for each wide or dominant plaid stripe, all along the seam line. Now you can cut out the piece. Remove the tissue carefully, and draw over the plaid lines so they're slightly darker.

4 Transfer these markings to the front pattern piece. In my example, I have a Bodice Front and Back piece. So I'll take the Bodice Back and lay it on top of the Bodice Front, matching side seams. You'll be able to see the plaid line markings through the tissue and trace them onto the front piece. Using a ruler, trace the plaid line markings onto the adjoining piece along the side seam or whichever seam it is you are matching. Use these lines to line up the next piece along the plaid fabric.

To sew, pin at intersections along each seam line, sew the seam and check your work after to ensure one side hasn't stretched out. For extra accuracy, baste the seams first.

Tips + Notes

Do you have to match every single plaid fabric? No. Fabrics with small-scale plaids, such as small checks or gingham, don't need to match up. The larger the plaid, the more important it is to match the plaid lines for aesthetic reasons.

It's easier to work with tissue patterns than white paper or traced patterns when you are cutting plaid fabrics. You can see through the tissue, which makes the plaid lines easy to find.

Pleats

WHAT IS IT?

Pleats are folds of fabric that are sewn in place at the top edge of skirts and trousers to add fullness or ease. Pleats can be partially sewn down inside the fold, edgestitched (page 69) on the surface or simply folded with the fold secured in a crossing seam and allowed to hang freely. Press pleats along the fold for a crisp look or leave them unpressed to create soft folds. Pleats can be sewn with an underlay fabric hidden beneath the pleat so when the pleat opens up, the contrast fabric is revealed. Sew pleats in groups or pairs, sew one single pleat or make pleats across the entire width of a skirt. There are different types of pleats, including box pleats, knife pleats and inverted pleats. The fabric is folded differently for each type of pleat, but they are sewn in the same manner.

Skirt with pleats (Simplicity 5803)

Pleat detail

▶ WHEN DO YOU USE IT?

Pleats add volume, take in fullness and add interest to the silhouette of a garment. Pleats work best made with fabrics that will hold a crease or have enough body to keep the shape of the pleat. Crisply pressed pleats require fabric that can be pressed to a sharp fold. Sew pleats instead of darts (page 63) for a softer look.

Tips + Notes

Pleats too puffy or adding too much volume? This can happen on pleated skirts where the pleats are secured at the waistline but open all the way down. Edgestitch (page 69) or topstitch (page 218) along the pleats from waist to hip to flatten them out for a yoke effect.

Change darts (page 63) to pleats by folding along the dart lines and basting across the raw edges. Or sew 1"–2" (2.5cm–5.1cm) down the dart line but leave the rest of it open to form a pleat.

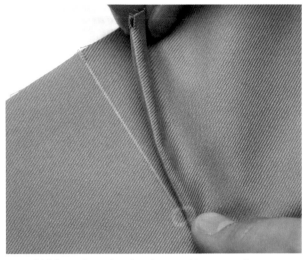

1 Fold fabric along the pleat line, and bring it to the placement line.

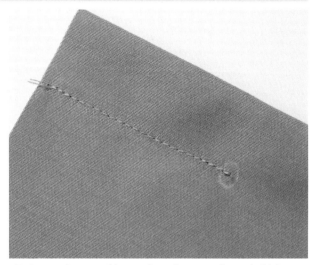

2 Pin in place, and baste along the raw edge to hold the pleat in place.

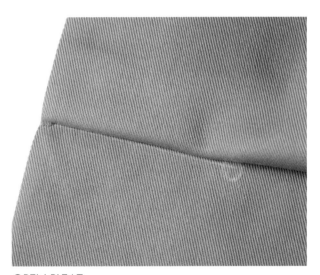

OPEN PLEAT

Some pleats are partially sewn along part of the pleat and open up to release the pleat. For these types of pleats, sew along the marked sewing line, backstitching (page 14) at both ends.

Pockets, Inseam

WHAT IS IT?

Inseam pockets are pockets sewn into the seam of a garment. The pocket bag is either cut as an extension of the seam or attached as a separate piece. Inseam pockets are flat and nearly invisible from the right side of your garment. They're also easy to add to any pattern with side seams or front princess seams.

Inseam pocket in Cambie Dress

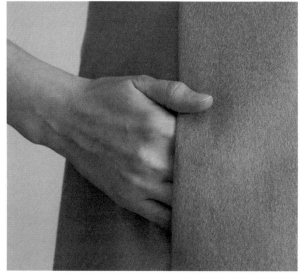

Inseam pocket in wool coat

WHEN DO YOU USE IT?

Inseam pockets are perfect to use when you don't want the pockets to be visible or obvious from the right side of the garment. Side seams are the most common place to put them; another option is on princess seams on the front of a garment. Inseam pockets are one of the easiest pockets to add when your pattern doesn't call for pockets, and they won't compete with the rest of the design.

There are three types of inseam pockets: with separate pocket bag pieces, with pocket bags cut as an extension of the seam allowance (cut-on) or with separate pocket bag pieces and a cut-on extension. They're all sewn the same way, with slight variations.

Tips + Notes

Want to add inseam pockets to a pattern without pockets? Use the inseam pocket piece from a pattern you already own. Simply borrow the pocket pattern piece and mark the pocket opening on the seam line where you want to add a pocket.

If you're adding inseam pockets to a pattern without pockets, be sure to choose a design with enough ease to get your hands in the pockets. Inseam pockets might not work well in a tight pencil skirt!

If you're sewing inseam pockets in a fully lined garment, skip the steps to finish the seam allowance. The seams will be enclosed in the lining and won't fray.

You may want to reinforce pocket openings with stay tape (page 204) to strengthen pockets that will be frequently used.

HOW TO SEW INSEAM POCKETS WITH SEPARATE POCKET BAGS

1 For each inseam pocket, cut two pocket bag pieces. If your fabric has a visible right and wrong side, make sure you have two pairs. Mark the pocket opening on both the pocket bag pieces and the seam. Snip ¼" (6mm) notches into the seam allowance. Finish the seam allowances of the side seam. Finish all seam allowances of the pocket piece. If serging or zigzagging makes the edges ripple, press to flatten them out. Pin the pocket piece to the seam, right sides together, matching notches.

2 Sew with a ⅜" (1 cm) seam allowance. Press the seam toward the pocket. Understitch (page 228) on the pocket side, if desired, to keep pocket bag seam secured in the right direction. Repeat steps 1 and 2 for the other side of the pocket bag.

3 Line up the pocket pieces on top of each other, right sides together, matching the top and bottom. Sew the seam with a ⅝" (1.5cm) seam allowance around the pocket bag and the remainder of the seam.

4 Press seam allowances and the pocket bag toward center or the direction that feels most comfortable when you place your hands in the pockets. The finished inseam pocket is flat and nearly completely hidden!

HOW TO SEW INSEAM POCKETS WITH CUT-ON POCKET BAGS

Simply place the two pieces right sides together and sew along the seam, pivoting around the pocket piece, and continue down the rest of the seam in one motion.

HOW TO SEW AN INSEAM POCKET WITH AN EXTENSION AND SEPARATE POCKET BAG

Sew the pocket piece to the seam extension, finish the seams and press the seams toward the pocket. Follow the same steps to sew inseam pockets with cut-on pocket bags.

Pockets, Patch

WHAT IS IT?

Patch pockets are pockets sewn to the surface of a garment, like a patch. Generally they are applied like a patch, with stitching around the edges, but they can also be sewn on invisibly by hand. Patch pockets can be any shape. They are easy to sew and only require one piece of fabric! If your pattern doesn't have patch pockets included, it's very easy to add your own.

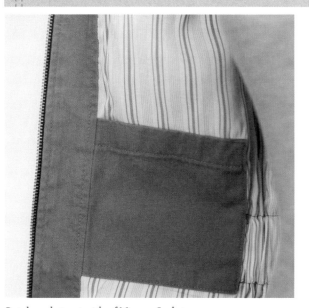

Patch pocket on inside of Minoru Jacket

Bias-cut patch pockets on Archer Shirt (Grainline Studio)

▶ WHEN DO YOU USE IT?

Patch pockets are perfect when you want to add visible pockets to a garment. You'll see patch pockets on blouses and dress shirts, suit jackets and coats, skirts, dresses and trousers. Patch pockets draw attention to the area where they are located. Therefore, you may not want patch pockets on your chest if you're busty, and you may not want patch pockets on your hips if you're pear-shaped. Patch pockets are great for embellishing, because you can add the embellishment to the pocket first, make sure you are happy with the look and then add it to the garment. Embroidery, appliqués or ribbon trim are all ways of embellishing a patch pocket. Patch pockets are an easy pocket to add to the inside of your garments, too, as you're simply sewing a piece of fabric to the lining. Make patch pockets out of contrast fabric or matching fabric.

For striped (page 208) or plaid (page 138) fabric, patch pockets can be turned diagonally for an interesting effect or matched to the lines of the garment so they're barely visible. Patch pockets can be added as an afterthought or removed without affecting the structure of the garment. You can place patch pockets symmetrically, on both sides of a garment, or place just one on the right side as a design detail. Sew pockets with contrast stitching, with one row of stitching or two, or with zigzag or decorative stitching.

HOW TO MAKE PATCH POCKETS

Patch pockets are easiest to sew before the garment is constructed. Sew pockets to garment panels while they are still flat. Decide on pocket shape and size. For decorative pockets, they can be any size. For useable pockets, make sure you can put your hand in them! Make pockets to fit specific items by measuring the item's width and height and making the pocket's dimensions slightly larger to fit the item. (Test the pocket size by making the piece, pinning it in place and placing the item in the pocket.)

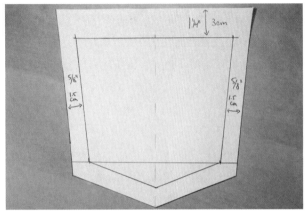

1 Draw the pocket shape on paper. Add ⅝" (1.5cm) seam allowance around all of the edges, and 1¼" (3.2cm) along the pocket opening edge.

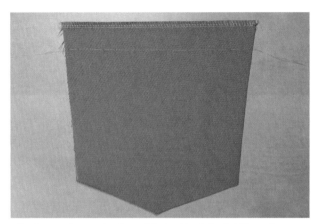

2 Cut out the pocket from fabric. Mark the fold line along the pocket opening by either hand basting (page 18) along the fold line or clipping the seam allowance at each end of the fold line. Finish the top edge. Serge (page 179), turn under ¼" (6mm) and stitch (page 181), zigzag (page 183) or bind (page 172) the edge.

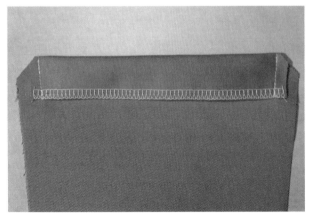

3 Turn under the top edge along the fold line, toward the front of the pocket, right sides together. Stitch across the sides of the top edge using a ⅝" (1.5cm) seam allowance. Trim (page 221) across the corners.

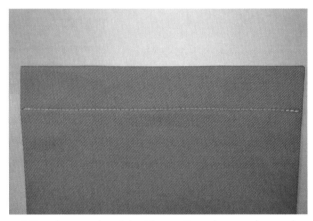

4 Turn the top edge right side out. Press the top edge, and press under all pocket edges. For curved edges, run a row of basting stitches (page 18) around the corner, and pull basting threads to ease in this edge. If desired, topstitch along the pocket opening edge.

5 Pin the pocket in position on the garment piece, then press the garment piece if necessary to remove wrinkles. Secure the pocket in place with pins or by hand basting (page 18).

If you use pins, pin in the direction you are going to sew, so the heads are closest to you. Or pin at right angles to the stitching line, with the heads on your right.

If you hand baste, use a contrast color thread so it's easy to see when it's time to remove. If you baste inside the stitch line, it will be easier to remove than if you have stitched through your basting.

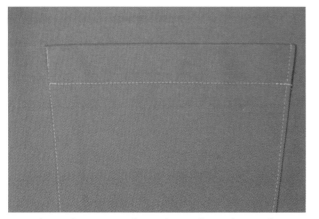

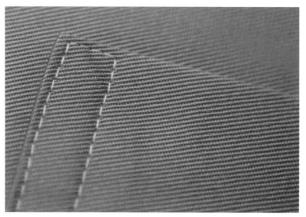

6 Edgestitch (page 69) the pocket in place. I line up the folded pocket edge with the groove of my presser foot as I sew. When you reach the corner, slow down and stitch until you are one stitch length away from the corner. Stop with the needle down and lift the presser foot. Pivot your work and lower the presser foot. The work should be lined up for you to edgestitch along the next edge. If it's too far away, turn your work back and take a half stitch toward the corner, then pivot again. To sew around curves, sew slowly and gently turn your work around the curve, without stopping and lifting the foot. You may want to shorten your stitch length for the pocket stitching to make it easier to sew around the curves.

7 Topstitch (page 218) with a second row of stitching if desired. When you reach the end point, sew across the top of the pocket for three or four stitches, then pivot again and topstitch parallel to the first row of edgestitching. When you reach the opposite corner with your second row of stitching, pivot at the top edge, sew across the top for three or four stitches and stop once you reach your starting point. Stitch in place to secure your thread.

8 Sew bar tacks (page 16) at corners of pockets for extra strength. As an alternative to bar tacks, sew triangular tacks. Sew across for a few stitches, then sharply angle your stitching to meet the edgestitching about ½" (1.3cm) down from the top edge. Repeat on both corners.

Pockets, Slash

WHAT IS IT?

Slash front pockets, or one-quarter top pockets, have a cutout on the surface of the garment and a pocket bag filling in that cutout and finishing the shape of the garment piece. A great example of this type of pockets is found on jeans; the front pockets are nearly always slash pockets. The opening can be curved (like jeans pockets), a straight line running diagonally at the hip or a right angle. These pockets are comfortable to put your hands in and easy to access. The pocket bag can be self fabric or a contrast fabric with a facing at the opening.

Slash pocket on Hollyburn Skirt

Slash pocket on Thurlow Trousers

▶ WHEN DO YOU USE IT?

Slash pockets are frequently used on the front of trousers and casual pants. I like to use them on dresses and skirts, as well, as they're easy to sew and add practicality to my garments.

Tips + Notes

If your pattern doesn't have pockets, but you want them, it's an easy add-on. Borrow the pattern piece from another pattern, trace the opening onto your skirt or trouser front and add the pocket. Reshape the part of the pocket that fills the cutout so it matches your original pattern.

HOW TO SEW A SLASH POCKET

If there are facings (page 74), sew the facings to the pocket bag. Finish the edges of the facings, place them right side up on the right side of the pocket bag and edgestitch (page 69) along the finished edges. Baste (page 18) the raw edges of the facings to the pocket bag and treat it as one piece from this point forward.

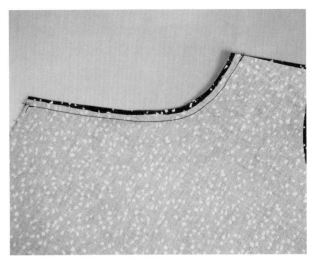

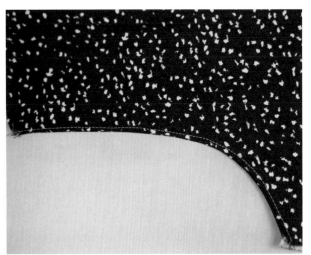

1 Pin the pocket bag to the garment opening. You may want to add stay tape (page 204) to the pocket opening so it doesn't stretch over time. Sew the pocket bag to the garment, trim and clip (page 221) the seam allowances.

2 Understitch (page 228) on the pocket bag side of the seam, and press the pocket bag to the inside of the garment.

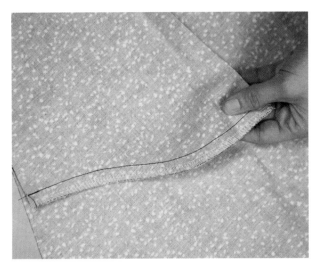

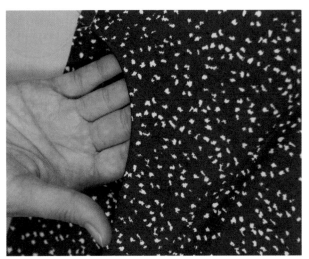

3 Fold the pocket bag along the fold line so that the lower edge of the pocket matches and the pocket bag fills in the cutout. Sew the lower edge of the pocket bag and finish the seam. This is a good place for a French seam (page 82) as it finishes the edge nicely.

4 Baste the pocket to the garment along the top edge and the side edge. Continue sewing the garment, treating the front and pocket as one piece.

Pockets, Welt

WHAT IS IT?

Welt pockets have a narrow rectangular bound opening on the surface and the pocket bag hidden on the inside. Welt pockets can be single-welt pockets, with one strip of fabric binding the opening, or double-welt pockets, which have two strips binding the opening and look like a large bound buttonhole (page 38). In fact, they are sewn nearly the same way, with the addition of a pocket bag. This is an advanced type of pocket construction. As with bound buttonholes, practice will help you master the technique!

Double-welt pocket

Pocket bag inside welt pocket

▶ WHEN DO YOU USE IT?

Welt pockets are used on the backs of trousers and shorts, on suit jackets and on coats. Welt pockets also make great interior pockets. Sew welt pockets either horizontally or vertically, depending on where you are placing them and the angle you'll be reaching from. They're more involved to sew than slash pockets (page 148), inseam pockets (page 143) or patch pockets (page 145), but they are flat and subtle. Their tailored look makes them excellent for menswear, suiting and tailored coats. Welt pockets work best in fabric that presses well, such as wool or other suiting fabrics, cotton twill and denim. Make sure you can press a nice flat crease in your fabric so the welts will be well defined.

Tips + Notes

Welt pockets cannot be moved once they are sewn, so be absolutely sure of the pocket position before sewing!

If your fabric is prone to fraying, you may want to add fusible interfacing (page 104) on the garment fabric behind the pocket placement line. Cut a strip 1"–2" (2.5cm–5.1cm) wide and slightly longer than the pocket marking. Fuse the strip in place before starting to sew the pocket.

For a casual look, and to hold the pocket bags in place, topstitch (page 218) around the pocket bag edges on the right side of the garment.

For faux welt pockets, sew the welts in place but skip the pocket bag. Sew the facing behind the welts to fill in the gap. I like faux welt pockets for a smoother line on dressy trousers, but it is nice to have functional pockets as well. It's up to you!

HOW TO SEW A WELT POCKET

In this example of sewing a double-welt pocket, the pocket is placed horizontally on the back of trousers, but the process is the same for vertical pockets. Welt pockets are sewn to the garment panels while they are still flat. Make sure the pocket line is clearly marked on the panel. If there is a facing on the pocket bag, finish the edges of the facing and place it on the pocket bag.

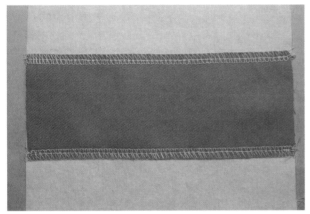

1 Edgestitch (page 69) the facing to the pocket bag along the finished edges. This will fill in the gap when the pocket opens, so the pocket lining fabric doesn't show.

2 Interface (page 104) the pocket welts, then fold them in half lengthwise, wrong sides together, and baste along the raw edges. Center the welts along the garment's pocket line, raw edges against the line, and sew down the middle of each welt parallel to the pocket placement line. Make sure the starting and stopping points on each welt are in line with each other.

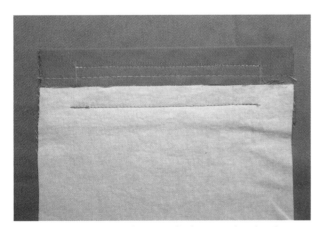

3 Sew the back pocket lining to the lower welt only, along the previous stitching, right side facing down, and finish the seam allowances. You might find it easier to flip over the piece and sew from the other side of the garment, where you can see the previous stitching.

4 Slash along the pocket line between the stitching lines. Clip diagonally toward the corners.

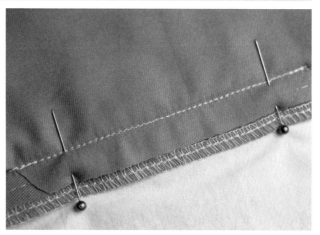

5 Turn the welts and back pocket lining to the inside. If there are puckers in the corners, you may need to clip further into the corner to release the fabric. Line up the welts so the folds meet in the middle of the pocket opening, and stitch the fabric triangles down on top of the welt ends. Baste across the triangles once, turn and check that the edges are square and that there are no gaps between the welts. Then stitch over the triangles several times. Press (page 155) the welts and the opening, and press the pocket bag down. Edgestitch (page 69) around the welt opening if desired.

6 Fold the pocket lining upward along the fold line, thereby lining up the raw edges. Sew the top welt seam allowances through the back pocket lining and facing. This ensures that items only go down into the pocket bag, not up above the welt.

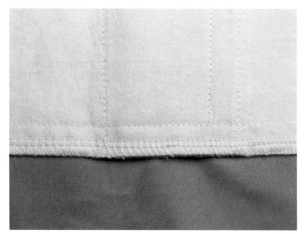

7 Sew the sides of the pocket lining and finish the seam allowances. If your pocket bag extends all the way to the top of the garment piece, baste the pocket lining to the garment along the top edge.

Press Cloth

WHAT IS IT?

A press cloth is a cloth placed in between the iron and the garment to protect the fabric when pressing (page 155). You can buy premade press cloths, but you can easily make your own by cutting a piece of fabric and finishing the edges.

Press cloths

Pressing with a press cloth

▶ WHEN DO YOU USE IT?

Press (page 155) with a press cloth when the surface of your fabric could be ruined by the iron. Wool fabrics can turn shiny when pressed, so a press cloth is especially useful when pressing wool. A press cloth can also reduce the heat that gets through to the fabric, protecting the surface from scorching. If your iron has buildup or glue from fusible interfacing on the plate, a press cloth will keep the garment protected from that, as well, when you don't have time to clean the iron.

WHAT FABRICS MAKE GOOD PRESS CLOTHS?

Unbleached cotton muslin is a good choice for a press cloth. It's durable, strong and can withstand heat and steam. It's easy to find in most fabric stores, and it's inexpensive. If you only have one press cloth, a muslin one is a good choice.

Bedsheets or pillowcases can be used as press cloths. A linen tea towel will also make a good press cloth because it's lightweight, can withstand heat and steam and is easy to wash. If there's an embroidery or design on the towel, you'll be able to easily tell the right side of the cloth. (Just don't press on top of the embroidery as it will leave an impression on your fabric.) Linen fabrics can be used for press cloths as well.

Silk organza is a popular choice because it's smooth and lightweight, drapes well and is mostly transparent, so it's easy to see your work through the press cloth. However, it may be hard to find silk organza in your local fabric store.

Use a wool press cloth for pressing wool garments to keep them from getting shiny. Cut a scrap piece of fabric from your leftover project fabric, if available, and use it as a press cloth.

HOW TO MAKE A PRESS CLOTH

Prewash your press cloth fabric (page 157) a couple of times so all of the finishing chemicals are removed. Cut a large piece of fabric, about 20" × 20" (50.8cm × 50.8cm). The measurements don't have to be exact. If you are using leftover fabric or garment fabric, try to get as large of a piece as you can cut. My sample cloths are about 12" (30.5cm) square.

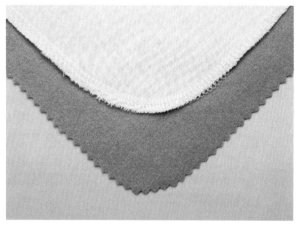

1 Finish the edges of the fabric. If you serge (page 179) the edges, serge with the same side up to make it easier to tell which side is the right side of the cloth. Does it really matter? It does if you end up getting adhesive from fusible interfacing (page 104) on the cloth. Having one side designated as the right side keeps all of the glue only on one side and never against your project. Round the edges to avoid serger tails and to make sewing faster. If you don't have a serger, pink the edges (page 177).

2 Cover the seam with the press cloth, and press!

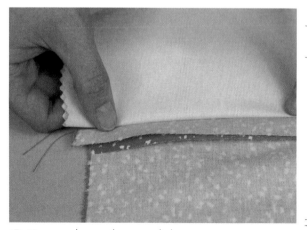

3 You can also use the press cloth to prevent seam allowances from showing through on the right side. Fold the press cloth and tuck it under the seam allowance. Press with the cloth underneath the seam allowance. (This also works with strips of paper.)

Tips + Notes

If you notice the press cloth is dirty or stained, wash it! Don't take a chance on ruining your next project.

A smaller press cloth may be easier to manage than a big one.

Sew a loop or ribbon to one side of your cloth so it's easy to hang.

Pressing

WHAT IS IT?

Pressing refers to using an iron with an up and down motion. Ironing is sliding the iron across the fabric. Pressing is lowering the iron, pressing, then lifting it up and placing it down in a new position. There's no dragging or sliding the iron in pressing.

Pressing a seam

Heat setting dial on iron

WHEN DO YOU USE IT?

Press as you sew! Each seam, dart (page 63) and pleat (page 141) will be pressed as you sew, before moving on to the next stage of construction. You'll also press the final garment when it's completed before hanging it in your closet. My least favorite type of pressing (although necessary) is pressing after laundering. Apply the same techniques to press your garments after each wash so they look their best. Press your fabric before cutting, and press to apply fusible interfacing (page 104).

GETTING READY TO PRESS

First, choose the right heat setting for your fabric. Generally synthetic fibers are pressed with low heat; cottons and linens on high heat; and wool in between. Modern irons have a heat dial labeled with fabric types, which makes it easy to choose the right setting for your sewing project. If your fabric is a blend, use the setting for the lowest fabric on the dial. For example, if your fabric is a cotton-polyester blend, use the polyester setting as it requires a lower heat setting than the cotton. Usually the steam and the temperature are both controlled by one dial, but there may be a separate switch for turning the steam on or off. Take a look at your iron before getting started, and test the iron on a scrap of your fabric before pressing your first seam.

If you are going to press curved seams or darts, you'll want a tailor's ham (page 212). A seam roll also comes in handy for pressing seams (page 185). One more tool that will improve your pressing is a press cloth (page 153). Gather these supplies, then make sure your ironing board is clean and your iron is working.

PRESSING FLAT SEAMS

After sewing, press seams and darts flat first, then press them open. Press all seam allowances open unless otherwise instructed. Press on the inside of your garment first, then on the outside. Use a press cloth (page 153) when pressing on the right side of your garment, and press with the grain (page 90).

PRESSING OVER A TAILOR'S HAM

Darts are curved, so it's best to press them over a curved surface. Using a tailor's ham (page 212), open up the darted area and find a place on the ham that fits the curve. Press on the wrong side of the garment.

PRESSING OVER A SEAM ROLL

It's challenging to press sleeve seams without flattening the rest of the sleeve. For narrow parts of a garment, like sleeves or pant legs, use a seam roll (page 185) to press just the seam allowances. Place the seam roll underneath the seam, tucking it inside the sleeve tube or pant leg. Press on the wrong side of the garment. This is also useful for pressing seams that might show through to the right side of the garment. The sleeve roll is curved just enough so you're pressing the seam allowances but not the garment itself.

Tips + Notes

Set up your iron and ironing board so they are easy to access while sewing. You might even want to lower the board to sitting height, so it's easy to switch between sewing and pressing.

Press only once you're sure the seams and darts are in the right place. It's hard to press out the creases if you end up letting out the seams or moving the darts.

If you have to pack up your project while it's in progress, fold the pieces as little as possible to avoid having to press them again when you start sewing.

Don't press over pins. You'll damage the iron, leave impressions on your garment and possibly melt the pins!

Fabrics with nap (page 121) need to be pressed very carefully so you don't flatten the surface. Some should not be pressed at all, for example, faux fur fabrics. Press velvet on a special pressing surface for velvet called a needle board.

Prewashing (Preshrinking)

WHAT IS IT?

Prewashing is basically washing your fabric before you start cutting or sewing. That's all there is to it!

Fabric to be prewashed

► WHEN DO YOU USE IT?

I recommend always washing your fabric before using it. Doing so eliminates the fabric's finishing chemicals, which can irritate people with sensitive skin. You're also reducing the chance that your fabric will shrink the first time the finished garment is washed.

WHY BOTHER PREWASHING?

* To avoid shrinkage! There's nothing worse than seeing your beautifully finished project come out of the wash shrunk. Luckily, you have control of the shrinkage if you wash the fabric before cutting.

* To remove sizing and finishing. After fabric is dyed, chemicals are used in the finishing process, including sizing, a substance that adds stiffness and smoothness. It's nice to wash the chemicals out of the fabric before you start working with it, especially if you have sensitive skin. On the other hand, these finishing chemicals are there to stabilize the fabric and might make it easier to work with, so your fabric might have more drape and softness after washing.

* To prevent bleeding. Fabrics like denim or dark fabrics are heavily dyed, and it can take several washes to get out the extra dye. That extra dye can rub off or "bleed" on to other fabrics. Without prewashing, these fabrics can stain your undergarments, your furniture and even your skin! Denim fabrics, dark navy and black fabrics and red fabrics are prone to bleeding and should definitely be prewashed.

* To make it clean. If you're not particular about used fabric, buying fabric from thrift stores and online is a great and eco-friendly way to go. Vintage and pre-loved fabric may smell musty from storage, so give it a wash so it's fresh to work with.

HOW TO PREWASH YOUR FABRIC

The general rule is to wash your fabric the same way you would wash the finished garment. If you plan to machine wash and dry your finished garment, then do the same to the fabric. That way the fabric won't shrink or change after the garment is washed.

Another theory is to wash it harder than you'd wash the finished garment. Even if you're going to handwash your finished garment, there's a slight chance someone might toss it in the dryer accidentally and shrink it. If you wash and dry the fabric beforehand, then the shrinkage will happen before you sew up your project.

One last thing to consider: Prewashing may change the feel and the drape of your fabric. Crisp fabrics like taffeta or linen may become soft and limp. If you're unsure, cut a large swatch (8" × 8" [20.3cm x 20.3cm]) and wash the swatch separately first, to see how washing will affect the fabric.

Prewashing cotton fabric

* Always prewash cotton fabrics! Cotton will soften up a little after washing, plus it's the most likely fabric to shrink later.

* For cottons, including denim, consider washing your fabric harder than you normally would. This means hotter temperatures than you might normally use, a more vigorous wash cycle and a hot dryer even if you might hang the garment to dry.

* For heavy cottons or denim, or when making garments where an exact fit is required, prewash your fabric more than once. Have you ever had a pair of pants that kept on shrinking each time they were washed?

* Rayon/viscose is very similar to cotton (both are plant based), so I treat them the same way. Rayon can shrink as much as cotton, and some rayons will shrink more! However, many rayon garments are dry-clean only. You may choose to always dry-clean the finished garment. Types of rayon fabric include bamboo, tencel and modal. Look for care instructions on the bolt of fabric and take note for your sewing projects.

Prewashing wool fabric

Most garments made of wool fabric are going to be dry-cleaned and not machine washed. How do you account for shrinkage? Here are some ideas on how to pretreat your wool fabric.

* Steam it. Working from end to end, hover the iron over the fabric and apply steam. Repeat until you've covered the entire length of the fabric.

* Get it preshrunk by a dry cleaner. You may be able to ask your local dry cleaner to preshrink your wool yardage. This is costly, but it reduces the chance that your finished wool garment will shrink and become unwearable.

Prewashing silk fabric

Silk fabrics are delicate, so handle with care. Silk can be washed, but it will often change the texture and sheen of the fabric. You can cut and sew it unwashed, knowing that you'll have to dry-clean the finished garment. If you'd like to be able to wash the finished garment, try handwashing a tiny piece and see how it turns out. Silk may get softer, more wrinkled and less shiny after it's washed, so you might not like how it looks. Or you might love it, and then you will be able to wash the finished garment.

Prewashing polyester, nylon and synthetic fabrics

* While synthetic fabrics are unlikely to shrink, you might want to prewash polyester and nylon fabrics regardless to remove any chemicals and to freshen them up if they've been in storage.

* Polyester dries really quickly, so you won't have to put it in the dryer very long, if at all. Polyester comes out of the washer just about dry!

Tips + Notes

To avoid your fabric fraying at the edges in the washing machine, finish the edges before washing. You can trim the cut edges with pinking shears (page 177), zigzag across the edges (page 183) or run them through the serger (page 179).

Prewash the trims and notions for your project. Check the packaging for notes on whether the trim is preshrunk.

Princess Seam

WHAT IS IT?

Princess seams are vertical seams used for shaping a garment. Princess seams start at either the shoulder or the armhole and extend across the bustline to the waistline. Tapering in at the narrow parts and out at the wider parts, the seam follows the curves of the body. If the garment extends below the waist, the princess seam can go all the way to the hemline. Princess seams are used instead of darts (page 63), as they're easier to fit and adjust than darted garments. They're simple to sew and very flattering. Princess seams are used on both the front and back of garments.

Princess seam on Pendrell Blouse

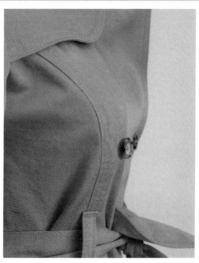

Princess seam on Robson Coat

Princess seam on wool coat

▶ WHEN DO YOU USE IT?

Princess seams are very flattering, as they curve to fit the body and create vertical lines. Choose princess-line styles for easier fitting. Princess seams are a good choice for heavier fabrics like coating, as there is no dart point to try to press flat. It's easy to make little adjustments to princess seams as you sew. You can change a pattern with darts into princess seams for a better fit.

Tips + Notes

When altering or fitting princess styles, be sure to make adjustments to all of the panels.

If you change a dart (page 63) to a princess seam, make a muslin test garment (page 118) to check the fit before cutting your fabric.

HOW TO SEW PRINCESS SEAMS

Both types of princess seams are sewn the same way, whether they start at the shoulder or the armhole. Your pattern will usually have notches or markings along the princess seam to help line up the curves. Make sure these markings are transferred to your fabric pieces, then staystitch (page 202) both sides of the princess seam just inside the seam line.

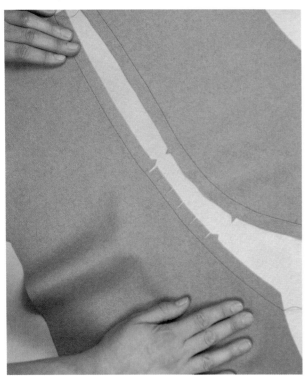

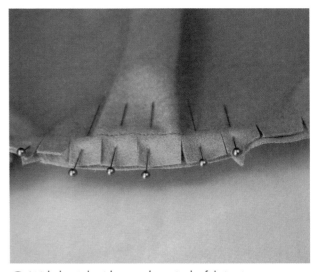

1 Compare the two sides of the princess seam between the markings. Clip (page 221) the seam allowance of the side with the inner curve, on the center panel, just between the markings that indicate the curviest part of the seam. This will allow the seam line to spread and to match the side with the outer curve.

2 With the right sides together, pin the fabric pieces together, matching notches and markings. Check the curviest section and spread the clipped part to match the curve. Make more snips, if needed, to ensure the raw edges meet on both sides of the seam.

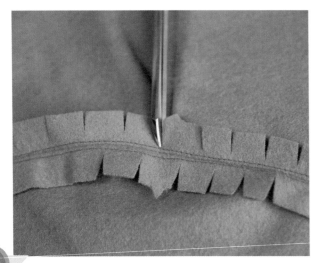

3 Sew the seam and press it open. Notch the seam allowance of the side panel so the seam allowance can lie flat without ripples. Snip the notches between the clips, so they are not in line with each other.

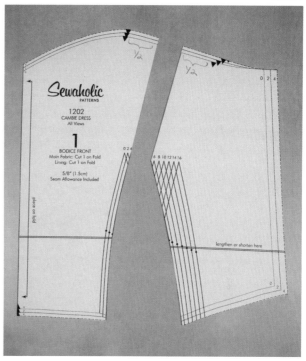

1 Take the pattern piece and draw a line from the dart point (page 63) toward the shoulder or armhole. For armhole princess seams, curve your line toward the armhole line, about one-third of the way up. For shoulder princess seams, extend the dart point up toward the middle of the shoulder seam. In this example, I'm going to extend it to the top of the bodice.

2 Cut out the dart along both sides of the dart and through to the extended line. My bodice piece is now two separate pieces. If there is a side bust dart, cut along one side of the dart line and fold the dart closed.

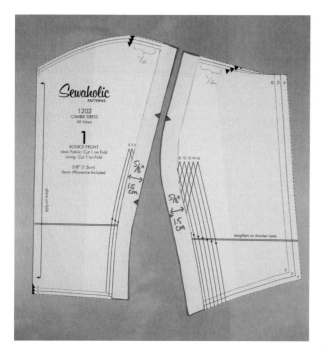

3 Round out any points or corners so the curve is smooth. Add a seam allowance to both sides of the new princess seam. Mark notches at the top and bottom of the curve to make the seam easier to match up and sew.

Printed Fabric

WHAT IS IT?

Printed fabric is fabric with a design on the surface. Prints can have many colors or just one or two. Often the print will sit on the surface of the fabric, and the wrong side will be white or another solid color. Prints can be large, small or in between, with defined edges or subtle transitions between colors. Florals, animal prints, polka dots and graphic prints are just a few of the endless possibilities!

Printed fabric bundle

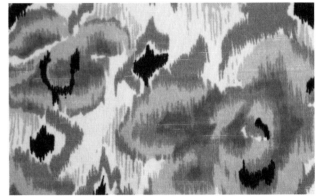

Printed fabric

WHEN DO YOU USE IT?

I use printed fabric all the time! I love prints. Choosing printed fabric is a wonderful way to work lots of color and personality into your sewing projects and wardrobe. Printed fabrics are great choices for tops, dresses and skirts. A couple of surprise bonuses come with sewing with printed fabrics, too. It's easier to tell the right and wrong side, and printed garments hide a little bit of dirt.

PRINT PLACEMENT

When you're cutting printed fabric, think about where the print is going to go on each piece. You want to avoid having two flower blooms placed on the bust or one flower bloom at the center front of your skirt. If you have a favorite section of the print, aim to cut the bodice front from that part.

CHOOSING A PRINTED FABRIC

My suggestion when it comes to picking a print? Choose prints you love. Don't worry so much about what the fashion magazines are saying about what's "in" or "out." If you love polka dots, then choose polka dots!

That said, you want to consider the pattern you're sewing. The larger the print, the fewer seams there should be in your chosen pattern. Otherwise the print will be sliced up and won't look quite the same as it does on the bolt. Smaller prints may look like solids from far away, which make your garment more interesting when people see you up close. If you're browsing in a fabric store, try wrapping the fabric around yourself and looking in a mirror. I've found that prints I love on the bolt may look a bit intense as a full garment.

It's easy to like a print when it's fabric but not like it when the same fabric is sewn into a garment. If you have a hard time choosing prints that you actually like to wear, window shop at the mall and look for prints you like in ready-to-wear garments. Or look online at clothing brands you like and note the colors, styles and scales of the prints they use.

HOW TO MATCH PRINTS

Do you have to match printed fabrics, like with stripes (page 208) and plaids (page 138)? It's up to you. I match prints only if it will be really distracting if I don't. If the print is small, it doesn't matter. Only when the print is very large or the lines are very distinct and there's an important seam, like the center back seam, do I like the print to continue across the seam line. If you are piecing together your fabric and want the seams to blend, matching the prints is a good idea. If you are placing a patch pocket (page 145) in printed fabric, you can make the pocket practically disappear if you match the pocket print to the background print.

To match prints along a straight seam line, cut out the first piece you need to match. In this case, I'm matching the center back seam. I have to cut two back pieces. Instead of cutting the piece once, through two layers of fabric, you'll be cutting this pattern piece twice through a single layer of fabric.

When I laid out my first piece, I had a general idea of where to place my second piece. You need to make sure if you're cutting a half-shape along the center back that you also have enough room to cut out the other half of the shape along the opposing seam line. Remember that when you cut a single layer, you'll need to flip the pattern to cut the second piece.

1 Here's my left back piece. I'm going to be matching the right edge to the right back piece. Press under the seam allowance along the center back seam or along the seam you want to match. This will be the line you need to match against your right back piece.

2 Lay the left back fabric panel on the fabric and match the print pattern as you go. See how I'm lining up the print across both sides of the seam? If your cut piece nearly disappears as you lay it on top of the fabric, then you're doing it right. Take a step back and look to see if any of the edges are out of line. Pin along the seam to match.

3 Take the pattern tissue and press under ⅝" (1.5cm) seam allowance. This will help you line up your right back along the matching line. Line up the folded edge of the pattern tissue along the left back fold line. The edges should meet, fold to fold, with no space between.

4 Pin the pattern tissue to the single layer of fabric around all edges. After pinning around the edges of the tissue, lift off the left back fabric panel. Unfold the center back seam allowance on the tissue piece, and pin along the edge. Cut out the right back piece.

5 All of this hard work and attention while cutting will pay off when you sew up the center back seam. From far away you can't even tell there's a seam, which is the ultimate goal. You may want to baste (page 18) the seam before stitching for even more accuracy. Baste the seam line, press the seam open to check the print matching, and if you're happy with it, stitch the seam.

Tips + Notes

You may need more fabric than your pattern asks for to match prints, especially large-scale prints.

Bring out the beauty of the printed fabric by adding contrast in one of the print colors. Add contrast piping (page 132) around the neckline, binding (page 28) or even contrast panels.

Unsure about wearing full-on printed garments? Choose prints for smaller garments, for example blouses instead of dresses, or use prints as accent fabrics on cuffs, collars and pockets.

Printed fabrics make great surprise contrast facings (page 74) and linings (page 113). It's especially fun to add printed pocket linings or facings on simple garments. No one will see it but you!

One-way designs are prints that are printed in one direction. These types of prints need to be cut with all of the pattern pieces facing the same way. See page 121 for more on nap.

Reinforce

WHAT IS IT?

Reinforce means to strengthen an area of your fabric piece. Often you reinforce a seam line by sewing a row of very short machine stitches.

Reinforced V

Yoke on Crescent Skirt that needs reinforcing

▶ WHEN DO YOU USE IT?

You will reinforce at the point of a *V*, at corners, narrow plackets or anywhere you are about to slash or clip into the seam allowance.

Tips + Notes

Draw in your stitching line with chalk or marking pencil before you begin. Doing so helps to ensure the reinforced stitching ends up in the right place, as it's very hard to unpick.

HOW TO REINFORCE WITH MACHINE STITCHES

Set the stitch length to a very small number, 1mm–1.5mm. Start a little bit ahead of the area to reinforce and stop when you have reached the end of the area to reinforce. No need to backstitch because these small stitches are tight and won't come apart. Clip the thread close to the stitching.

Ruffle

WHAT IS IT?

A ruffle is a piece of fabric that's been gathered or cut in a circle to add fullness. There are two types of ruffles: gathered ruffles and circular ruffles. Gathered ruffles are rectangular-shaped pieces that are gathered into ruffles; circular ruffles are cut from a circle so the outer edge is longer than the inner edge and soft folds result. Ruffles can be set into seams, sewn along edges of garments, such as necklines or armhole openings, sewn to hemlines or sewn on top of the garment's surface. Ruffles can be wide and deep or very narrow, very full or just slightly gathered.

Gathered ruffle

Circular ruffle

WHEN DO YOU USE IT?

Ruffles are a great way to add volume to areas of a garment or to bring attention to parts of the body. Add ruffles to the neckline to draw the eye to the face; add ruffles at the bustline to create volume on a smaller chest. Sew ruffles to hemlines for volume and swish, or to lengthen a skirt that's too short. Any fabric that isn't too thick to be gathered can be used for ruffles. Circular ruffles work better when made with lighter or drapier fabrics; fabrics that are too crisp will stand out stiffly and not hang very nicely. Try gathering your fabric in your hand to see what it will do as a gathered ruffle, and drape the fabric over your hand to see if it will have enough drape for circular ruffles. When in doubt, make a test ruffle out of scrap fabric to see how it will behave.

Tips + Notes

Cut the fabric for ruffles double, with the fold on the hemline, for extra body and to avoid hemming.

For gathered ruffles, soft and lightweight fabrics look better with more fullness. Thicker fabrics are best with less fullness, as they will get bulky and heavy when you gather them.

Pleat (page 141) gathered ruffles instead of sewing gathering stitches. Fold the top edge into even pleats and sew the ruffle in place.

To finish the edges of your ruffle and add more structure, add a facing. Cut two of each ruffle piece, sew right sides together along the hem, and turn it right side out. Your ruffle is hemmed and will have more body. You could even cut the facing layer in a contrast color for interest. This works for both circular and gathered ruffles.

HOW TO DETERMINE THE LENGTH OF A GATHERED RUFFLE

For a gathered ruffle, cut a strip on the crosswise or lengthwise grain (page 90), making the strip two to three times the length of the edge you are sewing it to. The length of the ruffle is up to you; make it however long you want. Add seam allowances (page 170) and hem allowances.

Ruffle twice the length of the edge

Ruffle three times the length of the edge

Ruffle four times the length of the edge

HOW TO MAKE GATHERED RUFFLES

1 Hem the lower edge of the ruffle. A narrow hem (page 123) is a nice way to finish the edges of a ruffle, as it doesn't add bulk and looks nice from both sides. Or finish the edge of the ruffle with binding (page 172). This adds a bit more weight to the ruffle but defines the edge nicely. In this example, I turned the edge twice and topstitched (page 218) the hem. Gather (page 86) the upper edge of the ruffle.

2 Divide the ruffle and garment into quarters so the fullness is evenly distributed, and pin the ruffle to the edge of the garment. Pull up the gathering threads. You want to smooth out the gathers so the whole ruffle is gathered evenly with no flat sections or densely gathered sections. If there are seams to be sewn after the ruffle is attached, try to keep the gathers out of the seam allowance so there is at least a 5/8" (1.5cm) flat section in the seam line. Sew the ruffle to the garment edge, finish the seam allowances together and press toward the garment.

CENTERED RUFFLE

For another ruffle idea, hem both sides of the ruffle, and gather with one row of gathering stitches down the middle. Pin the ruffle to the garment and sew along the middle of the ruffle. This is a good way to add ruffles when the garment edges are already finished or when you want to add ruffles where there are no seams or edges.

HOW TO MAKE CIRCULAR RUFFLES

To make circular ruffles, draw a circle with a circumference that is equal to the edge you want to add the ruffle to. This is going to be the inner edge of your ruffle. The smaller the inner circle, the more flared your ruffle will be. Draw a second circle around the first one, making the distance between the two circles equal to the length you want the ruffle to be. This second circle is going to be the lower edge of your ruffle. Add seam and hem allowances (page 96).

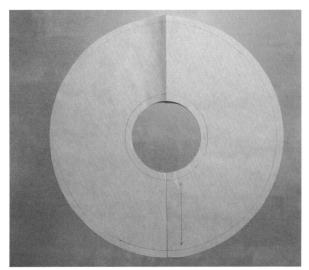

1 Draw a straight line from the outer circle to the middle of the inner circle; this is the line to cut along when cutting out the inner circle. Place this straight line on the straight grain (page 90).

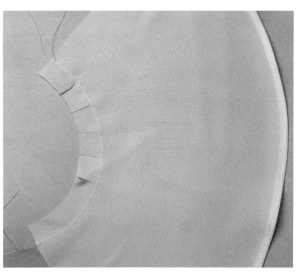

2 Cut out the circular ruffle piece. Staystitch (page 202) the inner circle after cutting, and clip (page 221) the seam allowance so the staystitching can stretch out into a straight line. Hem the outer edge of the ruffle using a narrow hem (page 123) or binding (page 172).

3 Sew the upper edge of the ruffle to the opening.

Tips + Notes

To make longer circular ruffles, cut several circles and piece them together before sewing to the garment.

Seam Allowance

WHAT IS IT?

Seam allowance is the margin of fabric added to pattern seam lines so that the pieces can be sewn together and pressed open. Turn a finished garment inside out to see all of the seam allowances.

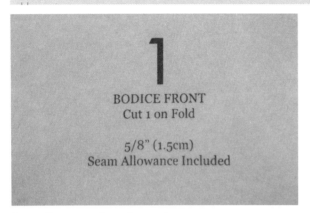

1

BODICE FRONT
Cut 1 on Fold

5/8" (1.5cm)
Seam Allowance Included

Seam allowance indicated on modern pattern

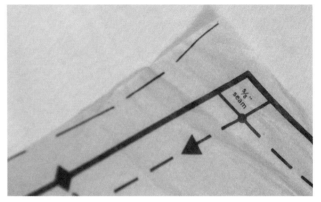

Seam allowance on vintage pattern

▶ WHEN DO YOU USE IT?

For every seam you sew, you must include a seam allowance. (The exception is abutted seams, page 8.) On most sewing patterns, the standard seam allowance is ⁵/₈" (1.5cm.) Seam allowances are marked on the pattern pieces or listed in the instruction sheet. Make sure you know what the seam allowance is before you start sewing.

Some patterns are sold without any seam allowance added, so you will have to add it as you cut out the pieces. This is convenient if you want to change the seam allowance, but it's an additional step to do before you can start sewing.

WHEN TO USE WIDE SEAM ALLOWANCES

If you have wider seam allowances on your fabric pieces, there is room to let out the seams. When making a muslin (page 118), you might want to cut the muslin pieces with extra-wide seam allowances for fitting. Leaving wider seam allowances on your finished garments gives you the chance to let out the seams later on, if needed. However, they may show through the garment and add bulk. You might want to keep the seam allowances wider than normal in certain areas of a garment, for example, at center back.

WHEN TO USE NARROW SEAM ALLOWANCES

Often sewing patterns for knit fabrics will have ¼" (6mm) seam allowances for sewing with a serger. If you are very short on fabric and know you won't have to make fitting changes, you could reduce the seam allowances on your fabric pieces. Also, on very tight curves, the seam allowance can be reduced to make it easier to sew. Sometimes strap or loop pieces will have narrow seam allowances since a wider seam allowance would have to be trimmed off. Narrow seam allowances don't allow any room for alterations later on.

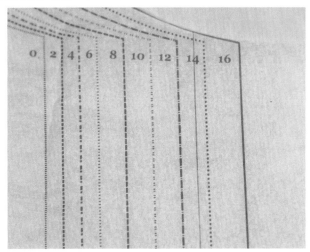

1 Figure out where your seam lines are. If your pattern has ⅝" (1.5cm) seam allowances, the seam line is located ⅝" (1.5cm) in from the cutting line. Draw in the seam lines on the pattern piece.

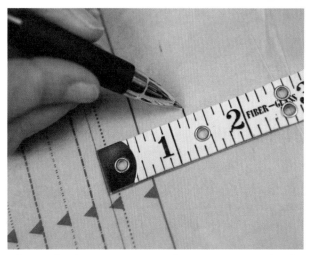

2 Decide what your new seam allowance is going to be. If you are adding to the seam allowance, tape a piece of scrap paper along the seam line for the extension. Or, if you haven't cut the pattern piece out completely, leave extra tissue paper where you plan to add. Add this amount to the seam line, measuring it off from the seam line at the beginning, end and several points in between.

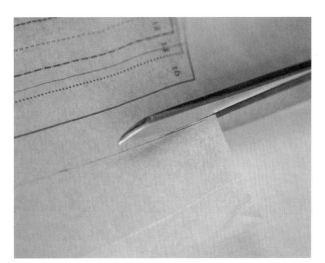

3 Draw in your new cutting line. When you sew this seam, remember to take the new amount of seam allowance instead of the original amount! Make a note of this in the pattern sewing instructions so you don't forget. Remember to adjust the seam allowances on both sides of the seam.

S Seam Finish, Bound

WHAT IS IT?

A bound seam finish has seam allowances that are enclosed with fabric strips, seam binding or bias tape. The seam allowances can be pressed open with each side bound separately or pressed to one side with both seam allowances bound together.

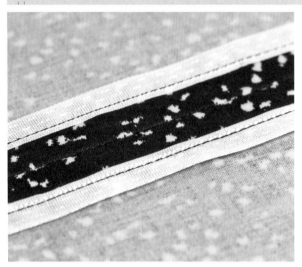

Bound finish with seam binding

Bound finish with bias tape

▶ WHEN DO YOU USE IT?

A bound seam finish is a great way to finish seams on unlined garments, when the inside may be visible. It's best for seams in which the binding won't be too bulky or show through to the right side.

Tips + Notes

If you can't find a perfect match for the seam binding or bias tape, go for a contrasting color instead!

If you do choose a contrast color, make sure it isn't unattractively visible from the right side of the garment.

Bias tape made from striped or plaid fabric will make very pretty binding with diagonal stripes.

A Hong Kong finish (page 175) is another type of bound finish that works well on unlined garments.

1 Sew the seam with a regular ⅝" (1.5cm) seam allowance. Press the seam allowances open.

2 Press the creases out of the seam binding. For each seam that crosses another seam at the top and bottom, you'll need two pieces of seam binding cut to the length of the seam. For each end that will not be covered by another seam, add ½" (1.3cm) to the length of the seam binding, so you can wrap the binding over the cut edge. Fold the seam binding in half lengthwise and press. Wrap the seam binding around the raw edge and push the fabric into the fold as far as it will go. Pin in place in the direction you plan to sew.

3 Arrange your piece so the garment layers are all to the left and only the seam allowance layer is underneath the presser foot. Edgestitch (page 69) the binding and seam allowance. It's better to be a little farther away from the edge and to catch both sides of the binding than to be superclose to the edge. As long as you've folded the binding down the middle, it should catch on both sides.

4 Repeat with the other side. Press the seam allowances. This is an attractive and sturdy edge finish. If you ever need to alter this seam, this edge finish will hold up and stay strong.

HOW TO SEW A BOUND SEAM FINISH WITH BIAS TAPE

1 Sew the seam with a regular ⅝" (1.5cm) seam allowance. Press the seam open.

2 For each seam, you'll need a piece of double-fold bias tape that's twice the length of the seam. If your bias tape is fresh from the package, press it to remove creases. If you are using single-fold bias tape, press it in half lengthwise. (To make your own bias tape, see page 25). Unfold one edge of the bias tape, and press. Line up the raw edge of the bias tape with the seam allowance, right sides together. Providing a ¼" (6mm) seam allowance, sew in the groove of the unpressed fold.

3 Press the bias tape away from the seam allowance. Wrap the bias tape around the seam allowance, and line up the fold with the stitch line. Pin in place. If your fabric is very thick, you may want to hand baste (page 18) instead of pinning.

4 Take your work to the sewing machine. Arrange your piece so the garment layers are all to the left and only the seam allowance layer is underneath the presser foot. Edgestitch (page 69) close to the edge of the bias tape.

5 Repeat with the other side. Press the seam allowances.

Seam Finish, Hong Kong

WHAT IS IT?

A Hong Kong finish is a type of seam finish that uses strips of fabric to enclose the seam allowances. It's similar to the bound seam finish (page 172) but is constructed in a different manner.

Hong Kong finish with solid tape

Hong Kong finish with bias tape

▶ WHEN DO YOU USE IT?

A Hong Kong finish is perfect for unlined garments, such as coats and jackets, in medium to heavyweight fabrics. It's also great for unlined summer garments. Use a Hong Kong finish on seams that will be pressed open.

Tips + Notes

You may find it easiest to work on both sides of the seam allowance at the same time. For example, you might sew the binding to both sides before proceeding to pressing.

HOW TO SEW A HONG KONG SEAM FINISH

Cut two strips of 1"-wide (2.5cm) bias tape (page 25) the length of your seam. You can use store-bought bias tape, if you like, or make your own. If the tape is already folded, unfold it and press it flat.

1 Sew the seam with a regular ⅝" (1.5cm) seam allowance. Press the seam open. Now pin one strip of bias tape to one seam allowance, right sides together. Sew with a ¼" (6mm) seam allowance.

2 Press the bias tape flat by pressing the seam toward the bias tape.

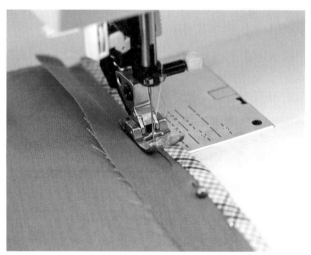

3 Arrange your piece so the garment layers are all to the left and only the seam allowance layer is on your work surface. Fold the bias tape over the seam allowance and to the inside. Press to set the fold.

4 Stitch in the ditch (see page 206) between the bias binding and the seam allowance only, not through the garment layer.
   Trim any extra bias tape from the underside of the seam. Repeat for the other side of the seam allowance.

S Seam Finish, Pinked

WHAT IS IT?

A pinked (page 131) seam finish is a quick and simple edge finish made using pinking shears. Pinking shears are special scissors that cut with a zigzag pattern. Use the shears to cut along the edge to be finished and the edge is finished!

Pinked edge

Stitched-and-pinked edge

▶ WHEN DO YOU USE IT?

This is a good seam finish for lightweight woven fabrics that won't fray. You'll often see this seam finish recommended in vintage sewing patterns, but it's not used as frequently in modern sewing patterns. It's great on tightly woven fabrics like cotton, when you want a quick and simple edge finish.

Tips + Notes

Before pinking the seam allowances on your project, cut on a piece of scrap fabric to make sure the pinking won't fray excessively. If it does, choose a different seam finish.

If you are having trouble pinking your edges, cut with strong, quick motions. Practice on scrap fabric to get comfortable with the pinking shears.

HOW TO DO A PINKED SEAM FINISH

1 Sew the seam with a standard ⅝" (1.5cm) seam allowance, and press the seam allowances open.

2 With the pinking shears, trim the edges of the seam allowances. With each cut, line up the blades with the zigzag pattern so the pattern isn't interrupted.

HOW TO DO A STITCHED-AND-PINKED SEAM FINISH

For extra stability, use a stitched-and-pinked seam finish in place of a pinked seam finish. This is also good for lightweight woven fabrics, but in the event that the fabric frays, the line of stitching will stop the fraying from traveling into the seam.

1 Just like the pinked seam finish, sew the seam with a standard ⅝" (1.5cm) seam allowance, and press the seam allowances open.

2 Arrange your piece so the garment layers are all to the left and only the seam allowance layer is underneath the presser foot. With a regular machine stitch, sew down the middle of each seam allowance, about ¼" (6mm) from the seam line.

3 Trim the seam allowances with the pinking shears. Stay close to the line of machine stitching.

Seam Finish, Serged or Overlocked

WHAT IS IT?

A serged or overlocked seam finish is an all-in-one seam finish that cuts, sews and finishes the edge. This seam finish requires a separate machine called a serger or overlocker. These machines use three or four spools of thread. One or two of these spools are threaded through needles sewing straight rows of stitching, and two loop over the cut edge to finish it off. As the serger sews, it cuts off the edge of the fabric, and threads interlock around the cut edge to stop it from unraveling.

Serged seam finish pressed open

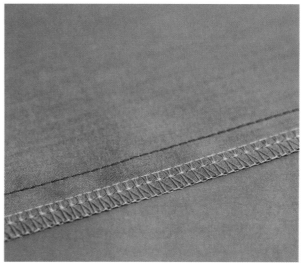

Serged seam finish pressed to one side

WHEN DO YOU USE IT?

This is the type of seam finish you'll see most often on ready-to-wear clothing, so it will give your sewing projects a store-bought appearance. People who own a serger likely use a serged seam finish on the majority of their projects. For knit fabrics, serging can be used to sew and finish seams in one step. Serging is very fast. You'll need to have a serger if you want to use this seam finish, as well as three or four spools of matching thread for your project.

Tips + Notes

Do not use pins near a serger! You'll damage the blade and risk broken bits of pin flying at your face.

Serging is fairly permanent, as it entails the trimming off of fabric. You can unpick serging if you must, but it is slow to do. If you do remove the serging, remember that the seam allowances are now much narrower than before.

Your regular sewing machine may have a stitch setting that imitates the look of serging called an overlock stitch or overcast stitch. It doesn't trim the edge like a serger would, but this does work as an edge finish!

HOW TO SEW A SERGED SEAM FINISH WITH THE SEAM PRESSED OPEN

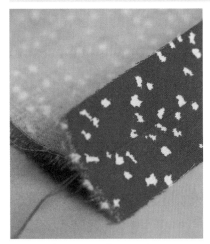  

1 Sew the seam with a regular ⅝" (1.5cm) seam allowance. Press the seam open.

   With the right side of the seam allowance up, separate one seam allowance from the rest of the garment so you are ready to sew through it as a single layer.

2 Serge this side of the seam allowance. Allow the serger to trim off a tiny amount of the seam allowance, about ⅛" (3mm).

3 Repeat with the other side of the seam allowance. Press the seam open again to flatten the serging. Trim the serged thread tails.

HOW TO SEW A SERGED SEAM FINISH WITH THE SEAM PRESSED TO ONE SIDE

 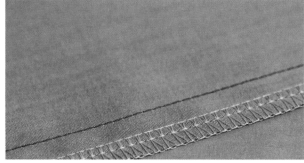

1 Sew the seam with a regular ⅝" (1.5cm) seam allowance. Do not press open.

2 Serge the seam allowances together. Allow the serger to trim off a tiny amount of the seam allowance, about ⅛" (3mm.) Press the seam to one side, and trim the serged thread tails.

Seam Finish, Turned and Stitched

WHAT IS IT?

A turned-and-stitched seam finish is a way to finish seams or edges by turning under the raw edges and edgestitching (page 69) them for a clean, flat finish. It may also be called an edgestitched seam finish.

Turned-and-stitched finish

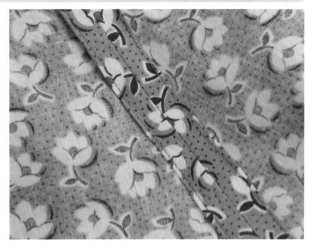

Turned-and-stitched finish

➤ WHEN DO YOU USE IT?

This seam finish is great for stable lightweight fabrics like cotton or linen. If your fabric presses well and holds a crease, this is a good solution for finishing the edges.

HOW TO DO A TURNED-AND-STITCHED SEAM FINISH

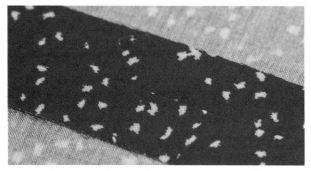 

1 Sew the seam with a regular ⅝" (1.5cm) seam allowance, backstitching (page 14) at the start and end. Press the seam open.

2 Tuck under the raw edge about ¼" (6mm) along one side of the seam allowance, and press in place.

3 Repeat with the other side of the seam allowance.

4 Take your work to the sewing machine. Arrange your piece so the garment layers are all to the left and only the seam allowance layer is underneath the presser foot. You'll be sewing a mini-hem on each side of the seam allowance in this step. Sew close to the folded edge, all the way from top to bottom, and backstitch at both ends.

5 Sew the other side. Backstitch at both ends again. Press the seam flat one last time to set the stitches.

Seam Finish, Zigzagged

WHAT IS IT?

A zigzag seam finish is a seam finish done with a row of zigzag stitching sewn on a regular sewing machine. The seam is pressed open or pressed to one side with zigzag stitching sewn along the seam allowances to keep them from fraying.

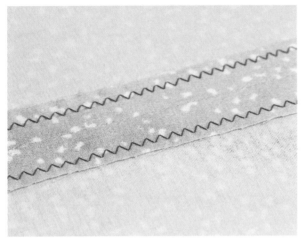

Zigzagged seam finish

Tips + Notes

Test your zigzag stitching on a scrap piece of fabric to see what it will look like on your project.

Make sure the zigzag doesn't pucker. If it does, loosen the tension or change the stitch length.

You many choose to zigzzg seam allowances before sewing the seam, especially on curved seams.

▶ WHEN DO YOU USE IT?

A zigzag finish is suitable for light- to medium-weight fabrics. Most people who don't own a serger (see Seam Finishes, Serged or Overlocked on page 179) will use a zigzag finish instead.

HOW TO SEW A ZIGZAGGED SEAM FINISH

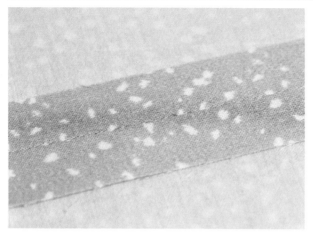

1 Sew the seam with a regular ⅝" (1.5cm) seam allowance. Press the seam open.

2 With the right side of the seam allowance up, separate one seam allowance from the rest of the garment so you are ready to sew through it as a single layer. Sew a zigzag stitch along this side of the seam allowance by lining up the edge of the presser foot with the edge of the seam allowance.

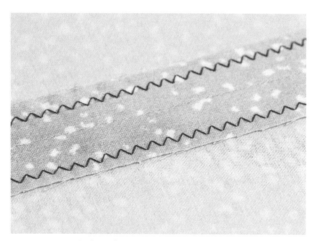

3 Repeat with the other side of the seam allowance. Press the seam again to flatten the stitching.

Seam Roll

WHAT IS IT?

A seam roll is a stuffed tool with a long narrow shape and rounded ends used for pressing (page 155). The most useful seam rolls are made with wool cloth on one side and cotton on the other. Seam rolls are stuffed with sawdust or commercial stuffing to keep their shape. Pair with a tailor's ham (see page 212) to cover most of your pressing needs. You can buy seam rolls, or you can make your own.

Seam roll

 ## WHEN DO YOU USE IT?

A seam roll is excellent for pressing hard-to-reach long seams on narrow areas, such as sleeves. You can also press seams with a seam roll when you want to avoid making an impression of the seam allowances on the right side of the garment.

Do you need a seam roll right away when you're learning to sew? You can get away without a seam roll until you run into one of the circumstances noted above.

HOW TO PRESS WITH A SEAM ROLL

Arrange your seam over the seam roll, with the seam line centered down the middle of the roll. Press. Slide the seam roll inside the tube, down the seam line. Continue pressing until you've pressed the entire length of the seam. Use the cotton side for high heat and the wool side for low heat.

Tips + Notes

Save extra stuffing to restuff the seam roll, in case it becomes deflated over time.

Make a hanging loop by sewing ribbon in the seam allowance at one end before you stuff it.

Stuff with cedar shavings found at pet supply shops instead of sawdust. You can also stuff it with wool fabric scraps or old nylon stockings.

Instead of making a seam roll, you can roll a narrow hand towel tightly and use it as a pressing tool.

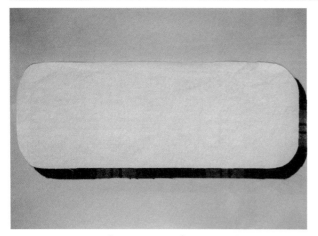

1 Cut out a rectangle approximately 14" × 5" (35.6cm × 12.7cm) from both wool and prewashed cotton fabric (such as muslin). Layer the two fabrics and round off the corners.

2 Sew around the edges with a ½" (1.3cm) seam allowance. Leave a 5" (12.7cm) opening for stuffing on one of the long sides.

3 Turn the seam roll right side out. Stuff the seam roll tightly with sawdust. It needs to be quite hard to hold its shape.

4 Turn under the seam allowance on one side of the opening, lap over the other edge and sew the opening shut.

Selvedge or Selvage

WHAT IS IT?

Selvedge, or selvage, refers to the edges of fabric that run along the lengthwise grain. Both spellings are correct. Selv-*edge* makes it easy to remember that the word refers to the *edge* of the fabric. On woven fabric, the selvedge is tightly woven and does not stretch. You may see tiny, evenly spaced holes running along the selvedge; this is from the machinery that stretches and finishes the fabric.

Selvedges of different fabrics

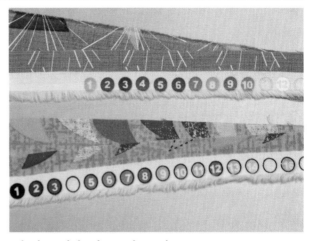

Selvedge with dots for matching colors

WHEN DO YOU USE IT?

When you are pinning your pattern pieces to the fabric, you can use the selvedge to line up the grain line (page 90). Fold the fabric in half, selvedge to selvedge. Pin one end of the grain line to the fabric, measure from the grain line to the selvedge and then pivot the pattern piece until the other end of the grain line measures the same to the selvedge.

Cut off selvedges and use them as stay tape (page 204). Because the selvedge is stable and does not stretch, it is excellent for reinforcing straight seams. It won't bend around curves well, so use it for straight edges like shoulder seams, pocket openings and waistlines. Selvedges of lining fabric are especially useful as they are lightweight and won't add bulk.

Tips + Notes

The selvedge is more tightly woven than the rest of the fabric, so do not cut any of your garment pieces with the selvedge included. Make sure the pattern piece is located off of the selvedge area.

Some fabrics will have information printed on the selvedge, such as the fabric's designer or the year it was produced. This information is useful if you want to locate more of the same fabric.

Little colored dots may be printed on the selvedge, one for each of the colors in the fabric print. Use these colored dots to choose matching or contrast fabrics or lining colors.

S Set-In Sleeves

WHAT IS IT?

A set-in sleeve is a type of sleeve that is set into the armhole, rather than being cut as part of the bodice. The bodice is sewn so the armhole is a round opening, the sleeve is sewn as a tube and then the sleeve is set into the armhole. (That's where the term set-in sleeves comes from, they are set in.) Set-in sleeves can be one-piece sleeves or two-piece sleeves. The sleeve pattern piece has a rounded curve at the top (called the sleeve cap) and narrows at the bottom. With set-in sleeves, the sleeve cap is shaped differently at the front of the armhole and the back of the armhole, so the left and right sleeves are not interchangeable.

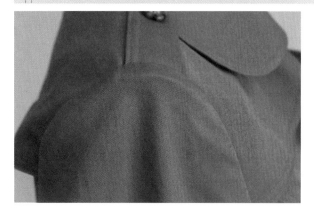

Set-in sleeve on Robson Coat

Set-in sleeve

▶ WHEN DO YOU USE IT?

Set-in sleeves are the best type of sleeve design for a close fit. Two-piece sleeves generally fit better than one-piece sleeves, as the sleeve seam curves along the natural shape of the arm. If you are making a tailored jacket or coat, look for a pattern with two-piece sleeves. One-piece sleeves work best for blouses and loose-fitting sleeves.

Tips + Notes

Use as many pins as you need when pinning the sleeve into the armhole. More pins will make it slower to sew, but you'll be certain that the sleeve is in the right position.

If you have time, I recommend basting (page 18) the sleeves into the armholes by hand. You'll have greater control over easing in the fullness, and when you sew the sleeve in permanently, you won't have to stop and remove the pins.

Sew the armhole seam with the sleeve side up, so you can check the gathers and make sure there are no puckers as you sew.

HOW TO SET IN A SLEEVE

Construct the bodice so the armhole is ready for the sleeve. Sew the sleeve seam and press open. I like to hem my sleeves or attach cuffs (page 60) before setting them in. But if you are not sure of the sleeve length, hem them after they are attached.

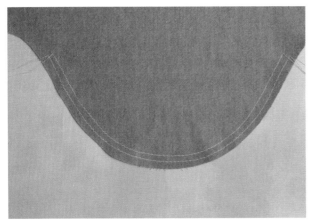

1 Easestitch (page 67) between the notches of the sleeve cap. Make two rows of easestitching, one just inside the seamline at ½" (1.3cm) and the other about ¼" (6mm) from the first row. For the demonstration, I left the sleeve seam open so it's easy to see where the easestitching is sewn.

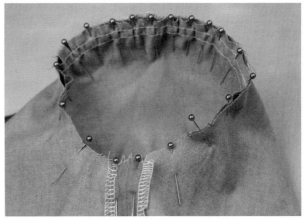

2 With the right sides together, insert the sleeve into the armhole and match the notches. Have the sleeve turned right side out and the body inside out, with the side seam facing you. Match the underarm seams, match the shoulder seam to the sleeve notch, then work on distributing the fullness in between. Pull up the easestitching to remove the fullness between the notches. You can pull the inner row of stitching tighter than the outer row, to pull in the extra fullness.

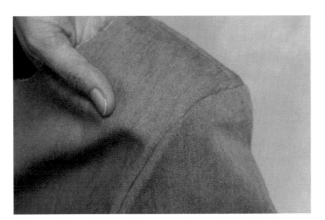

3 Baste (page 18) the sleeve into the armhole, either by hand or by machine, and adjust as needed to remove any tucks in the sleeve fabric. Turn the sleeve right side out, and check for puckers along the sleeve cap. If there are puckers, remove the basting about 1" (2.5cm) on either side of the pucker and restitch that section of the seam.

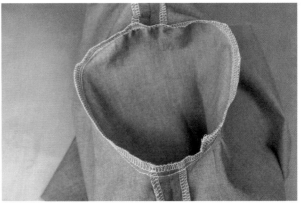

4 Sew the sleeve into the armhole permanently. For unlined garments, finish the seam allowance and press toward the sleeve. If the garment will be lined, sew a second row of stitching ¼" (6mm) away from the first, inside the seam allowance. Trim the extra seam allowance outside the second row of stitching, and press lightly toward the sleeve. If any of the basting stitches are visible from the right side, carefully remove them with a seam ripper.

S Shoulder Pad

WHAT IS IT?

Padding added to shoulders supports the garment, rounds out the sleeves and adds dimension to the shoulder area. You can buy purchased shoulder pads or make your own. Shoulder pads are sold in pairs and made of foam, felt or muslin with cotton, wool or synthetic padding, or a combination of these materials. These ready-made pads are shaped differently for set-in sleeves and raglan sleeves and will be thinner for lightweight dresses and blouses than for suits and coats.

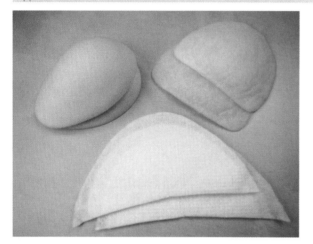

Assorted shoulder pads

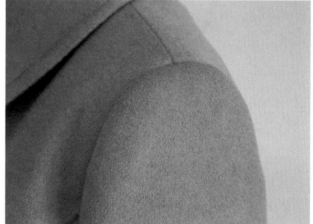

Shoulder pad in wool coat

▶ WHEN DO YOU USE IT?

Shoulder pads are used in tailored jackets and coats to define the shoulder area and support the sleeve. Usually shoulder pads are sewn in when the garments are lined, so the padding isn't visible from the inside. If you're sewing shoulder pads into an unlined garment, cover the pads with lining or garment fabric first for a cleaner finish. Shoulder pads can be used in blouses or dresses, as well, to add structure to the shoulders. If the pattern calls for shoulder pads, the pattern is drafted to include allowance for the shoulder pad. You can omit the shoulder pads, but you'll have to adjust the pattern before cutting your fabric.

Tips + Notes

Shoulder pads don't have to create an extreme silhouette like they did in the 1980s. Padding is important to create a tailored, structured look even when strong shoulders aren't in fashion.

Adding structure to the shoulders helps to balance out wide hips. Even a small pad will help define the shoulders and draw attention to the upper body.

Cover shoulder pads with fabric before sewing pads into unlined garments. Cut a circle of lining that's ½" (1.3cm) larger than the pad, fold it over the pad and finish around the edges.

Sew shoulder pads into unlined garments by tacking the pads to the top of the sleeve seam and the shoulder seam allowance and by tacking the edges of the pad to the armhole seam.

HOW TO SEW A SHOULDER PAD INTO A LINED GARMENT

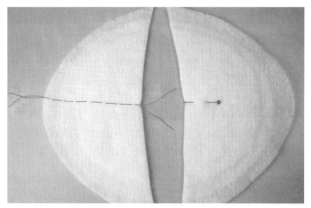

1 Construct the garment so the shoulder seam is sewn, the underarm seam is sewn and the sleeve is set into the armhole. Take the shoulder pad, fold it in half and mark the halfway point. You may find it helpful to mark the centerline all the way across the shoulder pad. Some pads may include a mark or notch indicating the shoulder seam placement.

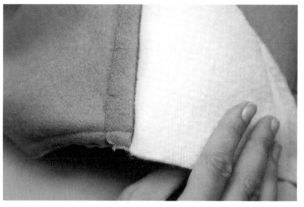

2 Place the shoulder pad inside the garment by matching the halfway point on the shoulder pad to the shoulder seam.

3 Extend the edge of the shoulder pad into the sleeve until the edge lines up with the armhole seam allowance. Pin the pad in place through all layers.

4 Try on the garment. You may want to rotate the pad toward the back of the garment slightly, depending on your body. Adjust the pad, and try it on again until the pad is in the right place. Once you're happy with the position, it's time to sew the pad in place. Thread a handsewing needle, and turn the garment inside out so the pad is on top.

Starting at one side of the pad, sew through the shoulder pad and the armhole seam allowance using a backstitch (page 14). When you get to the end, tie a knot.

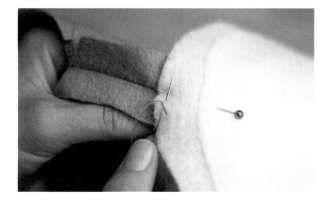

5 Tack the shoulder pad to the shoulder seam allowance.

Sleeve Head

WHAT IS IT?

A sleeve head is a strip of padding sewn into the cap of a set-in jacket or coat sleeve to support the sleeve cap and round it out. The sleeve head is sewn along the top of the armhole seam. It extends into the sleeve and fills out the rounded top of the sleeve cap. Sleeve heads can be bought ready-made, or you can make your own from cotton batting, thick flannel, lambswool or even polar fleece in a pinch. Sleeve heads are used along with shoulder pads to build structure into the garment.

Purchased sleeve heads

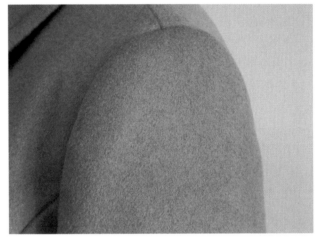

Sleeve head in wool coat

▶ WHEN DO YOU USE IT?

Sleeve heads are used in tailored, lined jackets with set-in sleeves (page 188). They're used in pairs with shoulder pads to add structure to a coat or jacket. When making tailored jackets, if you use a shoulder pad, you may want to use a sleeve head as well. It helps to hide the seam allowances at the top of the armhole and creates a smoother, rounder looking sleeve cap. The more structure you build into your coats and jackets, the better they will hold their shape over time. Are they necessary? Personally I'm in favor of anything that will improve the look of my projects and help them to keep their shape.

Tips + Notes

Not sure if your project needs sleeve heads? If it has shoulder pads and set-in sleeves, chances are it will look even better with the sleeve cap rounded out.

Make your own sleeve heads by cutting a 2"-wide (5cm) bias strip of lambswool or flannel. Cut two strips, each 9" (22.8cm) long, one for each sleeve.

Polar fleece can work as a sleeve head if you don't have any premade sleeve heads or lambswool on hand. Cut a strip as indicated and backstitch it in place. It's a nontraditional option, but the thickness and softness of polar fleece will do the trick.

HOW TO SEW IN SLEEVE HEADS

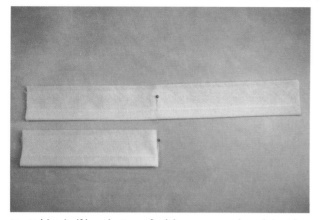

1 Fold in half lengthwise to find the center, and mark it with a pin.

2 Place the sleeve head in the sleeve cap. Line up the center marking with the shoulder seam, and line up one edge of the sleeve head with the armhole sleeve allowance. Pin the sleeve head into the armhole.

3 Starting at one end, sew the sleeve head in place through the sleeve seam allowance with a backstitch (page 14). Make the backstitches about ⅜" (1cm) long.

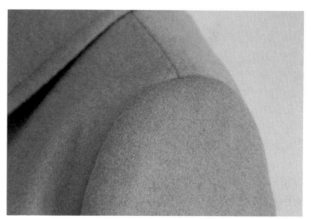

4 Here's what the sleeve cap will look like with a sleeve head inserted: rounded and smooth.

193

Slipstitch

WHAT IS IT?

A slipstitch is a nearly invisible hand stitch, often used when there's a folded edge to sew invisibly in place. You'll see this stitch used for hemming as well.

Slipstitched waistband

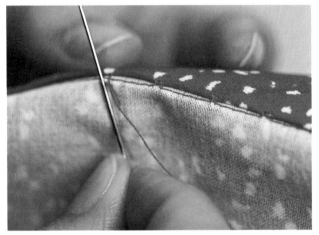

Slipstitches

▶ WHEN DO YOU USE IT?

Slipstitch to secure folded edges of waistbands and cuffs and when finishing a hem (page 96) or when closing openings left in belts or other enclosed parts for turning. Slipstitch to attach bias tape trim or bias binding (page 25) around necklines and armholes. Anytime you need to handsew a folded edge invisibly, a slipstitch is a good choice.

Tips + Notes

Instead of pinning before you slipstitch, hand baste (page 18) for greater control. Keep the basting away from the folded edge so you can slipstitch easily.

You can stitch away from yourself or toward yourself. Sewing toward yourself makes it easier to see your work as you sew.

For extra strength, use beeswax on the thread. Thread your needle and run it through a cake of beeswax, then wrap your thread in scrap fabric or paper and press (page 155) to seal in the wax.

1 Pin your folded edge in place. Thread the needle with matching thread so the stitches will be nearly invisible. Tie a knot at the end of the thread.

2 Poke the needle through the folded edge, about ¼" (6mm) from the end. This will help bury the start of your thread and hide the knotted end.

3 Catch a thread or two of the fabric on the right side, about ¼" (6mm) in from the end. It should line up more or less with where your needle comes out of the folded edge.

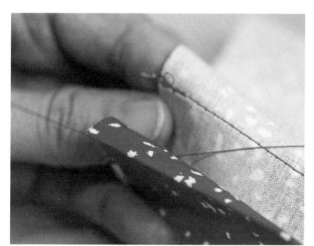

4 Bring your needle back into the folded edge, very close to where it came out of the fold the first time. Poke the needle into the fold so it comes out about ¼" (6mm) away.

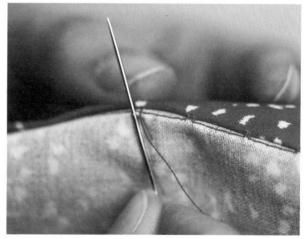

5 Pull the thread to bring the edges closer together. Don't pull too tightly or your work will pucker. Repeat these steps over and over again, and keep the stitches spaced evenly as you go. Pick up only a few threads of the main fabric, but feel free to take big bites out of the folded edge.

Snaps

WHAT IS IT?

Snaps are a type of closure used to secure garment openings. There are two parts to a snap: one with the ball and one with the socket. Snaps can be made of metal (coated or uncoated) or plastic, and they come in a variety of sizes from small to quite large. The larger the snap, the stronger the closure, but also the heavier it will be. Metal snaps are stronger than plastic ones.

Sew-on snaps are sewn to the garment by hand. Press-on or no-sew snaps have four parts; each side of the snap has a second piece with spikes that pierces through the fabric and clamps into the other half of the snap to permanently secure it.

If you don't like the metal or coated metal color, cover snaps with fabric to blend in with your garment fabric. You can also buy snap tape by the yard; this tape has snaps pre-attached evenly down the length of the tape.

Assorted snaps

Covered snaps

▶ WHEN DO YOU USE IT?

Use snaps when you want to secure an opening without buttons or zippers. Snaps are sewn on after the garment is complete, so you are able to decide last minute. Snaps work well for center front openings, pocket flaps, cuffs and self-fabric belts. You can also use snaps as part of a faux-button closure. Sew buttons to the top of the garment, but hide snaps underneath for faster opening and closing. Snaps can also be used in plackets in place of a zipper. This feature is often used in vintage dresses, but if you're used to zippers, this may not seem very secure.

Snaps open and close quickly, making them ideal for sporty garments or children's clothing. The only disadvantage is that they may pop open spontaneously. If you are busty, you may want to avoid snaps at the center front of blouses or dresses.

HOW TO SEW ON SNAPS

When sewing snaps to a garment, the ball side goes on the underside of the overlap and the socket side goes on the top side of the underlap.

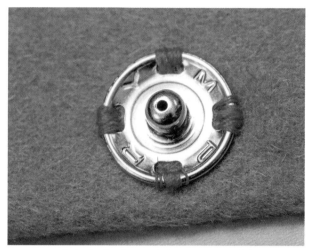

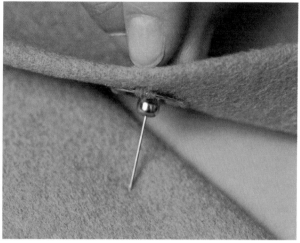

1 Start with the ball side. Mark the placement of the snap close to the edge of the garment. Sew through each of the snap holes. When you move from hole to hole, do not cut the thread. Instead carry it underneath the snap and up through the new hole. After sewing through the first snap hole, move to the hole directly across from it, so the snap is held in position and won't shift.

2 Use the ball of the snap to press into the other side and mark the placement. Try rubbing the tip of the ball with chalk and then pressing it to the other side to make a mark. Or, if your snap has a hole in the ball, insert a pin all the way through to mark the opposite snap placement.

3 Center the socket over the marking and sew through all of the holes, as you did for the ball side.

Tips + Notes

If you are sewing snaps through a waistband or facing, try not to catch the inner layer of the garment. It looks more professional if there are no stitches showing on the inside.

Press-on, or no-sew, snaps have sharp spikes that go through your fabric and clip into the ball or socket. Once these snaps are in, there's no moving them, so mark the position carefully!

For the top of a zipper opening, a hanging snap helps to close the top edge. You can use a hanging snap anytime the edges meet but do not overlap. To sew a hanging snap, sew the socket to the inside of the top edge. Make a thread chain (page 84) to attach the ball of the snap to the opposite side. Make the chain just long enough for the snap to reach the other side.

HOW TO COVER SNAPS

You can cover snaps with matching or coordinating fabric. If your fabric is thin, you can use self fabric to cover the snaps, but if not, choose a matching lining fabric instead. Cut two circles of fabric twice the diameter of the snaps plus a ¼" (6mm) seam allowance. If you are covering several snaps, make a circle template from cardboard for easier cutting.

1 Start with the ball side of the snap. Pierce a tiny hole in the middle of the circle or a slightly bigger hole if you are covering large snaps. The hole should be slightly smaller than the ball of the snap, so it fits snugly around the base of the ball. With the ball side up, cover the snap with the fabric circle and poke the ball of the snap through the hole.

2 Thread a handsewing needle with a single thread and gather (page 86) the outer edge of the fabric ¼" (6mm) away from the raw edge. End your gathering stitches with your needle and thread on the right side of the fabric. Pull the thread tight to fit the fabric snugly around the snap.

3 Wind the thread tightly around the gathered material a few times, then take a few stitches in the side of the bunched fabric and tie a knot. Trim the thread tails and extra fabric.

4 Place the socket part of the snap with the socket facing up and cover it with the second circle of fabric. Gather the outer edge of the fabric as you did for the ball part, and pull the gathering tight to fit the fabric around the snap. Secure the thread in the same manner, snap the ball and socket together, and sew the covered snaps to the garment.

Spaghetti Straps

WHAT IS IT?

Spaghetti, or shoestring, straps are narrow straps made of fabric. The straps are made by sewing a tube, then turning the fabric right side out. The seam allowances fill up the tube to make a slightly rounded strap. For flatter straps, trim the seam allowance before turning or sew the straps slightly wider.

Spaghetti straps on Saltspring Dress

Tied spaghetti straps

Double spaghetti straps

▶ WHEN DO YOU USE IT?

Lingerie, dresses, sundresses and camisoles are all common places to use spaghetti straps. If you want to add a little support to a strapless dress, spaghetti straps are easy to add and look delicate and dressy. They can be tricky to turn right side out. I recommend using a loop turner, an inexpensive tool, to help turn your straps easily.

Tips + Notes

Cut your strap pieces a little longer than necessary in case the ends get worn and frayed while turning.

As you start to sew the strap seam, hold on to the thread tails and gently pull them to keep the edge of your fabric from getting sucked into the machine.

When using a loop turner, it's important to keep tension on the strap as you turn it, otherwise the clasp will open up. You may be able to clip the clasp into the end, but if not, you'll have to start again. Don't let go of the turner; instead, pull it in one motion. Sometimes I loop the turner around my toe, so I can use both hands to get the strap going.

HOW TO SEW SPAGHETTI STRAPS

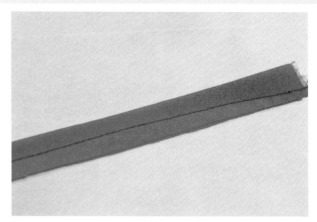

1 If the strap pieces are not included or if you want to change regular straps to spaghetti straps, cut the strap pieces 1" (2.5cm) wide by the length from the front to the back bodice plus 2"–4" (5.1cm –10.1cm) of extra length for adjustments. When in doubt, cut the straps longer than necessary, as you can always shorten them.

2 Fold the strap in half lengthwise, right sides together, and sew with ¼" (6mm) seam allowances. To make it easier to turn the loop, start by sewing a ⅛" (3mm) seam allowance at the edge of the strap and taper in toward the fold until you reach the ¼" (6mm) mark. For delicate fabrics, or to add extra strength, sew a second row of stitching on top of the seam.

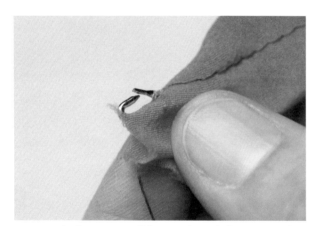

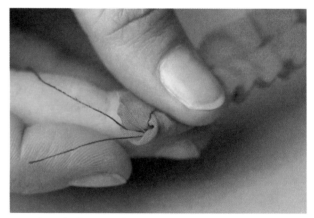

3 Insert the loop turner all the way through the strap, until the clasp is showing. Poke the hook of the loop turner through the edge of your strap fabric.

4 Close the lever, and with one hand on the strap and one hand on the circle-shaped end of the turner, pull the turner to turn the strap. It can be a little tricky to start turning the loop. Use your fingernails to slide the fabric toward the turning point and, at the same time, gently pull the turner.

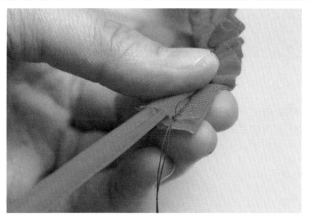

5 For long straps, you can remove the loop turner and turn the loop with your hands as soon as the turned edge appears through the turned loop. Hold the turned edge, and slide the fullness down toward the turning point. Work slowly and avoid letting it get too bunched up or it won't turn.

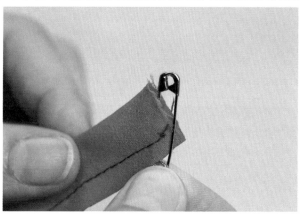

6 As an alternative, use a safety pin to turn the strap. Pin through one end of the strap, turn the safety pin into the strap and use your hands to work it through the tunnel.

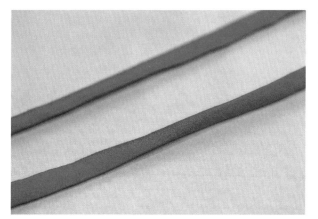

7 Press the strap. To keep the rounded look, steam it lightly without pressing on the surface. To flatten the straps, press flat with the iron.

Tips + Notes

If you're adding your own straps to a pattern, cut, sew and turn a small length of the strap to check that you're happy with the finished width. The straps end up quite a lot narrower than the pattern piece, which may be hard to visualize.

Sew multiple spaghetti straps to your dresses! Try two straps set farther apart that come together at the shoulder. Try braiding three straps together. Sew two separate straps to the front and back, and tie them in a bow over the shoulder. Sew several straps and cross them at the back for a pretty detail.

Staystitch

WHAT IS IT?

Staystitching is permanent machine stitching that is used to keep curved edges, such as armholes and necklines, from stretching out as you work with the pieces.

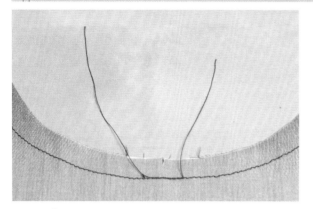

Staystitching

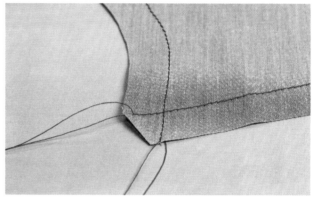

Staystitching

WHEN DO YOU USE IT?

You won't be able to see it on finished garments, but all curved edges should be staystitched so the fabric doesn't stretch out. This includes necklines, armholes and waistlines. Pattern instructions will usually tell you when to staystitch. It's generally one of the first things you do when the pieces are freshly cut. You may be instructed to staystitch after a section of the garment has been completed, such as on the skirt of a dress.

Tips + Notes

Make sure your staystitching doesn't stray outside the seam allowance or it will show when the seams are sewn.

Slow down around the curves if needed.

If it's hard to sew around curves evenly, draw a stitch line with chalk or marker and follow the guide as you stay stitch.

WHAT TO STAYSTITCH

* All curved edges

* Straight edges of fabric that frays easily

* Necklines, waistlines, armholes

* Princess seams

WHAT **NOT** TO STAYSTITCH

* Edges that will be eased (page 65) to fit another edge, for example, sleeve caps

* Edges that will be stretched to fit another edge

* Hems

* Outer edges of facings (page 74)

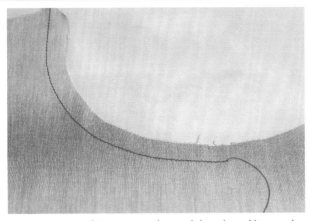

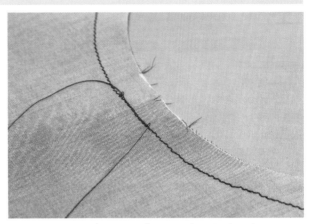

1 Set your machine to a regular stitch length and line up the fabric edge with the ½" (1.3mm) line.

Start stitching at the shoulder and work toward the center of the neckline. Stitch past the center front by several stitches.

2 Turn your work over, and start stitching at the other shoulder, working toward the center of the neckline. Overlap the previous stitching by two or three stitches and stop.

Follow the same staystitching method for waistlines, armholes and other curves, always working from the high point of the edge to the low point.

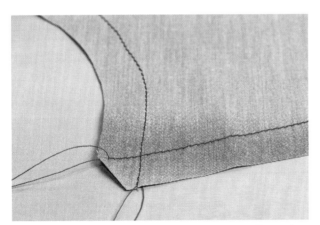

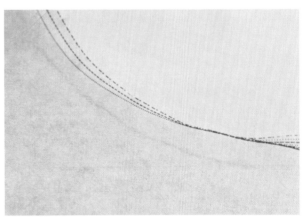

3 If you are staystitching around a corner, sew off the edge of the fabric and start again on the other edge, instead of pivoting around the corner.

4 Compare the fabric piece to the original pattern piece to see if you may have changed the edge after staystitching by either stretching it out or tightening it up. If the fabric has stretched, pull the staystitching threads until the fabric matches the pattern. If the fabric has pulled up, clip the threads at a few points to release the edge.

S Stay Tape

WHAT IS IT?

Stay tape is a thin, lightweight tape that is applied to edges and seams to stabilize and support them, so they don't stretch out and gape. Stay tape also prevents shoulder seams from stretching out. Adding quality details like stay tape helps the garment keep its shape and last longer. For stay tape, you can purchase a thin, sheer, flexible nylon tape labeled as Stay Tape, or you can use ribbon, seam binding or even bias tape (page 25), if you want a little bit of give.

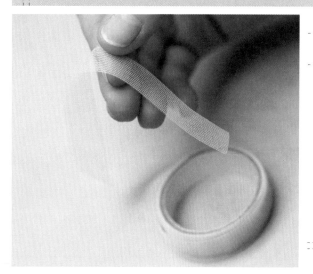

Roll of stay tape

Tips + Notes

Cut stay tape down the middle to double the amount. Stay tape won't fray, so this works well. Plus, I find it easier to work with the narrower tape, especially around curves.

Save your selvedges (page 187) from lining fabric and use them as stay tape on the same project or other projects. It's very thin and doesn't add bulk to the seams.

▶ WHEN DO YOU USE IT?

Stay tape is perfect when you want to stabilize a neckline, armhole, waistline or pocket opening. If your garment is going to be worn often, using stay tape will help it keep its shape. Using tape at the waistline of a dress will make it more rigid and structured; it will be less flexible in terms of fit, but it will not stretch out over time. If you have a neckline that gapes at the muslin stage (page 118), you can fit the neckline closer to the body by cutting the stay tape slightly smaller than the neckline to draw it in.

HOW TO APPLY STAY TAPE

Cut your stay tape the exact length of the seam or opening edge. If stay tape is specified in the pattern instructions, there may be a guide or a measurement to follow. If not, use the pattern piece as a guide. You can apply it to the seam two different ways: on top of the seam line or inside the seam allowance. I prefer to apply it just inside the seam line, in case the stay tape is not very flexible and doesn't allow the seam to be pressed completely flat.

1 With the wrong side of your garment facing you, pin the stay tape just inside the seam line. Line up the edge of the stay tape with the stitching line. Doing it this way makes it easy to trim along the edge of the stay tape. Pin in the direction you plan to sew, as this will make it easier to remove the pins as you go.

2 Sew on the stay tape. Stitch right down the middle of the tape. Backstitch (page 14) at both ends.

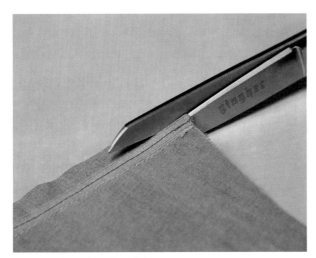

3 Trim along the edge of the stay tape.

Stitch in the Ditch

WHAT IS IT?

Stitching in the ditch refers to machine stitching that is sewn in the ditch of a seam so that it sinks into the seam and stays out of sight.

Seam stitched in the ditch on Crescent Skirt

Seam stitched in the ditch

▶ WHEN DO YOU USE IT?

You won't see it used very often in sewing patterns, which tend to favor hand stitching instead. It's very common in factory sewing. You can stitch in the ditch on waistbands, cuffs or anywhere where you would like to secure several layers together but don't want visible topstitching and prefer not to hand stitch. I like to stitch in the ditch on waistbands to secure the inside waistband without having to slipstitch. I also use it on the waistlines of lined dresses to close the lining and keep the layers from slipping or separating.

ALTERNATIVES TO STITCHING IN THE DITCH

As an alternative to stitching in the ditch, you can slipstitch by hand (page 194) for an invisible finish. If you prefer visible stitch lines, choose edgestitching (page 69), topstitching (page 218) or both!

Tips + Notes

Go slowly! It's better to slow down and sew more accurately than to have to rip out stitching in the ditch.

If you're using contrast topstitching on your project, stitching in the ditch is one place where you'll want to match the thread to the fabric. Darker is better, as it will hide in the shadow of the ditch.

Stitching in the ditch is less visible on thicker fabrics and fabrics with a texture. The thread will sink into these fabrics but will be visible on thinner, smoother fabrics.

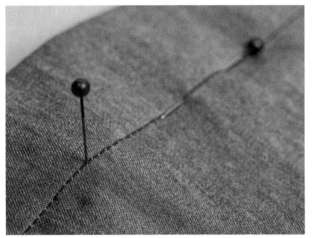

1 If you have the layers of your garment aligned properly, the actual sewing is very straightforward. Line up the seams—feel through both layers to make sure they're aligned. Place a pin through all layers in the ditch where the two pieces connect.

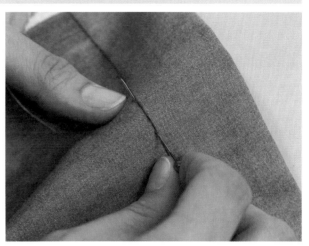

2 See where the pin is? That's the ditch you'll be sewing in. Pin all along the seam as you feel underneath to make sure the inner layer is lined up. You could also hand baste (page 18) for greater control, to keep the layers from slipping as you remove the pins.

3 The goal is to sew as close to the fold as possible, without jumping over the fold onto the other side of the ditch. Poke the needle into the ditch before lowering the presser foot, to be sure it's lined up correctly.

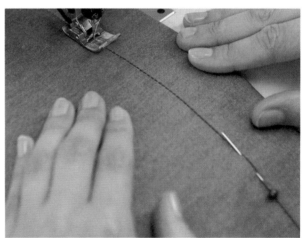

4 Stitch in the ditch. Stop when you reach the end. Gently pull apart the seam as you sew, so you can see the ditch clearly. Sew slowly. If your thread matches well, it's hard to see, but you should just barely be able to see the line of stitches in the ditch.

S Stripes

WHAT IS IT?

Striped fabric features vertical or horizontal lines. These lines can be printed on top of the fabric and merely sit upon the surface. You can tell a printed stripe fabric because the print will appear on the right side and be either faint or not visible at all on the wrong side. Stripes that are woven or knit into the fabric are visible on both sides. These are called "yarn-dyed" stripes. The yarn is dyed first and then the different colors of yarn are woven or knit into the striped pattern. Yarn-dyed stripes are generally a better quality than printed stripes. Pinstripes are very thin stripes that get their name because they are as narrow as a pin.

Striped fabric

Fabric that are treated like stripes

Stripes meeting at center seam

▶ WHEN DO YOU USE IT?

You'll see striped knit fabric for casual garments like T-shirts and activewear. Woven striped fabric can be used for day dresses, shirtdresses, skirts and sundresses, blouses and suiting. Menswear features a lot of striped garments: pinstripe suits, striped dress shirts, striped neckties and even striped pajamas and bathrobes. The stripes can be placed horizontally, vertically or diagonally. Striped fabric cut on the bias (page 23) will create a diagonal effect. Many garment designs will combine several directions of striping for visual impact. Sewing patterns will often include a note that says the pattern requires extra fabric for plaids (page 138) and stripes, or it might say that the design is not suitable for stripes.

HOW TO CUT STRIPED FABRIC

Just like border prints (page 36), plan out the stripe direction and placement before you start cutting.

When you place the pattern pieces, think about how the stripes will line up from piece to piece. This is called *stripe matching*. You'll also consider the *stripe direction* or the way the stripes will go on each piece. This is determined by the grain line (page 90) unless you change it.

Do you have to match stripes? Not if the stripe is fairly subtle and you're not concerned about having big bands of color ending up in strange places. Depending on the design of your pattern or the purpose of the garment, you may not be concerned about having the stripes match.

1 Fold your fabric according to the cutting layout. Before placing any of the pattern pieces, line up the stripes, from the top layer to the bottom layer. Place a pin through one stripe, and turn the fabric over to see if the pin passes through the same stripe on both layers. Yes? Good! If not, slide one layer of fabric and re-pin until they are properly lined up.

2 Pin every 6" (15.2cm) to keep the stripes lined up. When you get far away from the edge, check that the layers are aligned by lifting up the fabric edge to see if the pin went through the bottom layer in the right place. If not, slide the lower layer of fabric until it's lined up.

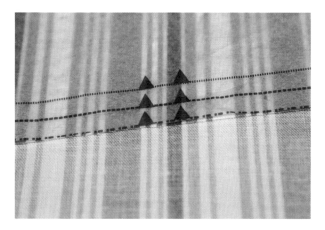

3 To match the seams, place the first pattern piece and line up one of the notches along the seam to match with one of the stripe lines.

When you place the second pattern piece, make sure the same stripe is in line with the same notch. If there are no notches, you can use the top or bottom edges of the piece as your matching point. When you sew the seam and match the notches, you'll be matching up the stripes at the same time.

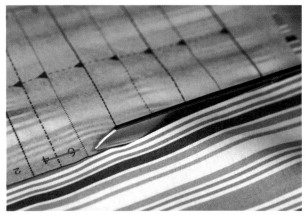

FOR PIECES ON A FOLD

Cut through the top layer only and remove the pattern tissue. Realign the cut edge with the stripe lines to ensure the piece is cut perfectly symmetrical.

FOR STRAIGHT PIECES

It's best to cut waistbands, cuffs and plackets with the fabric in a single layer. Line up the cutting line along a stripe. Once you start cutting, take the tissue off and focus only on cutting straight along the stripe line. You can replace the tissue to cut the other side, but at least you know you're staying on the stripe as you cut.

CUTTING IN A SINGLE LAYER

As an alternative to pinning the stripes, you can cut all of your pattern pieces on a single layer of fabric. This saves time on pinning and allows you to choose the placement of each piece. This is an especially good solution for cutting important pieces of the garment, for example, cutting shirt or bodice front panels when you want the stripe placement to be exact. If your stripe is really bold, large or distinct, cutting on a single layer lets you choose where each section lands. It also lets you choose the most flattering placement. Don't like orange next to your face? Don't cut the collar out of the orange section. And if you are short on fabric, cutting from a single layer wastes less fabric. Just remember to flip the pattern piece over when you cut the second piece!

SEWING STRIPED FABRIC

Here are some tips when it comes to sewing striped fabric. The cutting is the most labor-intensive part, and if you've cut with care, your seams will be easy to match and sew.

* Pin every stripe intersection on seams you want to match. Or pin every second stripe line. Pin as many times as you need to pin to feel confident about the pinning part. No one will know how many pins you used to sew each seam once your garment is finished.

* Baste your seam first. After basting (page 18), check to make sure the stripes match along the seam line. If you need to fix a slipped stripe, it'll be easier to unpick the basting than it would to undo permanent stitching.

* Be prepared to unpick and redo your basted seam a few times to get it right. If you nail it the first try? Awesome! Run your machine right over the basting stitches using regular-size stitches this time. If you expect to have some fixing to do, it doesn't seem so bad when it inevitably happens.

CHOOSING THREAD COLOR ON STRIPED FABRIC

When you're sewing a striped fabric, especially one with a strong contrast between the colors, what color thread do you use? Here are some factors to consider.

* What color is dominant? Are there heavy black stripes and thin white stripes? In that case, I'd pick black thread.

* What color are you serging, if you're planning to use a serger as well?

* What does the fabric look like from the inside? Some fabrics are bright and printed on the outside but all white on the inside. In that case, you might want to use white thread.

* Is there any topstitching (page 218)? If so, what color do you want the topstitching to be? If there is no topstitching, the color of your thread is less important as it's only going to be visible from the inside and maybe a little at the seams if they pull apart.

* Do you want to switch between thread colors? Perhaps there's a wide black stripe at the hem but you were planning to use white thread. It might look better if you switched to black thread just at that one spot.

* Can you find a good color match in thread? With some colors, it may be hard to find a matching thread color. Cream, white and black are all easy thread colors to find.

Tips + Notes

Buy extra fabric to make sure you can line up the stripes where you want them. The extra fabric will be handy in case you need to recut smaller pieces.

Know when enough is enough. If you've redone your seam three times, and it's still only 99 percent perfect, stop! Pat yourself on the back for getting it pretty darn close and move forward.

Not sure if your stripes are "good enough"? Put the project away, come back an hour later and see how you feel about the stripes. Do they match? Do you care? Make a decision and move on. Life is too short to agonize over possibly-not-matching stripes on a T-shirt.

Need validation on your stripes? Take a photo. It's the best way to look at your project from a distance and decide whether it's good enough to move on or needs to be fixed.

Striped fabric is a little tricky to cut but not as hard as cutting plaid fabric (page 138). If you're dreaming of sewing plaid fabrics but worry about the cutting stage, stripes are a good way to practice your cutting and matching skills before tackling plaids.

Tailor's Ham

WHAT IS IT?

A tailor's ham is a rounded, stuffed tool shaped like a ham, used for pressing curved areas. The most useful hams are made with one side of wool cloth and the other of cotton. Tailor's hams are stuffed with sawdust or commercial stuffing to keep their shape. Pair with a seam roll (see page 185) to cover most of your pressing needs. You can buy tailor's hams, or you can make your own.

Tailor's ham

Tailor's ham

▶ WHEN DO YOU USE IT?

A tailor's ham is used for pressing curved seams and darts. Making your own tailor's ham allows you to customize the size, which is great for making doll clothes or children's clothes. Press tiny darts on tiny hams!

Do you need one when you're learning to sew? It's hard to press darts on a completely flat surface without pressing creases into your garment. You'll need to use some sort of three-dimensional surface to press curved darts properly, so consider getting a tailor's ham as soon as you decide to tackle darts.

Tips + Notes

Snip notches at both ends of the fold line to make it easier to line up the two pieces of the ham.

Stuff with cedar shavings from a pet supply shop instead of sawdust. Both are naturally absorbent, which is perfect for pressing with steam.

You can also stuff it with wool fabric scraps cut into small pieces or old nylon stockings.

Save extra stuffing to restuff the ham in case it becomes deflated over time.

If desired, make a hanging loop by sewing ribbon in the seam allowance at one end before stuffing.

Make a smaller version of this ham for pressing children's clothing or doll clothes.

Instead of using a tailor's ham, roll up towels to use as pressing tools. You can reroll and shape the towel as needed to fit the curves of your project.

HOW TO PRESS CURVES WITH A TAILOR'S HAM

Arrange your seam over the ham, finding a curved part that suits the shape of your fabric piece. Press (page 155). Move the fabric around the ham as needed to use the curves that fit. Continue pressing until you've finished pressing the piece. Use the cotton side for high heat and the wool side for low heat.

HOW TO MAKE A TAILOR'S HAM

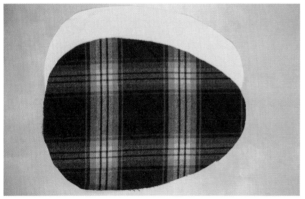

1 Cut out an egg-shaped circle from both wool and prewashed cotton fabric (such as muslin), making it approximately 14" (35.6cm) long, 10" (25.4cm) wide at the wider end and 8" (20.3cm) wide at the narrower end.

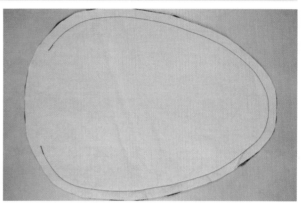

2 Sew around the edges with a ½" (1.3cm) seam allowance. Leave a 5" (12.7cm) opening for stuffing at the wider end.

3 Turn the ham right side out. Stuff tightly with sawdust. It needs to be quite hard to hold its shape.

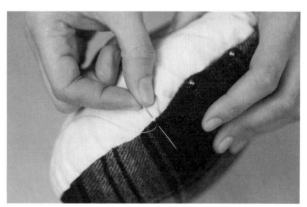

4 Turn under the seam allowance on one side of the opening, lap over the other edge and sew the opening shut.

T Tailor's Tacks

WHAT IS IT?

Tailor's tacks are thread markings done by hand, to mark darts, circles and other pattern markings. Tailor's tacks are little tufts of thread, usually in a thread color that contrasts with the fabric color. They are easily visible from both sides of the fabric, are easy to remove and don't leave a mark!

Tailor's tacks

▶ WHEN DO YOU USE IT?

Tailor's tacks are great for markings that you want to last, as opposed to fade-away marker and chalk. Tailor's tacks are done with many tufts of thread, so if one or two fall out, the remaining threads are still there to mark the spot. This is especially useful for markings that need to last during the construction of the garment, such as button placement or pleats that are sewn near the end.

Tips + Notes

Save nearly empty spools of thread and use them for sewing tailor's tacks.

Make all of the loops the same size. When you make the second loop, use the tip of the needle to pull both loops and adjust the new loop until it's the same size as the first one.

If you are making multiple tailor's tacks through the same piece, make all of the loops before pulling the layers apart and snipping the tacks.

Keep a handsewing needle near your sewing machine, threaded in a bright contrast color. Then, when you need to make a marking, it's all ready to go. Making tailor's tacks will seem quick and easy if the needle is ready and waiting.

HOW TO MAKE TAILOR'S TACKS

Start with your pattern piece still attached to the fabric. Thread a handsewing needle with doubled contrasting color thread. Line up the ends of the thread but do not tie a knot.

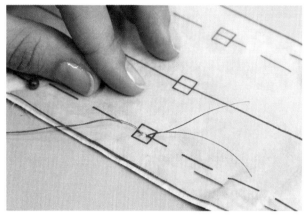

1 Take a few small stitches through the marking. If your pattern is printed, you can either poke a hole in the tissue to make your stitches or fold back the tissue paper to make your markings.

2 Take a small ⅛" (3mm) stitch through both layers of fabric and pull the thread until there is only 1" (2.5cm) of a thread tail left. Make a second stitch. Leave a loop of thread that is about half the length of the first thread tail. You can make your tailor's tacks thicker by making a few more stitches. Make at least two loops before finishing the tack. On fine or loosely woven fabrics, thicker tacks will last longer.

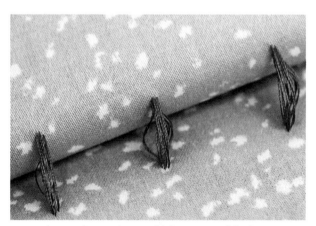

3 Peel apart the two layers of fabric. Spread the layers apart, as shown. In between the layers you can see the thread tacks are holding the two layers together.

4 Snip through the middle of each tailor's tack. You'll end up with a little tuft of thread on each side of your fabric. These tidy little thread markings show on both sides of the fabric. They won't stain or permanently mark your fabric, or fall out like pins do.

Thread Loops

WHAT IS IT?

Thread loops are thin loops made of thread used in place of button loops or buttonholes to secure buttons. Thread loops can also refer to loops of thread at the waistline of dresses and blouses used to hold belts in place.

Thread loop for securing a button

Thread loops at waistline to hold belt

▶ WHEN DO YOU USE IT?

For delicate garments, thread loops are a great option for a button closure as they're lightweight and subtle. Thread loops for belts are placed at the waistline side seams on blouses and dresses to hold fabric belts or purchased belts. These can be secured at the top and the bottom so the loop lies flat to the body; or they can be looped, with both ends secured in the same place so the loop can move up and down. Pattern instructions will tell you when and where to make thread loops, but you can add thread loops and a tie belt to any blouse pattern.

Tips + Notes

Instead of using this method for thread belt loops, you can also follow the directions for French tacks on page 84.

You can make button loops (page 44) instead of thread loops for a stronger closure on more substantial garments.

Run thread through beeswax for stronger thread loops.

Thread loops for tie belts are optional. If you don't like the idea of wearing a belt or if you will wear the garment without the belt more often than with, then skip the thread loops.

For thin fabric belts, make an extra thread loop at the center front to keep the belt from falling down.

HOW TO MAKE THREAD LOOPS AS BUTTONHOLES

1 Finish the edge where the loops will be sewn by sewing the facing or binding. Mark the top and bottom of each loop. Thread a handsewing needle with single thread. Bring the thread through the fold or seam line at the top loop marking. Insert the needle through the bottom loop marking, leaving a loop that will fit over the button.

2 Make two or three more looped stitches using the tip of the needle to pull out the threads. Make sure they're all the same length.

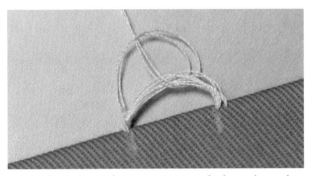

3 Work blanket stitches (page 31) over the looped strands from the top to the bottom until the strands are completely covered.

4 Secure the thread on the inside of the garment. Press loops flat.

HOW TO MAKE THREAD LOOPS AT THE WAISTLINE FOR HOLDING BELTS

Determine the waistline position and decide whether you want hanging loops (both ends secured in the same place) or loops that start and stop at different points on the side seam. Insert the needle through the side seam at the top loop marking. If you are making the hanging loop, insert the needle about ¼" (6mm) below the first marking. If you are making flat loops, insert the needle through the bottom loop marking. Leave enough space to fit the belt through the loop. Follow the steps above for making the thread loop.

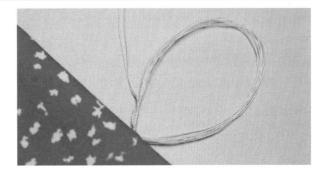

Topstitch

WHAT IS IT?

Topstitching is a row of stitching that's intentionally visible on the right side of your garment. Topstitching can be done in a contrasting color or in a color that matches and blends in with your garment. Use decorative stitching or just plain straight stitching.

Topstitching on shirt yoke

Topstitching on Minoru Jacket

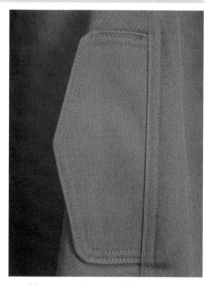
Double topstitching on Robson Coat

WHEN DO YOU USE IT?

Topstitching is a wonderful and easy decoration! Use topstitching to show off seam lines or to draw attention to areas of the garment such as the pocket opening, collar or neckline. Topstitching strengthens seams as well, so it's a great feature to use on garments that will be heavily worn like jeans. Topstitching also makes your fabric stiffer. This is great if you want to add structure to an area of the garment, such as a collar or waistband. Topstitching around the edge of a waistband will stiffen it considerably; topstitching several rows through the middle will add even more stiffness. Topstitching can also close up open areas of a garment, like waistbands. For fast, visible hemming (page 96) you can topstitch instead of handsewing.

Tips + Notes

When topstitching seams, you may prefer to topstitch first and then trim the seam allowances. That way your topstitching is going through all of the layers, and you're only trimming off the extra.

Use a triple stitch as an alternative to thick thread. This is a special setting on some machines that stitches three times over each stitch, so it's extra thick.

To change the width of your topstitching and still use the presser foot edge as a guide, move the needle position. Just make note of where you've moved it so you can keep the topstitching consistent.

Topstitch coats and outerwear with a slightly longer stitch length for a professional look. I prefer a slightly shorter stitch length for topstitching dress shirts and blouses.

HOW TO TOPSTITCH

Simply sew on the right side of your garment, making your stitching an equal distance from the edge all along the topstitching.

How far away should you topstitch? I like a ¼" (6mm) topstitch. It's close enough to the seam line to look clean and not too close that it disappears. Plus I can use the edge of my presser foot as a guide. This is often the width of the sewing machine's presser foot, so it's easy to maintain an even row of stitching by using the edge of the foot as a guide.

Depending on where the start and end points of your topstitching fall, you may want to backstitch (page 14) or you may not want to. Backstitch if the end point is going to be hidden or covered by another seam. If the end point is going to be visible, stitch in place to secure the end or pull the threads to the back and tie in a knot.

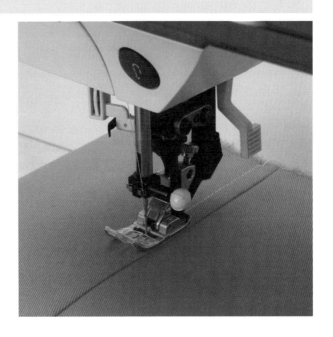

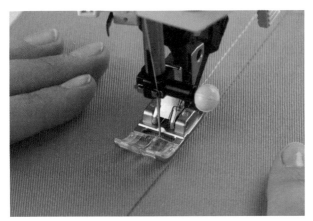

TOPSTITCHING A SEAM
To topstitch a seam, work from the right side of the garment. Pull the seam apart gently with your fingers, and line up your stitching with the seam line. Follow the seam line as you sew from top to bottom. Press the seam after topstitching.

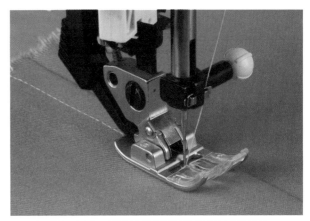

TOPSTITCHING WITH TOPSTITCHING THREAD
You can use special, thick topstitch thread. If you do, switch to a topstitching needle. These heavy-duty needles have an extra long eye for sewing with thicker topstitching thread or even with multiple threads. Use the thick spool on the top, and use regular thread in the bobbin. Press after topstitching.

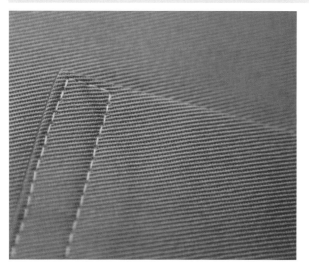

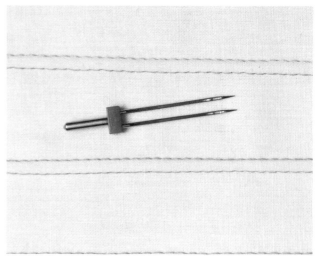

DOUBLE TOPSTITCHING

Double topstitching adds even more definition to the lines of your garment. Always topstitch the most important side first. If the topstitching is holding the pocket in place or closing the opening on a waistband, that's where the first row of stitching should be. Use the edge of your presser foot as a guide for sewing the second, decorative row of topstitching. Depending on the piece you're topstitching, it may look better to turn the piece to sew the second row, rather than stopping and starting. Patch pockets are an example of when it's better to sew the first row close to the pocket edge, then turn and sew a few stitches across the top of the pocket, then turn again to sew the second row of topstitching.

TOPSTITCHING WITH A TWIN NEEDLE

A twin needle sews two rows of stitching at once. It looks like two separate needles that are joined together at the top, and it fits into your sewing machine just like a regular needle. To sew with a twin needle, you will have two spools of thread on the top of your machine and one bobbin thread. Where do you put the second spool? If your machine doesn't have a place to put it, let it sit in a mug or bowl. It will bounce around while the thread unrolls. Thread both threads together as you would normally, and when you reach the needle, thread one thread through each side of the needle.

Tips + Notes

Go slow. It's not a race! No one will know how slowly you topstitched your seams, but everyone will know if it's crooked or uneven. (OK, they might not notice, but you will!)

Unsure of your topstitching skills or thread color choice? Test on scrap fabric. Compare a couple of thread colors if your fabric is hard to match. Stitch a couple of rows with different colors of thread next to each other and pick your favorite.

Lighter thread colors can look shiny. Darker is better if you want the stitching to blend in.

Trimming

WHAT IS IT?

Trimming is when you cut the seam allowances smaller or on an angle to reduce bulk. You'll need to trim to turn the piece right side out, if the seam allowances stop the piece from fully turning.

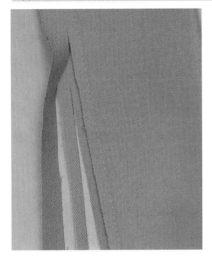

Trimmed seam allowance

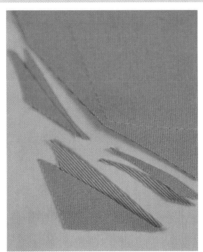

Trimmed corner

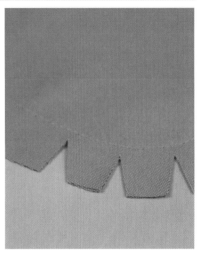

Notched curve

▶ WHEN DO YOU USE IT?

Trim anytime you are asked to trim the seam allowance in the pattern instructions. Trim inner and outer curves, and trim seam allowances on enclosed seams such as collars, tabs, pocket flaps and fabric belts. Corners must be trimmed to reduce lumps inside the point of the corner. Trim seam allowances on facings (page 170) so the garment edge lies flat.

Tips + Notes

Trim with pinking shears to quickly reduce bulk and finish the seams at the same time.

Trimmed too close? If so, go back to the machine and resew the seam a couple of millimeters away from the original seam line, only in the area where you trimmed too far. Use a short stitch length. If you snipped too close to the seam line, you could also apply a small piece of fusible interfacing (page 104) to reinforce the area and ensure it doesn't fray through the stitching line.

TRIMMING CORNERS

With corners, you want to remove as much as bulk as possible. All of the seam allowance needs to fit inside the point of that corner.

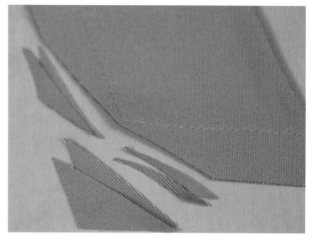

1 Trim diagonally across the corner first. Snip right across both sides of the seam. Get close to the point of the corner. Leave only about 1mm–2mm of space above the stitching.

2 Trim two more diagonal cuts with the scissors at a sharper angle toward the corner. Turn the corner right side out, and if there is too much bulk inside the corner point, turn it back inside out and make another angled cut on each side of the point.

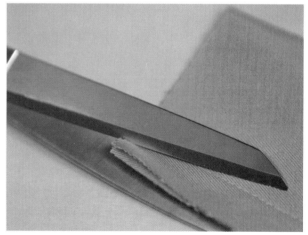

TRIMMING SEAM ALLOWANCES

Generally seam allowances start at ⅝" (1.5cm), and I trim them to ¼" (6mm). You can also aim to trim your seam allowances in half, which is easy to eyeball without having to use a tape measure. To reduce bulk even more, trim both seam allowances in half and then trim one of them in half again, so it's half the width of the other. This creates a smoother transition and reduces the chance of seeing the outline of the seam allowances on the right side of the garment.

GRADING SEAM ALLOWANCES

This is one thing I never quite got the hang of in high school sewing class! If you angle the scissors, tilting the blades toward you as you trim, you'll end up cutting one side of the seam allowance shorter than the other with a single cut. Grading takes practice, and the difference between the two sides is subtle. It ensures that there aren't two thick seam allowances with blunt edges sitting right on top of each other. The more you angle your scissors, the greater the variance between the two layers. Grading is faster than trimming the two layers individually, but it creates less of an obvious difference.

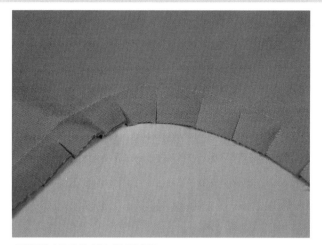

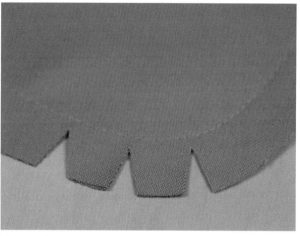

CLIPPING INNER CURVES

For inner curves, clip into the seam allowance, stopping about ⅛" (3mm) before the stitching line. Make your snips about ½" (1.3cm) apart or closer together in very curved areas. The snips release the seam allowance so the piece can be turned and pressed flat. Clipping the seam allowance makes it easier to do. If you turn the piece and it won't turn fully, turn it back inside out and make more snips.

NOTCHING OUTER CURVES

For outer curves, cut pie-shaped notches from the seam allowance, stopping about ⅛" (3mm) before the stitching line. Place these notches about ½" (1.3cm) apart from each other at the top edge. Make more notches around very curved edges. When the piece is turned right side out, the space between the notches closes as the seam allowance comes together. Without these pie-shaped notches, you would see lumps where the seam allowance bunches up inside the seam. If you turn the piece and there are lumps where the seam allowance overlaps, turn it back inside out and cut more notches.

Tips + Notes

Don't trim a seam that needs to be matched to another seam, because your trimmed seam will come up short. If you must, make sure the seam line is marked so you know where to line up the pieces.

Clip and notch curves at different points on the top and bottom seam allowances so they don't pull in the same spots. Doing so takes time, and it's more important for thicker fabrics and less important for thinner ones because bulk isn't as much of an issue.

After trimming, understitch (page 228) facings (page 74) to help them roll to the inside and create crisp edges.

T Tucks

WHAT IS IT?

Tucks are stitched folds of fabric used as decorative details or to hold fullness in place. Tucks can be narrow or wide, sewn in groups or as a single tuck. Pintucks are tiny tucks sewn in fabric that create a little ridge on the surface of the fabric. Tucks are more stable when sewn on the lengthwise grain (page 90) of the fabric but can also be sewn on the crosswise grain or on the bias (page 23).

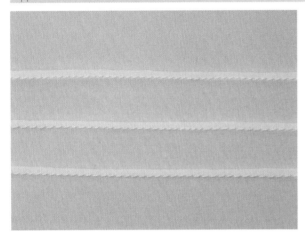

Tucks

 ## WHEN DO YOU USE IT?

Tucks are often used as design details. Tucks create lines across the garment, which draw attention to part of the body or create the illusion of length. Add tucks to blouses and dresses, placed either vertically down the bodice or horizontally across the hemline of skirts or sleeves. Tucks work best in lightweight fabrics; in heavier fabrics, they are too stiff. Choose solid fabrics for patterns with tucks and pintucks, as the tuck detail will be lost in printed fabrics and may look strange in plaid or striped fabrics.

Tips + Notes

Remember that all tucks take up fabric, even small ones, so if you make pintucks in a cut piece of fabric, the fabric will get smaller. Make the pintucks in a large piece of fabric first and then cut the garment piece. Or draw a horizontal line across your pattern piece for each tuck, cut along these lines and open up the pattern piece to add width for each tuck.

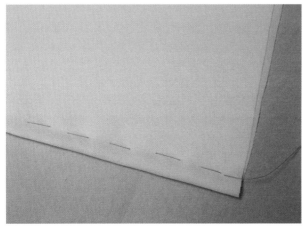

1 Fold the fabric along the fold line for the tuck. Pin or baste (page 18) in place. If you choose to baste, sew your basting stitches far enough away from the fold so they won't be caught in the tuck stitching.

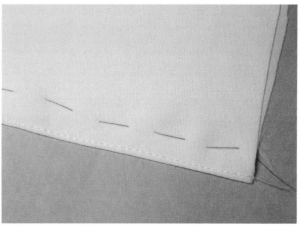

2 Sew the tuck in place from the side that will be seen. If the tucks are going to be pressed away from the center, sew on the center side of the tuck. If you are sewing very close to the fold to make pintucks, hold the thread tails tightly as you start to sew so the fabric doesn't get sucked into the machine.

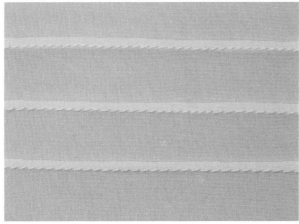

3 Press tucks from the wrong side of the garment to prevent making impressions from the fold on the right side of the garment.

Underlining

WHAT IS IT?

Underlining is a layer of fabric that's added behind the main garment fabric. It's different from lining (page 113) because instead of being sewn separately and attached around the edges, the main fabric and underlining are sewn as one. Underlining is used for sewing sheer fabrics as a backing to prevent transparency. Underlining is also used as support, to add stiffness and structure, or to change the drape of the main fabric.

White underlining under sheer fabric

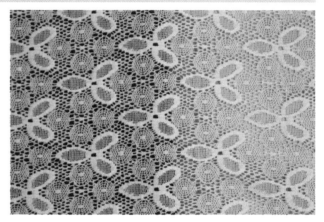

Dark underlining under lace fabric

WHEN DO YOU USE IT?

Underline sheer fabrics so you can't see through them. Add structure or stiffness with underlining when your main fabric is not supportive enough on its own. Underline with soft fabrics when the garment fabric is stiff or scratchy to add a softer inner layer against your skin. Change the color of your fabric by changing the underlining. Whites will brighten a white-based print, while ivory underlining will soften it. Underlining a black-and-white print with black will darken the look, while white will brighten the whites. Not only can it add structure or change the color, but underlining can make your project more comfortable to wear and extend the life of your garment. For lace fabrics, choosing a contrasting color for underlining will make the lace pattern show up more clearly than if you choose a matching color.

Tips + Notes

Prewash (page 157) underlining fabrics the same way you prewashed the main garment fabric.

If you underline the bodice, underline or line the skirt in the same color. Otherwise the bodice will look different in color than the rest of the garment.

As an alternative cutting method, cut the garment fabric first, then lay the cut piece on the underlining fabric. Baste the garment piece to the underlining and cut around the edges.

When basting the layers together, flatness is more important than lining up the raw edges perfectly. Smooth out the layers with your hands to ensure there are no bubbles as you work.

When hemming underlined garments, hand stitch the hem to the underlining only, not through to the garment fabric. This way the hem will be completely invisible!

HOW TO SEW UNDERLINING

Cut pieces of underlining using the same pattern pieces as the main garment fabric. If you are underlining a bodice, you will have a bodice front piece and a bodice back piece in both garment fabric and underlining. Place the underlining right side up on your work surface and lay each garment fabric piece on top of its corresponding underlining piece. Pin around the edges and smooth out bumps and wrinkles.

1 Baste around the edges of each piece. Run the stitching off the edges instead of pivoting at the corners. This helps to keep the layers smooth and stops the shifting that occurs when turning the fabric still attached to the machine.

2 When you're finished basting around the edges of all pieces, you will start working with each piece as a single layer. You can see how this is different from lining (page 113), for which each layer is constructed separately and joined around the edges. Give each piece a quick press after the basting is complete.

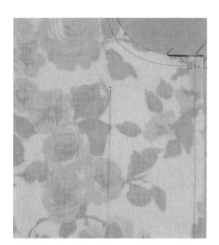

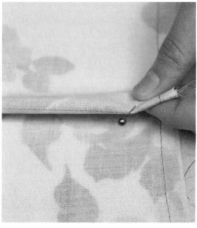

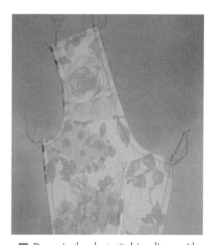

3 Sew the darts (page 63) through both layers of fabric together. Measure the center of the dart along the edge and mark it. Draw a straight line from the center of the dart to the dart tip using a ruler. Don't worry about the legs of the dart yet, just the centerline.

4 Stitch a line of machine stitching along the line you just drew. This will anchor the two layers of fabric together and prevent slipping when you sew the dart. Now your dart will be perfectly even through both layers. To sew your darts, fold along this newly stitched centerline and pin.

5 Draw in the dart stitching lines with a marking pen and stitch darts along the marked lines. A bonus of using underlining is that it's easy to see markings on the solid fabric. The lines don't get lost in the print. Press darts toward the center.

Make darts, tucks or pleats through both layers for the other garment pieces.

Understitch

WHAT IS IT?

Understitching is a row of stitching on the inside edge of a garment, usually a facing, sewn to keep the seam rolled to the inside of the garment. Understitching is never visible from the right side of the garment. Unlike basting, understitching is permanent. Understitching seems like a step you could skip, and just press the garment instead, but it makes a world of difference to the crispness of your edges.

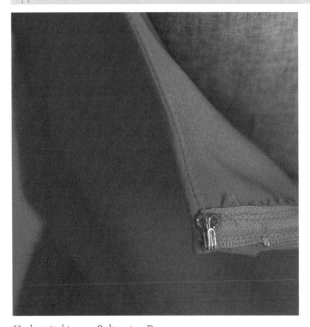

Understitching on Saltspring Dress

Understitching on Cambie Dress

▶ WHEN DO YOU USE IT?

Understitch after sewing the facing to the garment but before pressing the facing to the underside. Any garment that has facings can be understitched. Usually the pattern instructions will tell you when to understitch. But if they don't, feel free to add it! (Read to the end of the pattern instructions before adding it in to make sure it doesn't happen later in the construction.)

Tips + Notes

Understitch linings as well as facings if they start to roll to the right side.

You can also understitch by hand and thereby get into smaller areas like corners that the sewing machine can't reach. Thread a handsewing needle with a double thread, and sew tiny prickstitches (see page 240) to secure the facing to the seam allowance. It's time-consuming but adds a couture finish to gowns and formal wear.

1 Grade your seam allowances (see trimming page 221). Doing so helps reduce the bulk of your facing seam line.

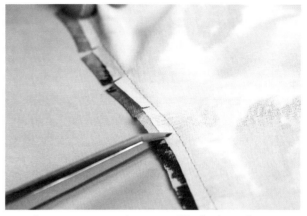

2 Clip inner curves so the seam will lie flat by making snips into the seam allowance about ½" (1.3cm) apart. Make more snips into very curved areas and less snips into less curved areas. Be careful not to snip into your stitching line. Once clipped, the curve can now be stretched into a straight line! You've made your seam more flexible. This is an important step, as otherwise it will be harder to understitch the facing.

3 Arrange your piece so that the facing is on top. Open up the seam line and stretch the seam as much as you can (gently!) with your fingers. You'll notice I didn't press the seam open with an iron. I find you get better results by stretching and understitching and then pressing the facing. This way there's no crease mark when you understitch.

4 Insert the needle into the facing, very close to the seam line. You want to keep this stitching very close to the edge, as close as you can maintain, while not crossing over onto the bodice front fabric. If you can manage to get at least ⅛" (3mm) away from the fold, that will work. Lower your presser foot and begin stitching slowly as you stretch the seam open with your fingers.

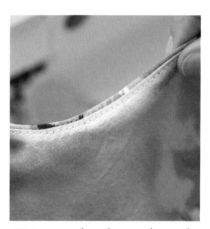

5 Continue along the seam line until you get to the end. Backstitch and trim threads. Now look at how nicely your facing rolls to the inside of your garment. You've made it want to stay in the right place. Pressing the facing will be so easy since you've created this lovely natural curve.

Waistband

WHAT IS IT?

A waistband is a band around the waistline, often seen on skirts, trousers and shorts. The waistband supports the garment, keeps it in place and, for loose-fitting garments, keeps it from falling down. Waistbands can be wide or narrow, curved or straight, interfaced or not interfaced, or even elasticized! Waistbands can be cut in two pieces, one for the inner waistband and one for the outer waistband, or they can be cut as one piece that's folded over along the top edge. Contoured waistbands have to be cut from two pieces because of the shaping at the waistline. This gives you an opportunity to use contrast fabric for the inner layer. Waistbands are cut with the grain line along the length, so the lengthwise grain goes around the waistline for the most stability.

Waistband on skirt

Waistband on skirt

▶ WHEN DO YOU USE IT?

A waistband is a great way to finish and stabilize the top edge of trousers, skirts and shorts. You need something to finish the top of the garment: either a waistband or a facing. If you have a pattern that has a facing, you can change it to a waistband and vice versa. Contour waistbands are great for garments that stop below the waist, as the curved shape fits the contours of the body. Straight waistbands are best for garments that sit at the natural waist or for men's trousers where the body is fairly straight from waist to hip. With a zipper closure, sometimes the zipper will extend to the top of the waistband, and sometimes the zipper will stop below the waistband with a button, snap or hook closure to secure the band.

Tips + Notes

To reduce bulk on two-piece waistbands, especially on thick fabrics like denim or corduroy, cut the inner waistband from a flat cotton fabric.

If your waistband seems too small for the garment, the garment may have stretched during handling. Sew a row of easestitching (page 67) along the waistline, and ease the garment into the waistband. Don't be tempted to cut a wider waistband to fit the stretched waistline.

Binding (page 28) is a nice way to finish the lower edge of the inner waistband, instead of turning it under. Bind the edge and don't turn it under along the seam allowance. When you topstitch (page 218) or stitch in the ditch (page 206), it will be easy to catch the inner edge, as it will be left longer than the top waistband.

HOW TO SEW A WAISTBAND

Interface (see page 104) the waistband. Prepare the garment so it's ready to have the waistband attached: darts are sewn, side seams are sewn and the zipper or other closure is complete. Make sure the fold line of the waistband is marked, either with basting (page 18) along the fold line or with ¼" (6mm) clips in the seam allowance at either end.

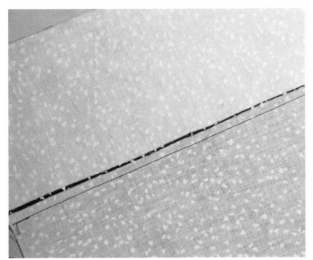

1 Match up the notches and pin the waistband to the garment. Sew the waistband to the garment. Trim (page 221) seam allowances, and press them toward the waistband.

2 Fold the waistband along the fold line (or seam, for two-piece waistbands), with right sides together, and sew across the ends. If there is an extension on your waistband (there is in the example above), pivot and sew along the lower edge of the extension until you meet the stitch line of the waistband-to-garment seam. Doing so finishes the edge of the extension without any handsewing.

3 Trim corners and seam allowances, clip curves and turn the waistband right side out. Fold the waistband along the fold line, wrong sides together, and turn under the seam allowance on the inside edge of the waistband. Baste the inner edge in place. Some pattern instructions ask you to turn under the seam allowance before sewing the waistband in place, but I like to do it at this point so I can be sure it's in line with the stitching.

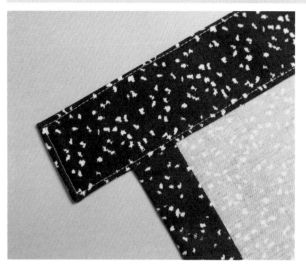 

4 To secure the inner edge of the waistband, you can choose to slipstitch (page 194) or topstitch (page 218). Slipstitching will be invisible, while topstitching will be visible from the right side of the garment. If you topstitch to close the waistband, continue the topstitching all around the top and sides of the waistband as well.

5 For a two-piece waistband, sew the inner waistband to the outer waistband along the top edge and down the short ends. Trim (page 221) seam allowances, and press open. Understitch (page 228) along the top edge as close to the corners as you can, so the inner waistband rolls to the inside, and press. Understitching is an especially good idea if you are using a contrast fabric for the inner layer, so it isn't visible from the right side. Follow steps 1–4 to sew the waistband to the garment.

Tips + Notes

To change a waistband to a facing, follow the instructions in the facing section (page 74). Fold out any darts or pleats from the waistline of the skirt. This will work for A-line skirts and slim skirts, but it won't work well for full, gathered or pleated skirts. Very full skirts need the support of a waistband to keep them in place.

For an elastic waistband, follow the steps in the casing section (page 56) for sewing a separate casing. Cut the waistband the same length as the garment, and use elastic or drawstring to pull it in and fit the waistline.

Whipstitch

WHAT IS IT?

A whipstitch is a quick hand stitch that is used to "whip" two edges together. This stitch is visible, so it's usually done on the inside of the garment or other places where it will not show from the right side.

Whipstitches

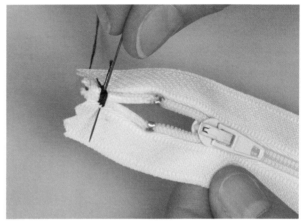

Whipstitch to close zipper tape

▶ WHEN DO YOU USE IT?

Use a whipstitch when you have two edges that need to be joined together quickly. Whipstitching can be used as temporary stitching as well. When inserting a zipper in a seam that is sewn both above and below the zipper opening, whipstitch the edges of the zipper tape together before inserting the zipper. (See lapped zipper page 245 for more.)

HOW TO SEW A WHIPSTITCH

1 Thread a handsewing needle with a single thread. Take a stitch through both sides to join at a right angle to the edge.

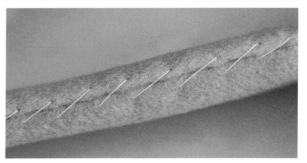

2 Repeat all the way across the edges. Sewing at a right angle makes the stitches slant as they enclose the edge.

Yoke

WHAT IS IT?

A yoke is a fitted garment piece at the shoulder or hips. Yokes on the shoulders cover the upper back and shoulders. Yokes at the hips cover the body from the waist to the hip. Shoulder yokes are often made of two layers of fabric, with the raw edges enclosed within the yoke. Yokes provide support around the neckline and shoulders and make it easy to fit the garment. They can also be a design feature, sewn in contrast fabric, on the bias (page 23) or cut into an interesting shape. Hip yokes may feature seaming or panels for shaping. Yokes are also used as a contrast to fullness: for example, a gathered skirt with a yoke at the hips or a blouse with soft pleats sewn to the shoulder yoke. Hip yokes are interfaced to support the skirt, while shirt yokes are not interfaced.

Bias-cut yoke on shirt

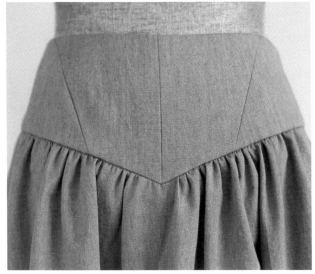

Yoke on Crescent Skirt

WHEN DO YOU USE IT?

Yokes are great for fitting shaped areas of the body. Sew a yoke to the rest of the garment with a plain seam or a lapped seam (page 111). Lapped seams are great for sewing shaped yokes with points, curves or corners that would be difficult to sew with a plain seam.

A yoke makes it easier to fit the shoulders, as there is no shoulder seam to fit and place on the shoulder line. It's easy to take out extra fabric at the front and back of the yoke lines, too. Yokes are comfortable for activewear, as there's no shoulder seam to rub on your shoulders. If you wear a backpack, it's better to have a flat layer of fabric underneath.

Tips + Notes

Cut yokes on the bias or use contrast fabric to add interest to your projects.

Use a contrast fabric for the inner yoke for an interesting detail that only you will see.

HOW TO SEW A SHIRT YOKE

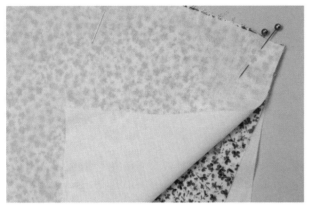

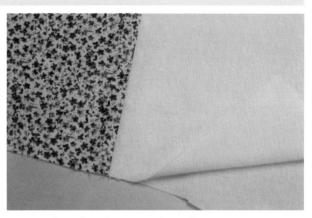

1 Sew the seams, darts (page 63), gathers (page 86) or pockets on the front and back shirt pieces, not including the side seams. Pin the outer yoke to the back, right sides together, and match the raw edges and notches. Pin the inner yoke to the back, with the right side of the yoke facing the wrong side of the shirt back.

2 Sew these three layers together with a ⅝" (1.5cm) seam allowance. Trim the seam allowances (page 221) and press the two layers of the yoke away from the back piece.

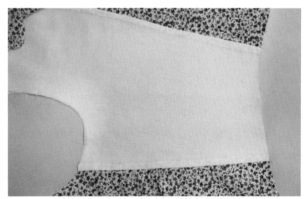

3 To attach the yoke to the front, pin the outer yoke to the front, right sides together. Twist the inner yoke so that the right side matches the wrong side of the shirt front.

4 Sew along the front yoke seam with a ⅝" (1.5cm) seam allowance. Trim the seam allowances, and turn the yoke seam right side out. Edgestitch (page 69) the yoke seams, if desired. Gently pull the yoke seam away from the shirt front and back along the seam line as you stitch. Press.

HOW TO SEW A HIP YOKE

A hip yoke is sewn like a very wide contoured waistband (page 230). Construct the panels of the yoke, and decide whether to sew a regular or a lapped seam (page 111). If the yoke is shaped or pointed, a lapped seam is best for producing crisp corners and points. Attach the skirt panels to the yoke.

Zipper, Centered

WHAT IS IT?

A centered zipper is a type of zipper insertion in which the zipper teeth are centered between the fabric opening. In this type of zipper application, the fabric covers the zipper equally on both sides, meeting in the middle of the opening, and the stitching is visible on either side of the zipper opening. The zipper teeth may be visible as you move and the fabric layers pull apart, but when the garment is flat, the folded edges meet to completely cover the zipper. To insert a centered zipper, you'll need a regular zipper, not an invisible zipper. (Can't tell the difference? If you can see the zipper teeth or coil as a ridge on the right side, it's a regular zipper. If the tape is flat and the ridge of the zipper coil is on the underside, it's an invisible zipper.)

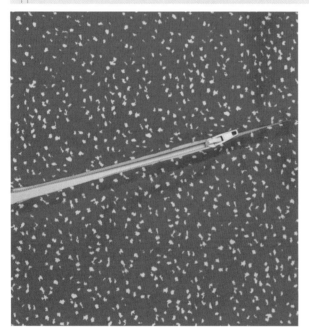

Centered zipper

Centered zipper on Crescent Skirt

▶ WHEN DO YOU USE IT?

This is a fairly simple zipper insertion method, so it can be used on several different types of garments, including skirts, dresses and blouses. It's most often used at center back and center front openings, and it can also be used at the side seams. I find that regular zippers are stronger than invisible zippers (page 242), so I recommend them for snug-fitting garments.

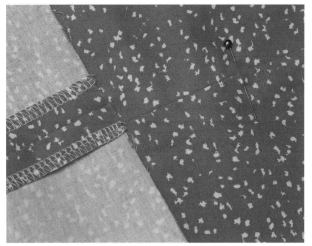

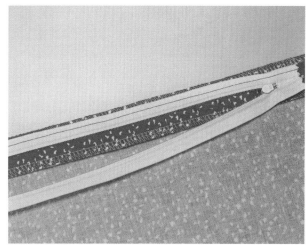

1 Sew the seam below the zipper. If the zipper is going into an unlined garment, finish the seam allowances of the zipper opening all the way down to the bottom of the seam. If the zipper is going in a lined garment, where the seam allowances will be enclosed, leave the seam allowances unfinished. Machine baste (page 18) the zipper opening above the seam closed, and press the seam allowance open.

2 Switch to a zipper foot. From the inside of your garment, with the top of the zipper opening facing you, open up the right seam allowance. Place the closed zipper face down on the seam allowance with the bottom stop at the top of the seam and the coil/teeth centered on top of the seam. Pin along one side of the seam allowance. Open the zipper and machine baste the zipper to the seam allowance only, down the middle of the tape. When you get close to the bottom, zip up the zipper a little so you can baste all the way to the bottom of the tape.

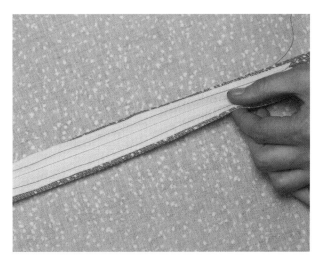

3 Zip up the zipper, and baste the other side of the zipper to the opposite seam allowance. A good way to ensure the zipper stays centered is to aim for the same amount of seam allowance showing on both sides of the zipper.

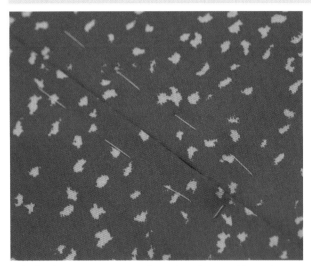 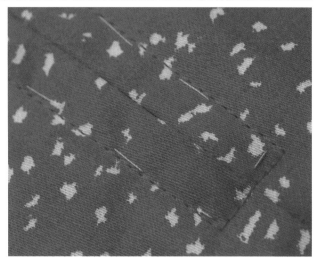

4 Flip the garment over to the right side. Hand baste (page 18) on either side of the seam, across the bottom just below the end of the zipper, and up the other side, ¼" (6mm) away from the seam. Make your basting stitches even, as you'll use them as a guide for topstitching in the next step. You can skip the hand basting and go straight to topstitching the zipper if you feel confident, but basting will keep everything in place so your topstitching is more accurate.

5 Starting at the bottom of the placket (page 135), topstitch (page 218) just outside of the basting line across half of the bottom edge, then pivot and sew up the side to the top. Start again at the bottom and sew up the other side of the zipper. Press the zipper opening, and remove the basting stitches.

Tips + Notes

If you prefer, you can topstitch starting at the top, across the bottom, and back up the other side in one motion. Starting from the bottom both times is good for fabrics that may ripple or shift.

For zippers in lightweight or shifty fabric, you may want to stabilize the zipper opening with fusible interfacing (page 104). Cut two 1"-wide (2.5cm) strips of interfacing the length of the zipper opening, and fuse along the zipper opening.

Zipper, Hand-Picked

WHAT IS IT?

A hand-picked zipper is a type of zipper insertion sewn with hand-stitches. From the right side, you'll see a series of tiny dots down either side of the zipper opening. This type of zipper insertion is surprisingly strong and makes it easy to replace the zipper if it breaks.

Hand-picked zipper on Cambie Dress

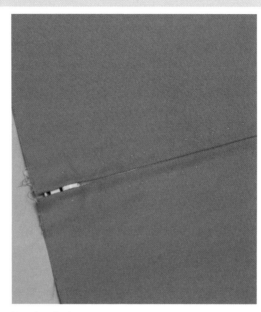

Hand-picked zipper

WHEN DO YOU USE IT?

A hand-picked zipper has vintage appeal, so it's great for sewing vintage-inspired dresses and skirts. You can use the same technique to sew both centered zipper (page 236) and lapped zipper (page 245). Instead of two rows of dots on either side, a lapped zipper will have just one row of stitches on the zipper opening. Because you're sewing by hand, you have a great deal of control over the zipper insertion. This is an advantage when there are a lot of horizontal seams to line up. If you plan to make hard-wearing garments, this type of zipper insertion makes it very easy to rip out an old zipper and replace it with a new one, without having to deconstruct the garment.

Tips + Notes

If your thread is getting tangled, or for an extra-strong zipper, you may want to strengthen your thread with beeswax. Thread your needle and run the thread through a cake of beeswax, then wrap your thread in scrap fabric or paper and press with an iron to seal in the wax.

For a decorative finish, add beads to your hand-picked zipper! Each time you start a new backstitch (page 14), thread a bead onto your sewing thread. Poke the needle through to form the backstitch, and pull the thread to secure the bead in place.

HOW TO SEW A HAND-PICKED ZIPPER

Prepare the opening for the hand-picked zipper. This can be as simple as finishing the edges with serging (page 179) or zigzag stitching (page 183). If you have a lining, you can sew the lining to the garment fabric along the zipper opening with the right sides together, and turn it right side out for a cleanly finished edge. Sew the seam below the zipper opening, and press the seam allowances open. Turn under ⅝" (1.5cm) along the edges of the zipper opening.

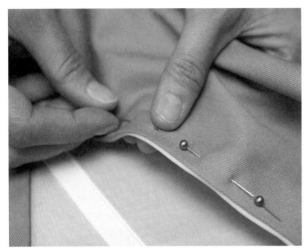

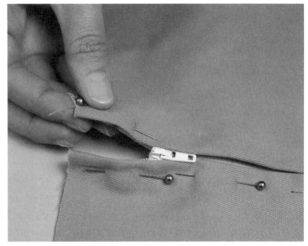

1 Take your zipper and unzip it 2"–3" (5.1cm–7.6cm). If the top edge of the garment is finished, turn under the top edge of the zipper tape toward the front, folding it down just above the metal stopper, and line up the fold with the finished edge. If the top edge is not finished, line up the metal stopper just below the seam line. Line up the zipper teeth with the folded opening edge, and pin through the garment and the zipper tape with the pin tips pointing up toward the top of the garment.

2 Continue pinning all the way along the zipper opening. Unzip the zipper as you go. Once you finish pinning to the bottom of the zipper, zip it up! Doing so will ensure that the top edges meet when you pin the right side of the zipper to the garment, and the edges of the opening meet in the middle of the zipper teeth. On the opposite side, pin the zipper tape to the top edge of the zipper opening. Make sure the edges line up.

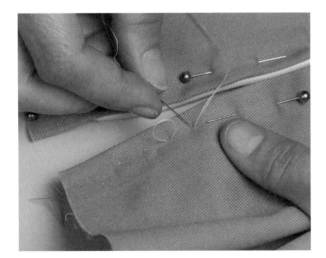

3 Pin all the way down the right side of the zipper opening with the pin tips pointing down.
 Thread a handsewing needle with thread, double it and tie a knot at the end. Start at the top on the left of the zipper, looking at the right side of the garment. Starting just below the zipper stopper, poke your needle through to the right side, about ¼" (6mm) down from the top edge or seam line, and ¼" (6mm) in from the center back opening. Make a tiny, tiny backstitch (page 14) in the zipper tape; this is also called a **prickstitch** (or pickstitch). The backstitch portion that shows should be super small, and the part where the needle comes back out through the fabric should be about ¼" (6mm) away from the first hole.

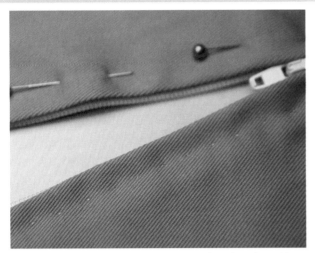

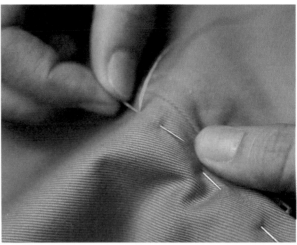

4 Continue making backstitches, or prickstitches if you like, spacing them about ¼" (6mm) apart.

5 Once you reach the bottom, zip up the zipper about 2"–3" (5.1cm–7.6cm). Make your last backstitch across the zipper, instead of continuing down. Now start working up the zipper, toward the top of the dress opening. I zip up the zipper only 1"–2" (2.5cm–5.1cm), so I can still get my hand in there to hold the edges together.

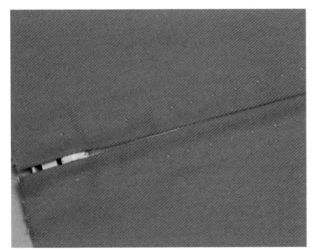

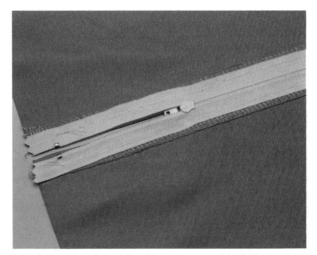

6 Keep going, all the way back up to the top. I like the hand-picked zipper method because it's easy to line up horizontal seams, especially waist seams. When your stitches get about 6" (15.2cm) away from the top, check how much fabric is left between where you've stitched and the top edge. Now is your chance to ease or stretch. If there's too much fabric compared to the zipper tape, ease in any extra fabric by pushing just a touch of extra fabric into each backstitch. If the zipper tape is longer than the remaining fabric, stretch the fabric just a tiny bit between each stitch.

Once you get to the top, poke the needle through all layers to the wrong side of the garment. Tie a knot and trim your thread. Give the opening a light press or steam.

7 This is what the inside of your zipper will look like, with large stitches along the zipper tape. The outside is the tidy part.

Z Zipper, Invisible

WHAT IS IT?

An invisible zipper is a special type of zipper that is designed to be hidden and nearly invisible from the right side of your garment. These zippers are sewn in differently than any other type of zipper insertion. To insert an invisible zipper, you'll need an invisible zipper, not a regular zipper. (Can't tell the difference? If you can see the zipper teeth or coil as a ridge on the right side, it's a regular zipper. If the tape is flat and the ridge of the zipper coil is on the underside, it's an invisible zipper.)

Invisible zipper on Cambie Dress

▶ WHEN DO YOU USE IT?

Use an invisible zipper when you don't want the zipper opening to be visible from the outside of the garment. Skirts, dresses and blouses are all good places for invisible zippers. It's rare to find an invisible zipper that separates at the bottom, so they're best for zipper openings above or below seams. Invisible zippers are great in side seams because both sides of the garment look the same. If you are having trouble finding a zipper color to match, know that very little of the zipper will actually show on the right side—only the little zipper pull at the top! I do find that invisible zippers are more delicate than regular zippers, so I don't recommend them for snug-fitting garments. They're great for loose-fitting or semifitted garments where there isn't a lot of stress on the zipper. Also, if the pattern you're using recommends an invisible zipper, follow pattern recommendations, as other construction steps can depend on this type of zipper application. Or read through the pattern instructions to determine whether you can substitute a regular zipper. You can use a standard zipper foot or buy a special foot for installing invisible zippers.

HOW TO INSERT AN INVISIBLE ZIPPER

When sewing an invisible zipper, the seam below the zipper needs to be left open. This is the opposite of most zipper applications, which have you sew the seam below the zipper first. If the zipper is going into an unlined garment, finish the seam allowances of the opening all the way down to the bottom of the seam. If the zipper is going in a lined garment, where the seam allowances will be enclosed, leave the seam allowances unfinished.

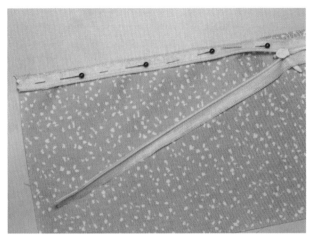

1 Place the closed invisible zipper along the right side of the seam allowance, face down with the zipper tab at the top. Open the zipper and pin or baste (page 18) the zipper tape to the seam allowance. Pin with the points facing the top of the garment, so they are easier to remove.

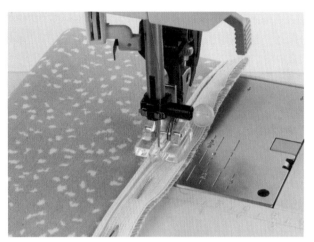

2 With a zipper foot, sew through the zipper tape and seam allowance, and make sure you don't catch the rest of the garment. Sew as close as you can to the teeth. A special invisible zipper foot comes in handy, as there is a ridge in the foot to allow the zipper teeth to pass underneath. It's possible to do it with a standard zipper foot, but it's easier with the invisible zipper foot. Roll the zipper tape back, and sew as close as you can to the teeth in the groove of the tape. Sew to the bottom of the zipper.

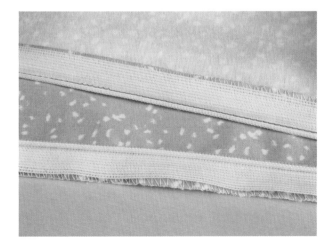

3 Pin or baste the other side of the zipper tape to the seam allowance on the other side of the opening, and line up any horizontal seams with the other side of the zipper. Sew with a zipper foot. Make sure you stop your stitching at the same point at the bottom of the zipper. This makes it easier to sew the seam below the zipper.

Close the zipper. Attach the regular zipper foot, and sew from the bottom of the zipper to the hem.

As an alternative to the last step, attach the regular sewing machine foot, sew upward from the hem to 1" (2.5cm) below the zipper opening, and backstitch. Then use the zipper foot to sew up the gap between the seam and the zipper stitching. Get close to the stitching along the zipper so the seam can be pressed smoothly below the zipper. Press the seam open, and lightly press the zipper opening from the right side.

SHORTENING AN INVISIBLE ZIPPER

Some fabric stores will have a variety of invisible zippers in varying lengths. Some will only stock short (8" [20.3cm]) and long (22" [55.9cm]), and you'll have to shorten them for lengths in between. Luckily it's easy to do!

Decide where to shorten the zipper, either by checking the requirements on the back of the pattern envelope or by measuring the length of the zipper opening. Measure from the top opening to the bottom and mark the new zipper length. Set your sewing machine to a wide zigzag and a short stitch length. I usually set my zigzag as wide as it will go, with a 0.5 stitch length. Start on one side of the zipper coil and use the handwheel to make sure that the next step of the zigzag is going to clear the zipper coil. If it's not wide enough, adjust the stitch width.

Zigzag over the tape about ten times until a nice thick bit of stitches secure the zipper coil. Cut 1" (2.5cm) below the stitching.

COVERING THE END OF AN INVISIBLE ZIPPER

If you shorten an invisible zipper, the cut end can be scratchy. Why not cover the end with fabric? Doing so adds a nice finishing touch and softens a stiff zipper end, making your garments more comfortable to wear! This works best with fabric that is lightweight. If your garment fabric is bulky, use a lightweight scrap fabric in a similar color to the garment or zipper tape.

Cut a small square from leftover garment fabric. Make it the width of the zipper plus two $^5/_8$" (1.5cm) seam allowances (about 2¼" [5.7cm] total). Press under the seam allowances on either side, so the zipper cover is the same width as the zipper tape. Press under the other ends as well. Sew to the zipper, with the inside of the zipper facing you, as shown. You'll wrap the tab up and to the front, so it's easy to sew from the right side.

Wrap the folded end around to the front, and line up the folded edge with the line of stitching you just sewed. Edgestitch (page 69) all around the zipper cover, pivoting at the corners. When in doubt, stop short of each corner, as it's easy to overshoot and sew off the edge. Trim the loose threads.

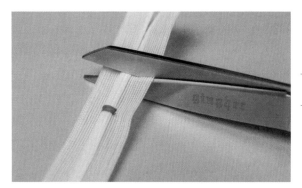

Tips + Notes

Invisible zippers take practice. It's OK if your first attempt at sewing an invisible zipper is less than invisible! If you can, sew a second row of stitching slightly closer to the teeth.

Buy an invisible zipper foot for your specific machine. The results are better than using the universal invisible zipper foot, and doing so makes inserting invisible zippers easier.

Be careful not to accidentally sew over the teeth of your zipper. If you do, remove the stitching carefully and make sure the teeth aren't damaged. If they are, switch to a new zipper. Broken or bent teeth on an invisible zipper can cause the zipper to burst when it's zipped or to stick when it's being zipped up.

Zipper, Lapped

WHAT IS IT?

A lapped zipper is a type of zipper application in which one side overlaps the zipper. The zipper is positioned so that it hides under this overlap. The zipper is harder to see from the overlap side of the zipper and easier to see on the side without the overlap. Instead of a centered zipper (page 236), for which the zipper is in the middle of the opening, a lapped zipper has one wide side that covers the zipper and one narrow side underneath. Lapped zippers are inserted after the seam below the zipper opening is sewn.

Lapped zipper

Lapped zipper

WHEN DO YOU USE IT?

A lapped zipper is a good type of zipper application for side zippers, because the overlap covers the zipper teeth. The lap also hides zipper teeth that are not a perfect color match. Use lapped zippers on skirts at the side seam, dresses at the side or at the center back, or blouses that have zippered openings at the top of the back neck.

Tips + Notes

Lapped zippers can be sewn into seams with a standard ⁵⁄₈" (1.5cm) seam allowance, but it works even better if the left seam allowance is slightly wider. Increase the left seam allowance to at least ¾" (1.9cm) so the raw edge of the lap is easier to catch in the topstitching (page 218).

For zippers in lightweight or shifty fabric, you may want to stabilize the zipper opening with fusible interfacing (page 104). Cut two 1"-wide (2.5cm) strips of interfacing the length of the zipper opening, and fuse along the zipper opening.

Instead of topstitching the left side of the zipper, why not hand pick it? Follow the steps for hand picking a zipper on page 239 and use this technique instead of the topstitching.

HOW TO SEW A LAPPED ZIPPER

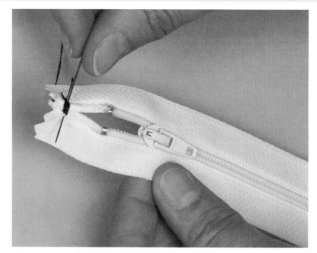

1 Start after the seam below the zipper has been sewn. If the zipper is going into an unlined garment, finish the seam allowances of the zipper opening all the way down to the bottom of the seam. If the zipper is going in a lined garment where the seam allowances will be enclosed, leave the seam allowances unfinished. Machine baste (page 18) the zipper opening above the seam closed, and press it open.

2 For a side-lapped zipper, where there is a seam below and above the zipper opening, place the top zipper tape edges so they are touching without overlapping, and whipstitch (page 233) the tape together at the top edge. In this sewing example, the zipper is open at the top, so I didn't whipstitch the end, as you'll see in step 3.

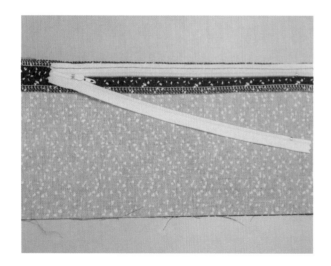

3 Switch to a zipper foot. From the inside of your garment, with the top of the zipper opening facing you, open up the right seam allowance. Open the zipper and place it face down on the seam allowance, with the bottom stop on the marking and the coil/teeth next to but not on top of the seam. Machine baste (page 18) down the middle of the zipper tape through the tape and seam allowance only, from top to bottom.

4 Switch back to a regular stitch length, zip up the zipper, and form a fold in the seam allowance but not in the tape. Bring the fold close to the zipper coil but not close enough to touch, and pin it in place. Edgestitch (page 69) the fold to the zipper tape, moving the slider out of the way as you sew.

Flip the garment over to the right side, and if you unzipped the zipper in the last step, zip it back up. The zipper now lies under the free seam allowance and a pleat is formed at the end of the zipper opening. Secure with pins. Hand baste (page 18) across the bottom of the zipper and up the left side about ⅜" (1 cm) from the seam. Make sure your hand basting is accurate, as you'll be using it as a stitching guide in the next step.

5 On the outside of the garment, just outside the basting lines, begin topstitching (page 218) at the bottom of the zipper, across the bottom, then pivot and sew up the side. For zippers that are going to open all the way up to the top, sew to the end of the tape. For zippers in the side seam, or any seam that is sewn at the top and bottom of the zipper opening, stitch to the top, pivot and sew toward the seam. Press the zipper opening, and remove basting stitches.

Resources

PATTERNS

Many of the patterns featured in this book are Sewaholic Patterns, designed by the author. Shop online at sewaholicpatterns.com or at retailers all over the world. A full list of retailers can be found online at sewaholicpatterns.com/retailers.

The best views of the Sewaholic patterns shown in this book include:

* Cambie Dress, page 6

* Crescent Skirt, page 111

* Hollyburn Skirt, page 54

* Minoru Jacket, page 60

* Pendrell Blouse, page 159

* Renfrew Top, page 109

* Robson Coat, page 66

* Thurlow Trousers, page 148

* Tofino Pants, page 132

* Saltspring Dress, page 10

Etsy.com is a great source for vintage patterns, and the site allows you to search by specific pattern number, by year or by pattern company. Vintage patterns usually only come in one size, and sizing has changed over the past hundred years. Check the measurements on the envelope back to choose the closest size for you.

Vintage patterns used in this book include:

* Simplicity 3965, page 63 and book cover

* Simplicity 5928, page 38

* Simplicity 4931, page 33

Other patterns used in this book:

* Grainline Studio, Archer Shirt, page 23

* Colette Patterns, Cinnamon Slip, page 23 and 86

* McCalls 5803, page 141

FABRIC AND NOTIONS

The fabric and tools you will need for these techniques are available from your local fabric store or sewing center or favorite online retailer.

Telio

Wholesaler of fashionable apparel fabrics. Contact them to find retail locations that stock Telio fabrics.
telio.com
teliotextures.com

Index

Dedication

To Ryan, my wonderful "Mr. Sewaholic," thank you for being there with a hug at the end of every long day. Couldn't have done it without you!

Acknowledgments

To Vanessa Lyman, Christine Doyle and the team at F+W Media, thank you for taking a chance on a new author.

To Leanne Scherp and Susannah Street, thanks for your talent in bringing my ideas to life!

To Caroline, thank you for your hard work and your enthusiasm to jump in whenever you were needed. Thanks also to Corinne for your energy, your endless hours cutting samples and your help with all the random needs that came up! I'm grateful to have such positive and inspiring women in my company.

To my parents, thank you for encouraging creativity from a young age. Thanks to you I grew up with the confidence that I could make anything I wanted if I put my mind to it!

To the readers of the Sewaholic blog, thanks for reading, for buying patterns and for being part of this journey. You are intelligent, helpful, kind and encouraging, and truly the best group of readers I could wish for. Thanks for sharing your wisdom and perspectives in the comments, and for asking great questions! Without your support, there would be no *Sewtionary*.

Other fine KP Craft books are available from your favorite bookstore, fabric or craft store or online *media* supplier.

18   17   16   15   14   5   4   3   2   1

DISTRIBUTED IN CANADA BY FRASER DIRECT
100 Armstrong Avenue
Georgetown, ON, Canada L7G 5S4
Tel: (905) 877-4411

DISTRIBUTED IN THE U.K. AND EUROPE
by F&W Media International LTD
Brunel House, Forde Close Newton Abbot,
Devon TQ12 4PU, UK
Tel: (+44) 1626 323200, Fax: (+44) 1626 323319
Email: enquiries@fwmedia.com

DISTRIBUTED IN AUSTRALIA BY CAPRICORN LINK
P.O. Box 704, S. Windsor NSW, 2756 Australia
Tel: (02) 4577-3555

ISBN-13: 978-1-4402-3832-1
ISBN-10: 1-4402-3832-4
SRN: U7397

Edited by **Christine Doyle**

Designed by **Kelly Pace**

Photography by **Leanne Scherp** and **Susannah Street/ ImageryWorks.ca**

Production coordinated by **Greg Nock**

METRIC CONVERSION CHART

to convert	to	multiply by
inches	centimeters	2.54
centimeters	inches	0.4
feet	centimeters	30.5
centimeters	feet	0.03
yards	meters	0.9
meters	yards	1.1

About the Author

TASIA ST. GERMAINE

Tasia is the founder and owner of Sewaholic Patterns. She launched Sewaholic in 2010 to offer pretty, versatile sewing patterns for pear-shaped women. Tasia has been sewing for twenty-five years; in high school she spent as much time working in the sewing lab as attending regular classes. Tasia completed a degree in fashion design and technology at Kwantlen University College, where she thrived in the company of other students who shared her passion for sewing, fabric and design. After graduation, Tasia honed her craft by working in the apparel industry for eight years. Sewing always remained her first love, so she decided to take the knowledge and experience she had gained and to apply it to the world of sewing patterns. This decision led to the Sewaholic blog, her successful Sewaholic Patterns business and this very book! Tasia's enthusiasm and love of sewing has inspired people all over the world to start sewing and to take pride in making their own clothing.

Tasia lives in beautiful Vancouver, British Columbia, Canada, with her husband, Mr. Sewaholic. When she's not sewing, she loves cycling, knitting, puzzles, traveling and quilting.

Visit the Sewaholic blog at www.sewaholic.com or Sewaholic Patterns at www.sewaholicpatterns.com.

Time to Get Sewing!

sewdaily | sewing made modern.

Interact with thousand of fellow sewing enthusiasts on SewDaily.com! Whether you sew clothing, accessories, home decor items, or just love the possibilities of fabric and thread, you'll find all sorts of great information....and make new friends, too!

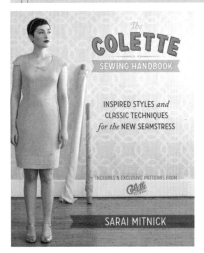

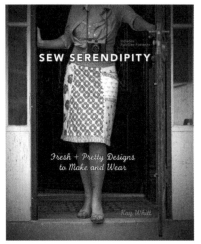

THE COLETTE SEWING HANDBOOK
Sarai Mitnick

Sarai Mitnick is the pattern designer to watch. Her line, Colette Patterns, is quickly gaining popularity not only for the beautiful, nostalgic designs, but also for their ease of use and thorough instruction. With *The Colette Sewing Handbook,* she takes the instruction even further, providing readers with the 5 fundamentals to the perfect sewing project—a great plan, a great pattern, a great fit, a great fabric, and a great finish. Five projects with tissue paper patterns (an $85 value) mean you can learn to sew and create a gorgeous project from one beautiful package.

SEW SERENDIPITY
Kay Whitt

Many readers are scared or nervous to sew clothes for themselves, but one taste of success is all they need to try more. Kay Whitt gives them that taste by gently introducing them to clothes-making. She shows readers that it's not a trade secret to alter a pattern to fit your figure and style—anyone can do it! Friendly math (½" seam allowance, not ⅝"!), solid coaching on how to measure for the best individual fit, and an overview of all the required sewing techniques ensures that readers will be on their way to making a coordinated, customized wardrobe.

STITCH BY STITCH
Deborah Moebes

So, you love all that gorgeous designer fabric and you really want to make something with it. Or maybe you've taught yourself a little sewing know-how but have become frustrated. Whatever your background, *Stitch by Stitch* guides you through everything you need to know to start sewing and make it to the varsity level.

In the book's unique format, skills and projects build upon each other so that you get instant gratification and motivation to progress. Whether you're a sewing novice or returning sewist, *Stitch by Stitch* will give you the confidence and skills to keep motivated, get great results and finally learn to love the process.